Francophone Cultures and Literatures

Michael G. Paulson & Tamara Alvarez-Detrell
General Editors

Vol. 34

PETER LANG
New York • Washington, D.C./Baltimore • Boston • Bern
Frankfurt am Main • Berlin • Brussels • Vienna • Oxford

Frank Rosengarten

The Writings of the Young Marcel Proust (1885–1900)

An Ideological Critique

PETER LANG
New York • Washington, D.C./Baltimore • Boston • Bern
Frankfurt am Main • Berlin • Brussels • Vienna • Oxford

Library of Congress Cataloging-in-Publication Data

Rosengarten, Frank.
The writings of the young Marcel Proust (1885–1900):
an ideological critique / Frank Rosengarten.
p. cm. — (Francophone cultures and literatures; vol. 34)
Includes bibliographical references and index.
1. Proust, Marcel, 1871–1922. I. Title. II. Series.
PQ2631.R63 Z8365   843'.912—dc21   00-030944
ISBN 0-8204-5126-6
ISSN 1077-0186

Die Deutsche Bibliothek-CIP-Einheitsaufnahme

Rosengarten, Frank:
The writings of the young Marcel Proust (1885–1900): an ideological critique /
Frank Rosengarten. –New York; Washington, D.C./Baltimore; Boston; Bern;
Frankfurt am Main; Berlin; Brussels; Vienna; Oxford: Lang.
(Francophone cultures and literatures; Vol. 34)
ISBN 0-8204-5126-6

The paper in this book meets the guidelines for permanence and durability
of the Committee on Production Guidelines for Book Longevity
of the Council of Library Resources.

© 2001 Peter Lang Publishing, Inc., New York

All rights reserved.
Reprint or reproduction, even partially, in all forms such as microfilm,
xerography, microfiche, microcard, and offset strictly prohibited.

Printed in the United States of America

To Lucy, with love everlasting

A Note on Translations

Everyone in the English-speaking world who deals critically with Proust's writings is faced with the problem of whether to cite quoted passages in the French original, on the assumption that serious readers expect this method, to cite the original French with accompanying English translations, or to use only English translations throughout.

I have opted for the third way, for the following reasons. First, I have noted the French sources for all translated passages, so that the reader can easily check the original if s/he feels the need to do so. Second, this study focuses primarily on questions of point of view and ideology, not on style, as fundamental as the latter undoubtedly is in Proust studies. Third, I envision a readership for this book that is somewhat larger than the usual one for scholarly monographs, since I believe that the issues with which I deal, from both a critical and an historical point of view, are of interest to people outside as well as within the academy.

Readers should be aware that, unless otherwise indicated, all passages from French, Italian, and German critical sources are mine. As for most of Proust's writings, adequate or excellent English transations are available. I have used these whenever possible. But there are letters, early stories and journalistic pieces, and several critical essays that, as far as I know, have not yet been translated. Hence my need to rely on my own English versions in some cases.

Acknowledgments

The process of writing this book was facilitated by Professor Mary Ann Caws, who was always available to me to talk about troublesome problems of focus, structure, and organization. Professors Robert Dombroski and Royal Brown were also careful readers and asked pertinent and probing questions.

Among friends who took the time to read several drafts, I am indebted in particular to Professors George Bernstein, Kate Crehan, and Joseph Buttigieg. All three pointed out ways of improving and developing arguments of central importance to this study.

For their assistance in giving me access to important Proust materials, I would like to thank the librarians and administrators of the Bibliothèque Nationale in Paris, the New York Public Library, the Columbia University rare book collection, and the rare book and manuscript collections of the University of Illinois library in Urbana. I am especially grateful to Caroline Szylowicz, the able administrator of the Kolb-Proust Archive for Research at the University of Illinois, who made me the beneficiary of her comprehensive knowledge of every aspect of Proust's life.

My thanks are due to the professors and staff of the Ph.D. Program in French at the Graduate School of the City University of New York. Their tutelage made it possible for me, after a professional career devoted primarily to Italian language and literature, to reinvent myself–at a rather advanced age–as an aspiring scholar of French literature.

Finally, the following publishers and individuals have given me permission to reprint copyrighted materials. They are Columbia University Press, for English translations of several of Proust's letters in Julius Edwin Rivers's *Proust and the Art of Love*; George Borchardt, Inc., U.S. agent of Editions Gallimard, for English translations of excerpts from *Pleasures and Days*, *Jean Santeuil*, and *Contre Sainte-Beuve*; the Bibliothèque

Nationale in Paris, authorizing me to cite manuscript and printed materials in its Proust collection; the Librairie Plon, for passages in Proust's *Correspondance*, edited by Philip Kolb; and Nathalie Mauriac-Dyer, authorizing me to cite manuscript materials in the rare book and mansucript division of the University of Illinois Library.

Abbreviations Used in the Text and in Endnotes

B.N.   Bibliothèque Nationale (Paris)

BSAP   *Bulletin de l'Association des Amis de Marcel Proust*

Corr.   *Correspondance de Marcel Proust* 21 Vols. Edited by Philip Kolb. Paris: Librairie Plon, 1970 . . .

CSB   *Contre Sainte-Beuve*

Dupee   *Pleasures and Days.* Edited by F. W. Dupee, translated by Louise Varese, Gerard Hopkins, and Barbara Dupee. Garden City: Doubleday, 1957.

JS   *Jean Santeuil*

Laget   *Les Plaisirs et les jours suivi de L'Indifférent et autres textes.* Edited by Thierry Laget. Paris: Gallimard, 1993.

PJ   *Les Plaisirs et les jours*

Recherche *À la Recherche du temps perdu*

UI ms.   The Proust manuscript collection at the University of Illinois library in Urbana.

Contents

Introduction		1
Part One	**The Socioliterary World of the Young Proust**	**25**
Chapter 1	Eros and Friendship at the Lycée Condorcet	27
Chapter 2	Three Parisian Literary Reviews in the 1890's: *Le Mensuel*, *Le Banquet* and *La Revue Blanche*	41
Chapter 3	With Reynaldo Hahn in Town and Country	63
Chapter 4	Young Proust, Robert de Montesquiou-Fezensac, and the Society of the Parisian Salons	73
Part Two	**Literary and Ideological Crosscurrents in *Pleasures and Days***	**89**
Chapter 5	The Vicissitudes of a Text	91
Chapter 6	Problems of Structure, Unity and Aesthetic Philosophy	101
Chapter 7	Elitism and the Primacy of the Spiritual	119
Chapter 8	A Profusion of Intertextuality	137
Part Three	**The Critic and the Novelist**	**157**
Chapter 9	Critical Principles	159
Chapter 10	Literary Text and Ideology in *Jean Santeuil*	185
Endnotes		213
Bibliography		225
Index		253

Introduction

For some Proust devotees, ideological criticism of their idol is tantamount to an unwarranted and even scandalous intrusion into a holy place. They maintain that Proust was above all a lyrical and contemplative writer devoted to the exploration of the human soul, not to the kind of political and social problems that lend themselves to ideological analysis. For these Proust lovers, À la *Recherche du temps perdu* is really a symbol-laden poem more than a novel, an evocative transfiguration of experience in which the dross of daily life is changed into the gold of a sublime work of art. In their view, Proust's signal accomplishments—the supple undulations of his prose, his vivid metaphors, his memorable portraits of men and women in the throes of obsessive impulses and desires, his insights into painting and music, his theory of memory, time, and artistic creation—cannot be appreciated if we place them in an interpretive framework that distorts or disregards their essential values. In sum, according to this primarily "poetic" reading of Proust, a stress on ideological analysis of his writings is a fruitless enterprise condemned to founder on its misunderstanding of his artistic methods and intentions. The same point of view has been expressed about Proust's early writings, which seem to be even less amenable to this type of analysis than the *Recherche*.

This study takes the position that such a "poetic" reading of Proust is not wrong but simply one-sided and incomplete. It does so, moreover, in the context of a literary critical history dating back to the 1930s, one that remains vital right up to our own time. The fact is that "ideological" analysis has long played an important role in opening Proustian texts to practical worldly concerns. Some of the critical voices that have helped to create this opening will be heard a little later in this introduction, where I shall provide a summary review of theoretical and critical works that have influenced my own approach to Proust and my attempt to do what Lauro

Martines calls "social literary analysis," meaning analysis in which literary texts are seen as inextricably interrelated with the society and history of their time.

Proust himself was in some measure responsible for the large number of incense burners who approach his work with hushed reverence. He was among those in the 1890s who worshiped at the altar of "art for art's sake." He adhered to an aesthetic philosophy according to which literary texts are ontologically distinct from nonliterary ones. Such a distinction rests on a premise this study does not share. Moreover, Proust himself honored it "more in the breach than the observance": the premise that literature and ideology, for example, belong to realms of expression so different in nature and aim as to make them incommensurable. My point is that if this were the case, to attempt a transposition of the language of literature into that of politics or philosophy, to cross over from one domain of expression to another, would be a violation of sacrosanct boundaries. But without the possibility of such "transgression" the various areas of critical inquiry would have to be considered inaccessible and irrelevant to each other. The result would be an impoverishment of intellectual activity in all of them. In this connection, Malcolm Bowie notes that Proust habitually used various "cross-over" terms such as "transition," "transposition," "transmutation" in order "to make disparate fields of human activity intelligible to one another" (Bowie 1998, 113–114).

In theory, Proust was committed to a spiritualized, quasi-religious conception of art and literature. In practice, however, it is my contention that virtually all of his writings, whether critical or fictional, personal or philosophical, were responses to specific moral, psychological, and sociopolitical problems of his time. His writing, together with its poetic and musical qualities, also served eminently practical ends. In the pursuit of relevance, he felt an irrepressible need to explore the world in many directions at one time, wherever this exploration might take him, irrespective of genres, modes, and preconceptions of any kind concerning the proper place of this or that style or type of writing. In a word, Proust thought of writing as an effective way to engage life and to confront human problems. Despite his avowed aestheticism, Proust was never a purist in his thinking or in his writing.

In 1971, Maurice Bardèche articulated the relationship between "the poetry of memory" and the prose of critical reflection in Proust's writing in the following manner:

> One understands . . . why Proust protested when his work was defined as a series of "memories." His "memories" had in effect certainly furnished the sub-

ject matter: but the transformation of these "memories" and their utilization as "examples" or "arguments" in a meditation on man and on social life, had been the main transmutation and the true labor of creation. (1: 13)

Gilles Deleuze had expressed a similar point of view somewhat earlier than Bardèche, when he observed that in Proust's writing, memory and the whole "nostalgic" return to places known and loved in childhood, despite their undoubted importance, are not the key to his work, even to the *Recherche*; that "Proust's work is not turned towards the past and the discoveries of memory, but towards the future and the progress of an apprenticeship." What is essential in the *Recherche*, Deleuze said, "is not memory and time, but the sign and truth. The essential thing is not remembering, but learning" (36, 111).

The learning process by which the young Proust came to an understanding of his literary vocation is to a considerable extent the subject of this study and what justifies its chronological boundaries. It was during the years 1885 to 1900 that Proust elaborated virtually all of the themes and pondered almost all of the literary and philosophical problems that were to reappear in his major work. For this reason, a thorough grounding in the events, trends, personalities, issues, and currents of thought that marked his youth and shaped his writing up to the turn of the century is a necessary precondition for adequate understanding of the *Recherche*. It is not a matter of a youthful "before" and a mature "after" in Proust's case. The material of his early writings—chiefly the collection *Les Plaisirs et les jours* (*PJ*, 1896), the unfinished novel *Jean Santeuil* (*JS*) written from 1896 to about 1900, and the early essays on John Ruskin (1899–1900)—is already the material of *À la Recherche du temps perdu*. It lacks only the transcendent vision of the *Recherche*, in which a single narrator views his own development and evaluates Parisian society from the last decades of the nineteenth century to World War I from a perspective that is at once more psychologically penetrating and more historically dense and textured than that of the earlier writings.

A second chronological consideration merits brief mention here. Proust was always closely affiliated with various Parisian social and intellectual coteries, but it was in his youth that his personal experiences were bound up inextricably with a socioliterary world that left its mark on his conception of life. However isolated and withdrawn he was for fairly prolonged periods after 1908, when he began writing the *Recherche*, the fact is that he was not a solitary Promethean genius towering over the heads of his merely mortal contemporaries, as he is sometimes pictured. From his student days at the Lycée Condorcet to the turn of the century he was an integral part of a network of personal and intellectual associations that needs to be scrutinized. In short, a study of young Proust helps us to situate him in a milieu, a culture, a moment in historical time. He was certainly an exceptional and original figure, but he was also very much a child of his time, a product of a civilization that provided him with a whole gamut of ideas and of modes and forms of literary expression. My aim is both to attach Proust to an established set of social and literary conventions and to indicate the ways in which he became independent of them. The young Proust, like the mature author of the *Recherche*, was at once a member of an elite intelligentsia and a severe critic of the social world that spawned this intelligentsia.

As far as I can determine, there have been no new, significant, in-depth investigations of Proust's early literary and philosophical development since the appearance in 1983 of Anne Henry's *Marcel Proust:Théories pour une esthétique*, to which I am indebted mainly for its insights into Proust's assimilation of German idealist thought. Prior to 1980, from the 1920s to the 1970s, numerous memoirs and biographies[1] looked at various aspects of his youth, and many worthy studies have dealt with such fundamental facets of his early life experiences as his education, his family background, his friendships, and his youthful writings.[2] Yet the special province of this study, which is the evolution and development of young Proust's conception of the world—his *Weltanschauung*—with emphasis on what I call its "ideological" constituents, has not been exhaustively cultivated. What I attempt to provide, therefore, is an analysis of Proust's youthful literary production—encompassing fiction, poetry, and criticism—primarily in terms of its ideological assumptions and beliefs. I have tried at the same time to situate these assumptions and beliefs in their sociohistorical context. My sources are Proust's correspondence, manuscript materials in special collections, memoirs, biographies, various editions of Proust's early writings, magazines and newspapers of the period concerned, and, of course, the relevant critical literature on Proust.

Since 1990, three new biographies of Proust have appeared that I would like to mention here. They are Jean-Yves Tadié's *Marcel Proust* (1996), a massive, richly documented volume that deals in considerable detail with Proust's teenage years; Edmund White's *Marcel Proust* (1999), an estimable work for the light it sheds on Proust's sexuality; and William C. Carter's *Marcel Proust: A Life* (2000). All three of these works refer to and quote from some of the same materials that I cite in this study, mainly letters, short stories, literary and art criticism, and journalistic pieces. Nevertheless, since I have utilized these materials for my own rather different purposes, I think that these new biographies and my monograph will easily and happily coexist in the libraries of Proust enthusiasts.

As opposed to the relative paucity of ideological analysis applied to Proust's early writings, the *Recherche* has received a considerable amount of critical attention stressing ideological and socio-historical questions. As I have already noted, some of it dates back to the 1930s, such as that of Anatoly Lunacharsky and several other Soviet critics,[3] Edmund Wilson's chapter on Proust in *Axel's Castle* (1931), and Walter Benjamin's essay "The Image of Proust." In more recent times, among important sociologically and ideologically oriented critical studies of the *Recherche* are Germaine Brée's *The World of Marcel Proust* (1966), Emilien Carassus's *Le Snobisme et les lettres françaises de Paul Bourget à Marcel Proust: 1884–1914* (1966), Seth L. Wolitz's *The Proustian Community* (1971), P.V. Zima's *Le Désir du mythe: Une lecture sociologique de Marcel Proust* (1973), Robert Sayre's chapter on "Swann's Way" in *Solitude in Society: A Sociological Study in French Literature* (1978), Antoine Compagnon's *La Troisième République des lettres* (1983) and *Proust entre deux siècles* (1989), Michael Sprinker's *History and Ideology in Proust: À la Recherche du temps perdu and the Third French Republic* (1994), and Anthony Albert Everman's *Lilies and Sesame: The Orient, Inversion, and Artistic Creation in* À la recherche du temps perdu (1998). The Compagnon and Sprinker studies will be discussed later in this introduction. The others will receive attention in subsequent chapters.

Let me try now to clarify the range of meanings of the word "ideology" and the phrase "ideological criticism" as I use them in this study, meanings drawn in large measure from literary and social theorists whose work I regard as essential for my own critical orientation. Such a clarification is necessary because the notion of "ideology" is so freighted with political baggage that comes down to us from the early decades of the twentieth century. It recalls the formulaic and dogmatic arguments that used to pass for Marxist and left-wing criticism. There is no need to feel overburdened by this particular history; we should think of it, it seems to me, as marking an inevitable stage in the development of twentieth-century historical-materialist thought. In any case, since the 1950s, often inspired by a select group of Marxist thinkers of the 1920s and 1930s (for instance, Mikhail Bakhtin, Walter Benjamin, Antonio Gramsci, and Georg Lukács), generations of thinkers on the Marxist left and others working independently of all schools have gone a long way to liberating the ideological criticism of literature from its troublesome associations with sectarianism and dogma. Raymond Williams was a key contributor to this liberatory process.

In *Marxism and Literature* (1977), Williams performs the vital service of historicising the term "ideology," which he treats as one of four "basic concepts," together with culture, language, and literature. After reviewing its uses by the Enlightenment *idéologues* and by Marx and Engels, Williams proceeds to argue that any and all reductionisms, whether materialist or idealist in origin, are inimical to the fundamental Marxist precept that consciousness and its products are parts of the total material social process. He points out that "thinking" and "imagining" are social processes that become accessible in tangible form such as works of art, "whether in sound, pigments on canvas, writing, or in worked marble or stone." He then takes note of the tensions never satisfactorily resolved in Marx's writing between the notions of science and of ideology, where the claims of the former to exactitude and disinterestedness conflict with the merely self-serving and partisan character of the latter, a troublesome dichotomy that sometimes appears in Marx's thought. It is responsible for the equation "ideology=false consciousness" (although Marx himself never actually used this phrase) that has had such a crippling effect on attempts to use the concept of ideology in literary study.

Although a little unsure whether the term "ideology" encompasses a sufficiently broad range of meanings for the purposes of literary study, toward the end of his essay Williams seems willing to concede that it serves reasonably well as a general term to designate "not only the products but the processes of all signification, including the signification of values." Again noting that the Marxist tradition had too often failed to see that "the fundamental processes of social signification are intrinsic to 'practical consciousness' and intrinsic also to the 'conceptions, thoughts and ideas' which are *recognizable* as its products," Williams believes that the key to understanding the validity of the term "ideology" in the study of literature and culture is to see it as part of "the material social process of signification itself." Thus, as Williams sees the issue, it is never acceptable to remove ideas and theories from their sociohistorical context, just as it is unacceptable to treat the production of material life as if it had no links with the process of signification.

Williams took long strides forward in the ongoing effort to grasp the complex relationship between literary texts and ideology, wherein ideology is understood as the ideas, feelings, values, and beliefs about the world that a writer brings to the act of literary creation, whether consciously and critically—as I think Proust did for the most part in his writing—or unconsciously.

The reflections on ideology in *Marxism and Literature* were influenced by Williams's reading of Antonio Gramsci, one of the earlier representatives of "Western Marxism" who helped Williams and others writing in the 1960s and 1970s to make a theoretically nuanced use of Marxist concepts in literary studies. Gramsci understood ideology as being "in its highest sense a conception of the world that is implicitly manifest in art, in law, in economic activity and in all manifestations of individual and collective life" (Gramsci 1971, 328). Behind this definition lies the all-important concept of "hegemony," which in the language peculiar to Gramsci's writing connotes a process through which the ideas and ideals of the dominant class of a society win acceptance by the subaltern classes. Williams sees hegemony as a concept that "goes beyond 'ideology'" in that he associates the latter with a relatively "conscious system of ideas and beliefs," while the former embraces "the whole lived social process as practically organized by specific and dominant meanings and values" (109). What matters most for the purposes of this study is the influence exerted on Williams by Gramsci's rigorously dialectical understanding of the relationship between society and culture, which Williams applied to his own work. Gramsci's concept of hegemony, and his formulations about the diffusion of ideology in modern societies, rested in part on the crucial role played by literary intellectuals, most of whom he saw as secular "priests" of bourgeois civilization. This prompts one to question whether and to what extent Proust saw himself consciously as part of a ruling class. There can be little doubt about his belief that the creators of literature and the other arts had a civilizing mission to perform, a calling, as it were, similar in spirit to earlier centuries when the priesthood assumed the responsibilites of providing moral and spiritual guidance to the masses. This idea is especially germane to Proust's writings on John Ruskin, which will be discussed in chapter 9.

A heterodox Soviet scholar, Mikhail Bakhtin, made a major contribution to building a different kind of literary-critical edifice on the foundations of historical materialism. His work entered Western thought somewhat later than that of Gramsci, but it was probably as influential once translations made it available to people outside of Russia.

Bakhtin conceived of literature and art as branches of what he called "ideological creations" linked dialectically both to the systems of economic production that underlie all societies and to various other "superstructural" branches of creative activity—science, ethics, religion, philosophy and so on.[4] Yet "ideology" as conceptualized by Bakhtin and his partners is not really a separable "superstructural" manifestation of a socioeconomic "base," as some Marxists have defined it, but rather a constitutive part of that base. This dialectical and interrelational manner of thinking is one of the qualities that give Bakhtin's writing its immense appeal. He agreed with an older generation of Marxists that, as "ideological creations," works of art demand sociohistorical contextualization and ideological analysis, but he parted company with them in calling for a discerning appreciation of what works of art offer that is distinctive and original, what makes them function specifically as art and not, let's say, as sociological treatise, political polemic, or philosophical reflection. In other words, while works of literary art may and often do contain many passages (as in the fictional writings of Proust) and even whole chapters (as in *War and Peace*) that are historical, sociological, or philosophical in character, what they do with those passages must be evaluated with a vocabulary and within a conceptual framework that are appropriate to literature.

In the course of working out the premises of his approach to literary studies, Bakhtin elaborated what he called a "historical poetics," which hinged on "forms of time and of the chronotope in the novel" whereby "Time thickens, takes on flesh, becomes artistically visible and space becomes charged and responsive to the movements of time, plot and history" (Bakhtin 1981, 84). The Russian scholar believed that, despite "the relative typological stability" of novelistic chronotopes in different historical periods, it was unproductive to interpret literary texts in accordance with generalized abstract standards and criteria of judgment, since each group of writers and artists operates from within its own particular matrix of ideas not only about what constitutes the true and the beautiful in art but also about the crucial concepts of time and space as understood historically as well as philosophically.

If for a moment we think of Proust in Bakhtinian terms, we can say that his conception of life was influenced by the new dynamic, rapidly changing scientific and technological civilization of the 1880s and 1890s, within which it was quite natural to think of the world in a "Hericlitean" and "kaleidoscopic" fashion, an attitude that Proust and many other writers of his generation shared with the impressionist painters. The interaction of chronos and topos in Proust's writing reflects the ceaseless changes in human affairs that one begins to feel, for example, in the first half of the nineteenth century in the novels of Stendhal and Balzac. In their work, society and history are not just backdrops with which to fill in the empty spaces left by the principal plot lines, but are integral to the plot and to the destiny of the main characters. Ideological questions, even if not called by that name, are of paramount interest to Stendhal and Balzac in that these writers present us with characters who embody ideological points of view and who live in a time of flux in which clashing socioeconomic interests compete for ascendancy.

Having noted the above, I must quickly add that literary forms and genres inherited from premodern times, such as mythic and fabular narratives, also had an impact on Proust's imagination and sensibilities. This side of his temperament is much in evidence in some of the stories of *PJ*, and is not entirely absent from the *Recherche*. We should be on guard against reading Proust in a single register. The "Hericlitean" view is predominant in his writing, yet at the same time he found the atemporal and universalizing qualities of the fable to be exceedingly attractive. Nor do I wish to give the impression here that this study is so tightly bound to Proust's own time or to other epochs as to make it impossible to see him from a contemporary perspective, in terms of the interests and passions that move us today at the turning point of the twentieth and twenty-first centuries. To adhere to a type of historicism that demands that we read a given work of literature and interpret a writer's style and ideas solely in accordance with what they signified in their own historical moment is to confuse philological rigor with antiquarianism.

Closely linked to the issue of historicism is the important question in literary study of the relationship between writers and their publics. This is a question of great interest to the French sociologist Pierre Bourdieu, for whom ideological criticism must pay careful attention to the ways in which class identification and affiliation determine every writer's choice of materials and his/her sense of where the potential readership for a specific work is to be found. Works of art have meaning and interest only for someone who possesses the cultural competence, that is, the code governing their composition. In the case of young Proust in the 1880s and 1890s, I shall argue that there is no reasonable and defensible way of detaching his writing from the belief systems of the aristocratic and bourgeois social worlds to which he belonged and with which he identified himself, even if he did so with some significant reservations and anxieties that are interwoven into the texture of many of his early fictional and critical writings.

Much of the work of Terry Eagleton is also pertinent to this study. Among the many definitions of the word "ideology" that he examines, the one that I think is most comprehensive and analytically useful is "the ideas and beliefs (whether true or false) which symbolize the conditions and life-experiences of a specific, socially significant group or class" (Eagleton 1991, 29). This definition has the advantage of tying the word down to sociohistorical interests and purposes. Literary production, as a fundamental signifying practice, enters the total social process via a writer's ideological assumptions, which in turn express themselves in diverse choices of genre, style, and mode of discourse.

Eagleton's conception of the relations between literary texts and ideology is marked by a powerful bias in favor of a "science" of criticism whose aim is to establish the grounds for a "materialist aesthetics." To this end, he sets forth six major "constituents of a Marxist theory of literature," six interrelated "levels" ranging from study of the general mode of production characterizing a society at a given moment in its history to a direct reconaissance of the text in question. Between these two categories or "levels" lie four others—the literary mode of production, general ideology, authorial ideology, and aesthetic ideology—that constitute intermediary stages of analysis (Eagleton 1976, 44). Such a scheme goes far beyond what I have tried to do in this study, but it is a reminder of how much more complex and nuanced Marxist literary theory has become since the 1930s, when Andrei Zhdanov and others of his ilk in the Soviet cultural bureaucracy were laying down the party line on literature and social change.

Louis Althusser's conception of ideology as alluding in the main to our affective, unconscious relations with the world, to the ways in which we are pre-reflectively bound up in a social reality, is not entirely congruent with the premises of this study. Where Althusser is relevant, on the other hand, is in his analysis of "ideology and ideological state apparatuses," for it sheds light on Proust's educational experiences and on his class-determined ideological affinities, which must, I believe, be taken into account in the attempt to understand the world view that permeates his early writings. Proust's respect for his family's middle-class heritage, especially on his father's side, whose origins could be traced back to the late sixteenth century, and his absorption of the idealist philosophical tradition imparted to him by several of his professors at the Lycée Condorcet and later at the Sorbonne, were also important in that they combined to give him a feeling of connectedness to a social history and an intellectual tradition that he came to believe were worthy of being upheld. At the same time, he assimilated and made his own certain values of the French aristocracy, some of whose representative figures, notably the poet Robert de Montesquiou-Fezensac, led him to think that there were enormous benefits as well as liabilities in the qualities of a social class whose prestige was by no means entirely eclipsed by bourgeois ascendancy from the Revolution of 1789 to the birth of the Third Republic.

The manner in which Althusser explicates the ambiguity of the term "subject," meaning both (1) a free subjectivity that individually chooses and elaborates its own ideology, and (2) a subjected being who submits to a higher authority (whether religious, political, intellectual, or all together), is what endows his thinking with its particular theoretical value for our purposes. Every subject in the first sense must be related to a Subject in the second sense; the relationship between the two, Althusser maintains, is "speculary" and mutually necessary. In other words, there can be no subjectivity without a superior authority or value system to refer to, and which may assume different names in different historical periods (Althusser 170–183).

What this has to do with young Proust can be summarized as follows. First, as an intellectual and writer with impeccable bourgeois credentials, and as a highly educated individual with the sophistication, the personal charms, and the fund of knowledge to allow him to circulate in the upper echelons of Parisian society, Proust sought out and aimed to reach a highly particular readership that more or less shared his world outlook, was interested in what he had to say about literary and intellectual matters, and in general responded at the very least with a sense of amusement and recognition to the idiosyncrasies of his temperament and style. Second, his family background and connections were such that he had ample access to all of the resources from which his class and his literary associates drew for their sense of personal and group identity. Third, and perhaps most important for the line of inquiry taken by this study, Proust was a superbly gifted "subject" whose ideological choices depended on his relationship with an ultimately spiritual Subject for whom body and soul, matter and spirit, the visible and the invisible, while not parts of an abolute dichotomy, required a supreme act of artistic and philosophical synthesis to be finally brought into touch with each other and reconciled. Proust was not religious in a conventional sense and may not even have believed in any abiding way in God, but he did depend, for almost everything he thought and wrote, on the notion of a soul and of transcendence that expressed itself through, if not religious belief per se, then its nearest contemporary substitute, namely Art. If we were to remove the idea of the soul, of the inner spiritual self, of the individual as the ultimate arbiter of life choices, and of works of literature (like all works of art) as "the children of silence," that is, the products of solitude and arduous moral self-scrutiny, it seems to me that what we most associate with the Proustian world view would simply collapse.

The point here is that Proust's life as a writer hinged in tangible ways on his sense of belonging to a specific social milieu, to an educational establishment, to various elite intellectual coteries, to a family history and traditions, to a heritage of philosophical idealism, and to a long unbroken continuity of literary achievements in genres bequeathed to him by writers in whose work he found inspiration. To these ties I would add his sense of a political destiny that, broadly speaking, was transmitted to him and to many of his friends and colleagues by and through centuries of French nationhood and patriotism. Edmund White aptly describes Proust as "a fierce patriot" (77) who took great pride in his military service (1889–1890) because it was a way of fulfilling his personal responsibility to a collective national cause.

A framework of analysis such as the one provided by Althusser is therefore helpful for a general understanding of where and how Proust fits in the society of his time and of his place as a "priest" of bourgeois-aristocratic high culture in the last two decades of the nineteenth century.

Among literary scholars and theorists who have shaped their Proust studies in accordance with the theory of historical materialism, Michael Sprinker occupies a unique place inasmuch as he bases his analysis of the *Recherche* in *History and Ideology in Proust* almost entirely on the specifically Marxist concepts of "base and superstructure," "class and class struggle," "ideology," and "revolution."[5] These are the titles of Sprinker's book's four chapters and constitute the intellectual framework within which he conducts his critical inquiry. He acknowledges his debt to earlier Marxist and historically oriented interpreters of Proust such as Walter Benjamin, Alfred Cobban, P.-V. Zima, and Seth L. Wolitz, but clearly his book is in a class by itself in terms of its close adherence to Marxist theory. Sprinker tends to throw the weight of his analysis more in the direction of the historical than toward the specifically literary, so that one occasionally feels that some of the qualities of Proust's writing are pushed to the margins within the book's historico-theoretical framework. But this is a pitfall of all historically and ideologically grounded literary study, one I think is well worth risking.

In chapter 1, "Base and Superstructure," Sprinker takes note of different forms of interclass collaboration in France in the early decades of the Third Republic, dwelling on class compromises, the birth of the mass press, the ideological role of the salons, and the sense conveyed subtly yet persuasively by Proust of the ever more rapid erosion of long-established social hierarchies in France up to World War I. In this chapter, Sprinker provides a useful review of the ideological positions taken by the main characters and, reflecting an Althusserian influence, of the "principal state apparatuses portrayed in the novel": the military, the police, the schools, the diplomatic corps, and the salons—the last of which Sprinker sees as "the quintessential institution for ideological elaboration and social stratification in the *Recherche*" (47).

In chapters 2 and 3, "Class and Class Struggle" and "Ideology," Sprinker focuses on the *Recherche* as a "monumental funerary edifice" to the aristocratic world Proust so much revered and whose deserved loss of prestige and ideological hegemony after the Dreyfus Affair he felt compelled to acknowledge. The burden of Sprinker's analysis in these two parts falls on allegorizing each of the important characters who are made to represent or typify widely diffused attitudes and mentalities. Thus, for Sprinker, Swann's jealous love for Odette is an allegorical figure for "the chronic social and political instability over the first two decades of the Republic's life." The love affair between Swann and Odette "is not merely about sex and gender relations, it is at the same time a story of class relations, or more properly, class struggles." Swann's incapacity to control Odette, his jealousy over her infidelity, can be construed, Sprinker maintains, in "straightforwardly political and historical terms to indicate the bourgeoisie's tenuous hold over governmental—and to some extent social–power."

Sprinker makes some interesting observations about the politics and culture of Proust's social world and about the psychosexual aspects of his depiction of character. Much of chapter 3, "Ideology," is devoted to the Dreyfus case as a major event in French political history and as it is treated in the *Recherche*, which Sprinker relates especially to the "patriotism" of Saint-Loup and to the passionate Dreyfusism of the Jew, Charles Swann. He leans on Althusser in this chapter, while taking issue, it seems, with the unhistorical way in which he feels Malcolm Bowie and Paul De Man interpret the theme of jealousy in the *Recherche*, namely as a permanent existential fact of human life. But there are theoretical differences alluded to here that are not made entirely clear. The chapter concludes with a provocative section on the relations between "science" and "ideology," the second term connoting in the main that part of human consciousness that obscures or inhibits genuine understanding of oneself and the world. But Sprinker refuses to accept this dichotomy. He argues that "the reign of ideology does not come to an end with the emergence of science. But neither is the possibility of scientific knowledge forever banished by the unavoidable fact of ideological conditioning. Ideology and science name two permanent potentials of human consciousness" (153).

In chapter 4, "Revolution," Sprinker makes an argument whose point of departure is historical rather than literary; that is, he takes his understanding of the historical facts and claims that the *Recherche* "presents an image of French society that is broadly in line with the historical record of class struggles during the period 1871–1914" (156). Controversy about that history is implicitly obscured by such a blanket statement. Is literature to be evaluated only in terms of its adherence to a particular interpretation of history? Fredric Jameson reasons that "history is *not* a text, not a narrative, master or otherwise, but that as an absent cause, it is inaccessible to us except in textual form, and that our approach to it and to the Real necessarily passes through its prior textualization, its narrativization in the political unconscious" (35). While Jameson's statement does assume that, in the final analysis, "all literature must be read as a symbolic meditation on the destiny of community" (70), it does so in a manner very different from that of Sprinker, in whose formulation the complex mediated relationship between history and literature seems at times almost to disappear.

Sprinker dwells in the book's final section on Proust's dim consciousness of the working-class movement and comments, allegorically once again, on Robert de Saint-Loups's death, together with Charlus's decline, as symbolic of the French aristocracy's loss of its historic role in French society. The "revolution" depicted in the *Recherche* is therefore the definitive triumph of the bourgeois revolution, which began in 1789 and ended almost one hundred years later, culminating in the birth of the Third Republic.

Among critical studies that are eminently sociohistorical in their basic orientation but that eschew all explicit connections with Marxism or with any other ism is Lauro Martines's *Society and History in English Renaissance Verse,* a work I regard as especially important in that it takes as its province not the customary prose genres such as the novel that have long been the subject of ideological criticism, but poetry—and often highly personal and idiosyncratic poetry at that. Martines argues theoretically and demonstrates concretely that

> history holds nothing in airtight compartments. Social life—society—is a vital whole or unity of some kind. The truth of this is measured in the innumerable interconnections among the diversities of individual, group, community, and national experience. In semiotic terms, this suggests that meaning can be "transcoded"— transposed from one network of signs to another. (4)

Two underlying premises of Martines's project with which I am in basic agreement are, first, that every society "is a vital whole or unity of some kind" that "engages all who live in it;" (5) and second, that no literary text, no matter how lyrical, lofty, or subjective, should be seen as somehow ideologically innocent. These premises place him and myself in disaccord with proponents of the fragmented vision of life and language associated with postmodernism. It is not my intention to take up cudgels in this debate except to say that I am indebted to scholars who have sought to overcome the mutually hostile relationship that has long separated Jacques Derrida and his disciples from others, such as Martines, who continue to view society as an organic whole that can be studied in a scientific or social scientific manner. The dispute hinges on a whole range of unresolved differences, particularly different conceptions of language as used in literature, a realm of expression where postmodernist thinkers find a "playfulness" and an "indeterminateness" that are irreducible to interpretive certainty of any kind whatever.

One outcome of this dispute, since the 1970s, is the emergence of a new type of critical methodology that has arisen mainly in the Academy and that reflects the general crisis and breakdown of the political universe in which the older dogmatic Marxism could still function. Representatives of a neo-Marxist generation that came of age amidst the ferment of the 1960s and 1970s have tried to engage other disciplines, to show in what ways an historical-materialist criticism not only borrows necessarily from other schools of thought and other disciplines but depends on them for its own critical vitality and relevance. In his *Marxism and Deconstruction*, Michael Ryan was one of the first American scholars to attempt "a critical articulation" of Marxist theory and deconstruction. His example has been followed by many writers in such fields as sociology, anthropology, social and literary theory, and philosophy. In *Film, Politics, and Gramsci*, for example, Marcia Landy has tried to bridge the differences between Marxist and poststructuralist methods. While deriving her main critical categories from the "open Marxism" of Gramsci, she makes a strong case for the relevance to Gramscian Marxism of poststructuralist analyses applied to narratives hinging on concepts such as nation, patriotism, family, and religious rituals. Another example of neo-Marxist interdisciplinarity is Randy Martin's *Socialist Ensembles: Theater and State in Cuba and Nicaragua*, which borrows techniques of analysis from cultural anthropology to shed light on the ways in which both street theatre and professional theatrical companies have interacted with the larger political communities of revolutionary Nicaragua and Cuba. Martin's work is one of many similar attempts to work with Marxist methods and concepts as a living tradition that must continually grow in many different directions.

Two other categories of critical writing that help us to see some of the ways in which imagery, plots, themes, and character types are often the bearers of implicit ideological assumptions are those of feminist and queer studies. Teresa De Lauretis and Eve Kosofsky Sedgwick are among the thinkers who have mined these rich fields.

In *Alice Doesn't: Feminism, Semiotics, Cinema* and in other writings, De Lauretis maintains that feminist thinking necessarily involves political intervention in institutions and in the practices of everyday life. She argues that feminist criticism finds itself faced inexorably with the need to interrelate literary and film studies with society and politics, not only because such interrelations are required by the vicissitudes of everyday life but also because an activity such as literary or film production draws its vital energy from its embeddedness in specific social and historical contexts.

De Lauretis looks at forms of social life and their representation in cinema and literature as embodiments of "ideological formations." Her critical approach is shaped largely by semiotics, but there is a Marxist component of her analysis as well. Of particular importance is the manner in which she speaks of "codes and social formations" as these define "the positions of meaning" one finds in narratives of all kinds. As social beings, De Lauretis argues,

> women are constructed through effects of language and representation. Just as the spectator, the term of the moving series of filmic images, is taken up and moved along successive positions of meaning, a woman (or a man) is not an undivided identity, a stable unit of "consciousness," but the term of a shifting series of ideological positions. Put another way, the social being is constructed day by day as the point of articulation of ideological formations, an always provisional encounter of subject and codes at the historical (therefore changing) intersection of social formations and her or his personal history. (14–15)

This notion of interrelatedness between cinematic or literary representations and "the shifting series of ideological positions" taken by filmmakers and authors has a definite applicability to Proust's methods of characterization. Both the male and the female characters of *PJ* are seen from various and surprising perspectives, a technique that Proust will employ profitably in the *Recherche*. Some of the female characters of the *Recherche*, especially Albertine, change and metamorphose in unpredictable ways. Yet at the same time, they are also "constructed" according to a moral code that young Proust seems to take for granted, one that derives ultimately from his adherence to a Judeo-Christian belief system.

For her part, without addressing herself directly to the question of ideology, Eve Kosofsky Sedgwick performs an illuminating deconstruction of certain concepts and practices in contemporary culture. Building on Foucauldian foundations, but steering some of Foucault's techniques of analysis in new and startling directions, Sedgwick takes as her particular province in *Tendencies* the current construction and deconstruction of sexuality as seen in a context at once social, political, and cultural. Her key term is "queer," which she distinguishes from the words "gay" and "lesbian" in a philologically as well as politically suggestive manner. The words "gay" and "lesbian" have become, for her, objective, empirical categories, while the word "queer" "hinges more on a person's undertaking particular, performative acts of experimental self-perception and filiation" (12).

Tendencies contains a number of observations about Proust's attitude toward homosexuality that are pertinent to the concerns of this study, since it seems quite clear that his homosexual experiences and views on the subject heavily conditioned his world outlook and influenced his pessimistic understanding of human relationships. These experiences and views are only fleetingly present in his writings of the 1890s, but I think that they nonetheless colored his depictions of love and sex in both *PJ* and *JS*.

Sedgwick's comments on Proust deal with the *Recherche*, but they are useful for our purposes in that they reveal the extent to which he was a child of his time and class and borrowed from available contemporary sources—usually without crediting them—for many of the ideas which an earlier Proust criticism had ascribed to his intellectual daring and originality. She discusses several examples of Proust's borrowings. One concerns the "inversion trope," which he used in the *Sodom and Gomorrah* section of the *Recherche*, where a long disquisition on male homosexuals as "women trapped in a man's body" drew its basic concept from a widely known treatise by the German sexologist Karl Heinrich Ulrich, "who defined the homosexually oriented man in the Latin formula 'anima muliebris virili corpore inclusa,' the soul of a woman in a man's body," a definition Proust adopted for his own literary purposes. Ulrich reversed the order for lesbianism. Proust's thinking on this subject, Sedgwick trenchantly observes, "is famous as a thicket of pseudo-scientific self contradiction" (*Tendencies*, 59 n. 9). Another example concerns Proust's place in the ranks of thinkers who, at the end of the nineteenth century, despite their Kantian idealism, were strongly attracted to a certain form of positivism, or better, scientism. In the wake of Darwinian thought, Proust was very susceptible to theories of inherited dispositions and tendencies, and in general to a type of thinking that had many features in common with late twentieth-century biological determinism. In this sense, he and Zola were kindred spirits.

Sedgwick places Proust among thinkers who, in the 1890s, were interested in "articulating explicitly gay subjectivities, or ideologies that would defend anyone labeled homosexual against the grossest punishment" (90). To accomplish this, it was necessary to replace the still predominantly criminal model of homosexuality with a medical model, which is essentially what Proust did in his early short story "*Avant la nuit*" (Before the Night) and later in the *Recherche*. This viewpoint held that homosexuality had nothing whatever to do with violating any laws except those which a dominant legalistic and moralistic civilization chose to impose on a form of natural behavior, natural, that is, for the person who feels homosexual desire, which springs from a "disturbance" of the nervous system, not from any antisocial impulses. Young Proust expounded this point of view by having Leslie, the narrator of the short story "*Avant la nuit*," recall to his distraught friend that Socrates, in *The Symposium*, "happily approved" same-sex desire among his close friends.

One of the most provocative chapters of *Tendencies* is "Nationalisms and Sexualities," where Sedgwick makes a connection between Proust's Dreyfusism and his efforts on behalf of "gay recognition" which, she thinks, are the two "organizing principles for one another as they are for the volumes through which they ramify" (152).

While distancing herself from the perspectives of historical materialism, Sedgwick offers the kind of psychological and sociohistorical insights from which the ideological analysis of literature must draw.

The two titles *La Troisième République des lettres* (The Third Republic of Letters) and *Proust entre deux siècles* (Proust Between two Centuries) reveal the temporal, and therefore historical, coordinates of Antoine Compagnon's critical approach to Proust. In *La Troisième République*, Compagnon identifies Flaubert and Proust—the two writers to whom the book is devoted—as the embodiments of two different conceptions of literary study, the one, Proust, for whom criticism was still regarded as a literary form not yet given over to history, the other, Flaubert, as marking the transition of criticism to history. In this sense, Compagnon argues, the Third Republic of letters situated itself somewhere between the two novelists. But he acknowledges that these terms are insufficient to capture the nuances of difference implicit in them. What matters in his argument is that Proust becomes a precursor of critical formalism, while

Flaubert, often associated with a nineteenth-century formalism, foreshadows a later turn to a historicising criticism, as exemplified by Sainte-Beuve (1804–1869) in the first half of the nineteenth century and by Gustave Lanson (1857–1934) in the years that spanned the nineteenth and twentieth centuries.

Compagnon clarifies Roland Barthes's distinction between two types of literary study, the one interested in literature as an institution, where historical perspective is necessary, and the other in literature as "creation," the realm of the subjective and the psychological, from which historical categories are to be rigorously excluded. But Barthes thought of history in positivist rather than dialectical terms, and for this reason felt that literary history would have to be limited to areas of "sociological" and "institutional" interest such as sources, influences, functions, programs, and manifestoes, in short what Lucien Febvre called the collective and supraindividual side of literary production. The "individual" core of literature must remain in a sphere apart from all "historical" contaminations. It is not entirely clear to me where Compagnon himself stands concerning the concept of history that understands literature primarily in empirical terms, according to the positivist model, and the historical materialist or Marxist concept, where, at least as formulated by "the philosophy of praxis" in the Gramscian and Bakhtinian senses, the notion of a "total" historical process incorporates all forms of "ideological creation," including the literary, but does so in such a manner that the peculiarly literary forms retain their specificity and uniqueness.

Seen from a certain angle, Proust was "the incarnation of literariness," according to Compagnon, but at the same time he also displayed many traits that identify him as a conservative thinker on social and intellectual issues. Yet paradoxically, in his literary practice, instead of being just another exponent of the "Third Republic of letters," he was really a part of the literary avant-garde, whose adepts did not believe in a "national" literature but were convinced rather that "literariness depends on universality" (216). Thus Proust's relationship with the critical currents of his time was complex, a point Compagnon further demonstrates by noting that, in certain respects, there were elements of agreement between the thought of Proust and that of a figure such as Gustave Lanson, who in his history of French literature and studies of individual writers insisted on "clarity, good sense, and intelligence" against "mystery" and "incomprehensibility," as Proust also insisted in his 1896 essay "*Contre l'obscurité*" (Against obscurity).

But Compagnon also notes that the difference between Proust and Lanson was radical, that the *Recherche* was conceived as much against

Lanson as against Sainte-Beuve in its call for a literature that inquires into the soul, leaving "faddish" concerns such as nationalism, populism, and class struggle to the propagandists. Compagnon touches on various facets of Proust's thinking as they affected his literary practice, such as his ambivalent attitude toward "reading" and "erudition," his dislike of libraries, which he felt hindered rather than abetted the "spiritual" appreciation of literature, his analysis of artistic fetishism and idolatry (as shown for example in Swann's way of appropriating the iconography and imagery of certain paintings), and his views on rendering the thought of others, as he himself had done in his translations of John Ruskin. When he began the *Recherche*, Compagnon observes, Proust ceased translating Ruskin in order to "translate himself."

In his exegeses of passages where these facets of Proust's intellectual and creative life are of paramount importance, Compagnon adds considerably to the reader's historical as well as textual grasp of Proust's writings. Compagnon's primary contribution is to textual analysis, but it is highly problem-oriented; that is, its points of departure are motivated by contemporary concerns reaching "outside the text" in which such concepts as "genetic" criticism, terms such as "androgyny," and questions such as Proust's place in the history of modern culture both mirror the debates of the 1970s and 1980s and prefigure the interests Compagnon was to manifest in *Proust entre deux siècles*, published in 1989.

This title is itself a token of Compagnon's sensitivity to a powerful emerging current of thought that rejects all established forms of disciplinarity, all conventional lines of demarcation between this or that behavior, this or that mode of literary or sexual expression in favor of an attitude that allows for much more porous boundaries between different behaviors, much more intimate interrelations between seemingly disparate phenomena. Thus, the words *entre deux* in the title, which allude literally to the chronology of Proust's life (1871–1922), are also pertinent to the structure of the *Recherche* and its various languages, which reveal it to be a "mixed, hybrid, intermediary" work that occupies a space between the novel and criticism, between literature and philosophy.

Although Proust's aesthetic theories belonged to the nineteenth century, Compagnon continues, his work was also prophetic. He was the last writer of the nineteenth century and the first of the twentieth. Thus, having been born between two centuries was but one of many ambiguous features of Proust's life and work, another of which was his "androgynous" conception of human nature.

One of the most stimulating sections of Compagnon's work is devoted to an exploration of the ways in which Proust was attached to Racine, Baudelaire, Huysmans and the painter Gustave Moreau by reason of his need to place his own psychosexual and literary insights in a context of aesthetic theory and practice. What these pages accomplish is a kind of literary and cultural history that, while stopping short of broader sociohistorical contextualization, illuminates Proust's poetics as a product of a certain cultural milieu where the devices of "disguise" and "dissimulation," and the theory of the "enigmatic" sexuality of the artist make him a representative of the "decadent" movement in fin-de-siècle Europe. As Compagnon sees it, Proust's conception of the artist's deep sexual ambiguity was manifested in his portrait of Charlus, which revealed a strong reciprocal connection between "perversity" and "artistic creativity." How original all of this was in Proust's time remains uncertain. It would seem that such a connection was a common feature of "decadent" thinking about the interdependence of art and "madness," which had its antecedents in Plato's conception of the poet, reappeared in certain strands of Renaissance thought, and later found a congenial environment in some Romantic notions about artistic creativity.

Compagnon ends his study with a refreshingly irreverent observation concerning Proust's failure to subject the narrator of the *Recherche* to the same stringent moral standard he applied to Mlle Vinteuil and her lesbian friend, to Saint-Loup and his first lover, to the actress and ex-prostitute Rachel, and to Charlus and Jupien. The narrator never questions himself about the meaning of his own "repeated voyeurism;" in other words, he is treated with an indulgence not granted to other characters. "The narrator lies," Compagnon maintains, "he covers up the hero instead of exposing his 'vices.' Because the narrator is vicious, because the narrator conceals it from the reader, the novel is based on a lie. The search for truth is a disguise imposed on the reader: it is the major transposition of the novel" (278–279).

I shall have occasion in all three parts of this study to return now and then to the body of critical work that I have just reviewed. Although comprising only a small part of the immense critical literature on Proust, it fulfills an important purpose, that of helping us to situate Proust's writing in its sociohistorical context. In doing so, it suggests that while innovative and original, Proust's writing was not deeply subversive of established models and norms. His literary practices paralleled his "ideological" commitment to defend what was valuable in France's classical heritage while at the same time using and shaping that heritage for a task of psychological, philosophical, and spiritual inquiry into the conditions of modernity.

The first part of this study looks at the social world within which Proust came to an awareness of himself as a thinker and as a literary intellectual, from his student days to his début and subsequent participation in a number of Parisian salons. In this section I have kept the interactive nature of his personal and professional relationships in mind. Intellectually and literarily speaking, Proust was the first among equals at the Lycée Condorcet, and in the 1890s he acquired a prominent place in the ranks of the Parisian intelligentsia, but he was also engaged in a learning process; he willingly acknowledged what he had taken from his teachers and paid homage to his literary mentors. In short, by focusing attention in part 1 on the group of budding writers at the Condorcet, on the main literary periodicals with which he was associated, on his relationship with the composer Reynaldo Hahn, and on several of the salons he frequented, I hope to have shed some light on the experiences that contributed to the formation of Proust's world view.

Part 2 is an analysis of Proust's most important fictional writings published in the 1890s, the anthology *Les Plaisirs et les jours*. This book is the bearer of an extraordinarily heavy load of literary and philosophical referentiality. For this reason, it is quite difficult to know with certainty where Proust's sources end and he begins. But this is precisely the point, especially in a study of the traces left by ideology in works of literature. In Proust's case, it is never possible to separate his response to and use of other writers from his own interpretations and innovations with respect to these writers. He was attached to them, yet at the same time broke free from them. I am referring here not only to his French but also to his English, Russian and American models. He found "elective affinities" in many different times and places. Through an examination of how these affinities manifested themselves in *PJ*, it becomes possible to extrapolate from them in order to draw some conclusions about his ideological orientation with regard to such issues as social class, religious sentiment, political loyalties, and the role of art in society.

Part 3 concerns the ever more intimate reciprocal relationship in Proust's evolution during the 1890s between his work as a critic and his work as a writer of fiction. The inseparability of these two functions in Proust's case is as evident as it is in that of Charles Baudelaire, whom Proust regarded as the greatest poet of the nineteenth century and a critical mind of the highest order. With such a master, Proust first engaged in writing an ambitiously conceived novel, *Jean Santeuil,* and then, when that project failed to materialize in the way he had hoped, devoted himself to a critical appraisal of John Ruskin. This is the moment when, for all practical purposes, Proust's aesthetic philosophy assumed its mature form and his general ideological orientation became relatively stable.

While I believe that what I offer in the following pages sheds new light on the early evolution of Proust's conception of the world, I must also restate my acknowledgement that nothing I say here can somehow be detached from its moorings in existing scholarship and criticism. My study is part of a critical continuum, a collective project that connects each fragment of research to its counterparts in this country and elsewhere in the world. Criticism is an international undertaking; each contribution to it will, it is hoped, both resonate with similar or like-minded projects and suggest new perspectives to those who have traveled along different critical paths.

Part One

THE SOCIOLITERARY WORLD OF THE YOUNG PROUST

Chapter 1

Eros and Friendship at the Lycée Condorcet

The early education Proust received from his family and his seven years of schooling at the Lycée Condorcet[1] (1882–1889) engendered in him a strong attachment to three interrelated concepts.

The first was love of country, the conviction that transcending all divisiveness and egoistic self-interest there existed a union of people belonging to all classes who shared a commitment to the defense, honor, and glory of France. Patriotism for young Proust had little to do with economic or narrowly political aims; it was the living expression of a spiritual and cultural consensus, a natural organic connection between people rooted in their common memories, struggles, aspirations, defeats, and victories. It was a sentiment quite different in origin from the kind of rabid nationalism that gripped millions of Frenchmen after the debacle of the Franco-Prussian War. As these new postwar nationalists viewed the world, the French political order of the 1870s and 1880s had fallen prey to a degenerate middle-class republicanism. For them salvation could come only from a revival of faith in God, the Monarchy, and the Church, all three seen as bulwarks against further encroachments by a corrupt egalitarianism. Proust's family was republican as well as faithful to an essentially liberal-conservative outlook on the body politic, and he himself supported the Republic throughout his life, except for a possible brief flirtation with Boulangism.[2]

A second concept in the incipient world view of young Proust was the heroic ideal with which he came into contact in his classical studies and especially in his readings of the tragedians Racine and Corneille under the tutelage of Maxime Gaucher and several other respected lycée professors. From these readings he drew a conviction that personal honor should always take precedence over mere material self-interest. Proust's early literary exercises formed part of an educational curriculum designed not only to form character, which was the primary aim, apparently, of Proust's favorite instructor, the philosopher Alphonse Darlu (Ferré 221–230), but also to sharpen a young person's critical faculties so that he (girls were not yet admitted to lycées in the 1880s) could build an argument from different points of view, with appropriate rhetorical strategies. For this reason we cannot be absolutely sure when the neophyte writer was honestly expressing his own personal viewpoint and when he was simply performing a rhetorical exercise. Nevertheless, I think it is reasonable to assume that the prevalence in his early writing of this heroic ideal, along with his compassion for the downtrodden, the forgotten victims of human indifference and cruelty, reveal the extent to which his readings contributed to a deeply felt value system. "Literary studies," said young Proust, "allow us to disdain death, they elevate us above the things of the earth by speaking to us of spiritual things" (*CSB* 324).

Young Proust thought of Corneille's *Le Cid* as one of the most eloquent dramatic representations of moral truths existing in French literature. Although he was later to look upon Racine as a more important predecessor than Corneille, in his teens Proust revered both playwrights. To love Racine and Corneille, he wrote at about age sixteen, means "to love in the former the most tender, the most sorrowful, the most sincere intuitive understanding of so many charming and martyred lives, just as to love Corneille passionately is to love in all its integral beauty, in its unalterable dignity, the highest realization of the heroic ideal" (*CSB* 332).

A third component of young Proust's conceptual universe has been touched upon quite often by scholars and historians of the *belle époque* in France, namely his tendency to transfer to the realm of the aesthetic the impulses and ideals customarily associated with religion or with politics. The "religion of beauty" that characterized the belief systems of large sectors of French intellectual and literary society in the 1880s and 1890s had an ardent advocate in Proust, and not only during his student days. For Proust, the existence of beauty as perceived and created across the full spectrum of artistic forms was a permanent rebuttal to materialist conceptions of life. His early repudiation of materialism remained firm throughout his life, which helps to explain why he never once, in all his voluminous writings, makes explicit reference to Marx and why he makes only one perfunctory reference to Freud, almost at the end of his life (*Corr.* 21: 447). The importance to Proust of this idealist orientation cannot be overestimated. In fact, one could argue that the totality of his literary and critical work is one vast idealist response to the challenge of materialist thought. This difficult problem in Proust's intellectual development will be discussed at various points later in this study.

One catches a first glimpse of Proust's spiritual conception of art in the 1880s in a description he wrote for *La Revue lilas*, one of two or three ephemeral literary reviews he helped edit with his friends at the Lycée Condorcet. One of the distinguishing features of this brief description is the idea that the ordinary things he sees around him in his bedroom derive their beauty and mystery from the qualities he invests in them rather than from any intrinsic qualities they may possess themselves. Like the seer in earlier times who infused the ordinary world of things with his transforming and luminous vision, he, young Marcel Proust, endowed the objects in his room with an ethereal and magical charm:

> My lamp next to my bed on a little table, amidst glasses, little bottles, fresh drinks, small preciously bound books, letters of friendship and of love, dimly illuminates my bookcase in the background. The divine hour! Usual things, like nature, I have made sacred, being unable to conquer them. I have adorned them with my soul and with intimate or splendid images. I live in a sanctuary, in the midst of a spectacle. I am the center of things and each one causes me sensations and feelings that are magnificent or melancholy, which give me pleasure. I have splendid visions before my eyes. It is sweet in this bed. I fall asleep. (*CSB* 334)

Faith in art and beauty did not entirely supplant conventional religious belief in Proust's case, as we shall see in some of the guilt-obsessed stories of *PJ*, where one finds a full panoply of Catholic philosophical and theological concepts built into the lives of his characters. But it was not so much the fine points of Catholic doctrine and liturgy that won his early allegiance as its core belief that there is a spiritual essence in each human being called the soul that lives not only through ritualized religious practices but also in works of art, in philosophy, in diverse forms of creative expression.

Young Proust did not, however, assume a renunciatory attitude when it came to the sensual and intellectual pleasures of life. Indeed, there was a strong worldly component of his personality and outlook that emerged during his teenage years, one that we need to look at now in the context of his experiences and relationships at the Lycée Condorcet.

The prevalent image of Proust as a recluse ensconced in his cork-lined room, feverishly writing his masterpiece while coping with a serious asthmatic condition, is true, up to a point, of his life after 1908–1909, when he finally settled down to writing his great novel, but has very little (excepting the asthma, whch was a lifelong affliction) to do with the period treated in this study. From his teens to his late twenties, he was part of at least four overlapping but fairly distinct groups: his immediate family; his friends and professors at the Condorcet; the social world composed of both aristocrats and wealthy bourgeois who frequented the trendy Paris salons, cafés, concert halls, and theatres; and the intellectuals who gravitated around numerous literary reviews and occasionally took positions on public issues of the day.

Young Proust's indebtedness to his country's political, cultural, and literary heritage was no doubt influenced by the unusual attributes of his parents. Proust biographers have found archival documents showing that his father's family had been established in French provincial society since the late sixteenth century, in the town of Illiers, about fifteen miles south of Chartres (*Corr.* 1: 35). But while perusing a volume of archival documents one day in 1913, Proust himself claimed to have found a record of the Proust family dating back still further, to the fourteenth century (*Corr.* 12: 209, 210 n. 4). Thus for at least three hundred years, and perhaps even five hundred, the Proust clan had done its share of the town's administrative work, managed small farms, and pursued modest careers as priests, bailiffs, court recorders, and shopkeepers, always maintaining a solid if never especially brilliant level of attainment until the arrival of Proust's father, Adrien, who was born in 1834 and became the first member of his family to leave the Beauce region (Borrel et al., *Dining with Proust* 19). It was Adrien who gave a boost to his family's status when, instead of choosing the priesthood, as his parents had hoped, he opted for a career in medicine, becoming one of France's most esteemed epidemiologists. Among many other honors, he was admitted to the Legion of Honor for his work on cholera. His approximately twenty books, the best known of which, *La Défense de l'Europe contre la peste* (1897), is regarded as a classic work in the history of modern epidemiology and placed him at the vanguard of the new experimental science whose strict empiricism somehow coexisted in him with an old-fashioned respect for the religious faith of his ancestors. He was quite literally a self-made man who, in 1870, at the age of thirty-six, lacked only significant wealth to make him a fully acepted member of Paris's upper-middle class. This he obtained by marrying Jeanne-Clémence Weil, the attractive twenty-one year-old daughter of Nathé Weil, a Jewish stockbroker who offered Adrien a dowry of 200,000 francs. While Adrien's education was primarily practical and scientific, Jeanne excelled in the humanities. She had a good reading knowledge of Latin and classical Greek, spoke German and English, was widely read in French literature, and was also musically cultivated. She was a loving but often possessive and authoritarian figure in Proust's life, and there can be little doubt that her enveloping presence was at once troublesome and seductive to him. Her attitude toward unconventional forms of sexual behavior such as homosexualty was that it should be controlled and transcended, never indulged.

The marriage of these two rather exceptional scions of their respective families on September 3, 1870, and their subsequent move to an expensively if somberly furnished apartment in Paris's fashionable 8th *arrondissement*, at 9, boulevard Malesherbes, where they lived for more than thirty years, consolidated a substantial heritage of cultural and finance capital. Upon the death of his mother in 1905, Marcel received a substantial inheritance that allowed him to live rather comfortably for the rest of his life, despite the upsetting vicissitudes of the stock market.

The Weils were Reform Jews whose forebears had moved to Paris from the town of Niederwille in the Moselle region of Alsace-Lorraine in the late eighteenth century after previously emigrating to France from Wurtemburg, Germany. Although attached to Jewish custom and culture, Jeanne's parents did not practice their religion, and apparently had no problem with Jeanne marrying outside the faith. Adrien on the other hand wanted his family to follow his religion, but he did not demand that Jeanne convert, and she never did so. Marcel and his younger brother Robert were raised as Catholics; despite Jewish law, they did not regard themselves as Jews. However, for reasons having to do with the times and with the circumstances of the milieus in which the Proust family moved, many of young Proust's closest friends were Jewish or half Jewish, and several of the salons he began frequenting in the late 1880s were presided over by Jewish women, notably that of Geneviève Straus.

We need to consider here how young Proust responded to the ever more imperious demands of his burgeoning libido, which probably assumed a primarily homosexual character when he was quite young, early enough certainly to add elements of acute desire and pain to his fledgling efforts as a writer and thinker. The pain was not initially the result of guilt or self-doubt. On the contrary, in his teenage years Marcel Proust displayed a truly remarkable self-confidence in the realm of erotic feelings, and never wavered, at least in the letters and poems that express these feelings, from a conviction that boy-to boy-love was just as natural and just as pleasurable as boy-to girl-love. His feeling of strangeness derived not from his own instincts but from the disdain and mockery of schoolmates whom he regarded as his trusted friends at the Lycée Condorcet: Jacques Bizet, Daniel Halévy, Robert Dreyfus, Fernand Gregh, Robert de Flers, Louis de La Salle.[3] Like Proust, these young men were part of a social elite—Anne Borrel thinks of them as members of a "bourgeois aristocracy of the right bank" (*Ecrits de jeunesse* 11)—able to afford the reasonable but still, for most families, prohibitive cost of a lycée education (less than 3 percent of French children attended lycées in the late nineteenth century).

The excerpts cited below from two love letters Proust wrote to Jacques Bizet and to Daniel Halévy are the aspiring writer's first conscious steps in a life-long process of struggle toward seeing his homosexuality not as an aberration or a mental disease but rather as an expression of what Carolyn Heilbrun has called "an androgynous vision" of life. In his 1980 study *Proust and the Art of Love*, Julius Edwin Rivers, whose English translations of the letters in question I cite here, believes that if we fail to grasp the centrality of Proust's androgynous vision to everything he wrote— culminating in the so-called "sexual transpositions"[4] of the *Recherche*, where we are at first astonished to learn that many of the characters we had thought were heterosexual turn out to be bi- or mainly homosexual— we risk missing a key component of the Proustian ideological universe. What Proust hoped to achieve, writes Rivers, was a "transcendent unity" (229) in which previously polarized and mutually mistrustful forms of psychosexual life would be reconciled. In developing this idea, Proust used his own insights, supported by copious reading of all kinds of texts, from Plato's *Symposium* to contemporary medical treatises. He often vacillated in his attitude toward homosexuality, at one moment relegating it to the realm of "nervous disorders" and at another folding it into an essentially bisexualized conception of human life, but I think Rivers is right in saying that his basic impulse remained what it was when he was sixteen years old, one aspect of which he expounded a few years later in the short story "*Avant la nuit* " (Before the night), but from a tragic rather than hopeful point of view.

The first letter, which was evidently a response to Jacques Bizet's rejection of Proust's recent sexual advance, reads as follows:

> I have just read your letter at frightened and breakneck speed, under the watchful eye of M. Choublier. I admire your circumspection but also regret it. Your reasons are excellent, and I am glad to see how alert and strong, lively and penetrating your mind is becoming. But the heart—or the body—has reasons of which Reason is scarcely aware. I therefore accept with admiration for you (I mean for your mind, and not for the matter you refuse, for I am not [vain] enough to think my body is such a precious treasure that one needs great will power to do without it) but also with sadness the superb yet cruel yoke you impose on me. Perhaps you are right. However, I still think it is unfortunate not to pick the delightful flower

> which very soon we shall no longer be able to pick. Because by that time it will have turned into forbidden fruit. I realize that even now you think of it as a poisonous flower. So let's not think about it or talk about it any more: prove to me through a very long and very affectionate friendship—as will be, I hope, mine for you—that you were right. (Rivers, 57; *Corr.* 1: 103–104)

Young Proust was clearly saying in this letter that the sexual desire he felt for Bizet was not a poisonous flower but rather a beautiful and "delightful" one that promised joy to those able to pick it. He attributes the prohibitions of society to a notion of guilt about homosexual love that youth has no reason to share. Bizet seems to have felt that he and Proust could continue to be friends only if they renounced indulgence in Proust's fantasy of a homosexual garden of delights.

The larger issue at stake in this letter to Bizet is that young Proust was struggling to overcome what could easily become a crippling self-consciousness about his "difference" from his friends. He was intent on feeling whole, on integrating into his self image emotions that could otherwise carry him to paroxysms of frustration and anger.

The letter to Halévy was written in Proust's last year at the Lycée Condorcet, when he was studying under the tutelage of his philosophy instructor, Alphonse Darlu. It makes a frank defense of erotic and sensual pleasure that may have embarrassed its recipient but that perfectly expressed its author's admirable effort to attain an integrated, joyful acceptance of his own sexuality. The difficulty of such a struggle in the 1880s, and its still troublesome aspects today, are evident in Proust's need, on the one hand to assert the naturalness of his sexual feelings for his friend, and on the other to deny that what he felt should be categorized as "homosexual" since, as he argued also in the letter to Bizet, one had to distinguish between the natural expansiveness of adolescent sexual energy, which could flow in various directions, and the habits and relationships of adult males often driven to homosexuality as much by boredom with the women in their lives as by true desire. After asserting his "ethical beliefs" that allowed him "to believe that sensual pleasure is a very good thing," Proust went on to compose a flowery love letter that the guardians of Proust's literary estate did not approve for publication until 1970. Rivers is correct: the letter to Halévy "is a testimony to the philosophical and aesthetic importance Proust attached to homosexual love even at this early stage of his life":

> You take me for a blasé, worn-out person, but you are wrong. If you are delightful, if you have clear, beautiful eyes, which reflect the fine grace of your mind so

> purely that it seems to me that I do not love your mind completely unless I also kiss your eyes, if your body and your eyes are, like your mind, so graceful and supple that it seems to me that I can mingle better with your mind while sitting on your lap, if, finally, it seems to me that the charm of your you, the you in which I cannot separate your lively mind from your nimble body, would refine for me, by increasing it, "the sweet joy of love," there is nothing in all that which causes me to deserve these contemptuous phrases which would be more properly addressed to a man tired of women and seeking new pleasures in pederasty. I know some very intelligent boys of—and I pride myself on this—a high moral refinement, who once had a good time with another boy they knew. That was when they were very young. Later they turned back to women. If that was their end what great gods!—do you think they are, and what do you think I am, and especially what do you think I will be if I have already finished with love pure and simple! I will gladly speak to you of two Masters possessed of refined wisdom who all their lives picked only "the flower," Socrates and Montaigne. They allow very young men to "have a good time" in order to gain a little familiarity with every kind of pleasure and to find release for the fullness of their affection. They believed that friendships which are at once sensual and intellectual are better than relations with stupid and corrupt women when one is young and yet also has an acute awareness of beauty and also of the senses. I think that these old Masters were mistaken, and I'll explain why later. But I retain only the general character of their advice. So don't treat me like a homosexual, that causes me pain. Morally, I try, if only by means of elegant conduct, to remain pure. You can ask M. Straus what kind of influence I have had on Jacques [Bizet]. And it is by one's influence that one's morality should be judged. (Rivers 58; *Corr.* 1: 123–124)

Proust's intellectual and literary superiority was freely granted by all of his friends at the Lycée Condorcet,[5] but their attitude toward him sometimes bordered on dislike and even ridicule for what they saw as his "strangeness," his cloying politeness and affected mannerisms, his extreme sensitivity, and his need for what another boyhood friend, the painter Jacques-Emile Blanche, called "tyrannical and total possession" of a friend's affections (Blanche 96). The mixture of admiration and discomfort comes through, for example, in Daniel Halévy's portrait of the teenage Proust:

> Dear Proust, so wise but already mixing with his wisdom a nascent and painful strangeness. He appeared among us to be a sort of restless and disturbing archangel. We loved him dearly, we admired him, yet we remained astonished, troubled, by our sense of a difference, a distance, of a real and invisible incommensurability between us. (Halévy 121–122)

Halévy recalls in his memoirs of the years he spent at the Lycée Condorcet that, despite the embarrassment caused by Proust's personal manners and mannerisms, when it came to matters literary and philosophical no one ever doubted that it was he, Proust, who persuaded the others to go beyond the classics to embrace the poets and novelists of modernity—Shelley, Baudelaire, France, Nerval, Poe, Verlaine, Mallarmé and others—the writers who had opened up new ways of exploring the human soul through richly and highly personal symbolic language free of the constraints imposed by academic models of excellence. According to Halévy, a sort of pleasant anarchy reigned at the Condorcet, an atmosphere of discovery based on only two common points of agreement: a rejection of naturalism, of whose triumphs they were unaware or to whose virtues they were indifferent, and an openness to originality. In literary matters, as in painting and the other arts, Halévy recalls, "our teacher, our professor of taste in this lycée filled with functionaries was Marcel Proust" (118).

The lesson that young Proust imparted, by group consensus, was a belief in individuality in all matters having to do with the arts and philosophy. He demanded that each of his friends express his own unique voice, whose authenticity depended in turn on finding one's own truth, independently, no matter how difficult or painful such a search might be. Received truths, he warned, were worthless unless earned by their recipient; they might originate outside oneself, but their assimilation and expression had to be the creation of the individual writer or thinker. In the same vein, Proust was an eclectic; he never liked isms and schools, always insisting on the composite nature of truth whenever a fellow student or colleague seemed to be leaning too far in the direction of intellectual or sectarian exclusiveness.

Fernand Gregh (in *L'Âge d'or* and *Mon Amitié*) remembered that Proust had a number of disquieting traits. He could be snobbish and sycophantic when trying to impress someone of higher social station, especially someone with an aristocratic title, and his gift for humor and mimicry had its cruel side. These were aspects of the fashionable Proust, the man-about-town, the person that Blanche captures so well in his portrait of Proust at age twenty-one, the dandy with a flower in his buttonhole, the perfectly parted hair, the elegantly tailored jacket. But Gregh also recalls the teenage Proust's exceptional generosity and his spontaneous enthusiasm that overflowed whatever psychological boundaries his sometimes formal manner and attire might suggest.

When it came to pursuing a life in literature, Gregh and others agree, Proust established only two criteria for writing about something: that it convey an impression of "poetic enchantment," and that it lend itself to the formulation of a general truth. Such was the deeply personal code by which Proust began to live even before he had won his *bachelier ès lettres* in the summer of 1889. It was a code in harmony with the tenets of symbolism that were coming into renown precisely in the mid-1880s, when Proust began to think seriously about becoming a professional writer.

Young Proust paid a price for his difference, and for his first groping attempts to work out a theory of sexuality and of personal identity that avoided the pitfalls of conventional psychological and ideological dichotomies. The price was a growing pessimism about the nature of both love and friendship, which characterizes his writing almost from the beginning of his literary career. It is difficult not to attribute at least some aspects of Proust's jaundiced conception of love to his early sexual frustration and disappointments, and to the less than sympathetic responses he had elicited from his friends to what he considered to be perfectly natural feelings. Moreover, coming from a privileged, overprotective, cossetted family environment, where his parents and domestic servants ministered to his every need, fearful lest his asthma and generally delicate constitution lead to life-threatening health crises, Proust was often subject to agonizing episodes of insecurity not only about his literary ambitions but also about the integrity of his spiritual as well as his physical self. On October 2, 1888, the second day of his philosophy course under Alphonse Darlu, seventeen-year-old Proust wrote a letter to his philosophy professor asking for help in understanding and resolving a sense of being two separate individuals, the one who reacted spontaneously to experiences, and the other who dissected and analyzed them to the point of vitiating his enjoyment of them. His critical faculties, he said, had destroyed even the pleasure that at other times had been his "supreme joy, works of literature" (*Corr.* 1: 121–122). This, he said, had caused him to suffer intensely.

Eventually, young Proust was to overcome this split, what he called this *dédoublement* of his personality, in a satisfactory manner, and no doubt he owed his recovery to a variety of factors, not the least of which was his growing circle of literary friends and acquaintances that, by the time he graduated from the Condorcet, included one of the elder statesmen of French letters, Anatole France. When he left the Lycée Condorcet and soon thereafter began a year of military service in Orléans, young Proust had completed a significant period in his life, a period of self-discovery and selfdefinition whose impact on his literary sensibilities cannot be overestimated.

Nothing that happened to Proust in his student days, no loss or disappointment, not even the disillusionment he had experienced concerning love and friendship, are of sufficient magnitude to warrant our thinking of him as being in any way an "alienated" writer and intellectual comparable, for example, to James Joyce and Henry James, both of whose early years were marked by ruptures with home and country. Proust found sustenance in the literature and philosophy of his native country. He belonged to the elite Parisian intelligentsia by reason of birth and intellectual attainments, and had a strong sense of affiliation not only with people who shared his concerns and passions but with certain representatives of France's working and peasant classes as well. If there was sadness in his life, and constant fear of death, he was able to surmount these emotional difficulties without sacrificing what was most essential in his nature.

That his allegiance to an established way of life involved a significant degree of compliance with rules on his part cannot be denied. But his was a critical compliance, a voluntary but always alert submission of himself to literary and cultural values that he was able to assimilate and utilize in original ways. Proust was neither a rebel nor a conformist, neither an avant-garde exponent of the new nor a conservative defender of the old. His was an "ideology," a world view, that reflected what was at once most valuable and most in need of questioning in the bourgeois heritage.

Germaine Brée's *The World of Marcel Proust* provides a useful critical commentary on some of the problems of personal identity mentioned in this chapter. She is especially acute in her analysis of how and why young Proust felt himself to be so closely connected not only to his own family but also to what she calls "a collective past and future" that made sense to him. This side of Proust's personality, his feeling of rootedness in the French national culture, and his commitment to certain values— family solidarity, patriotism, a community of intellectual and political concerns—has not always received the attention it deserves. Brée contributes to our understanding of this Proust, the "national-popular" Proust, to use Gramscian terminology, far more thoroughly than most. Echoing Brée in this respect, Emilien Carassus notes that it was in his early years that Proust acquired the ideological attitudes and biases that were later to assume literary form in such characters as the family cook Françoise, on the one hand, and the heroic (even if deeply flawed) Saint-Loup on the other. Carassus points out that for Proust, these two characters embodied the most authentic and enduring qualities of the French peasantry and aristocracy. In this judgment, Carassus anticipates Michael Sprinker's allegorized interpretations in that he, Carassus, felt that there was an emblematic story implicit in Proust's portraits of these and other characters in the *Recherche*, a story of enduring loyalty and resistance to the encroachments of a rampant, abhorred "materialism."

While young Proust's views on great questions such as patriotism, honor and tradition may have been perfectly consonant with the dominant philosophy of his social class, his views on sexuality placed him in a small minority that spoke an oppositional and subversive language.[6] Rivers and others who have studied Proust's theory of homosexuality make it clear that he never fully resolved its contradictions, as can be seen, for example, in the opening section of *Sodom and Gomorrah*. Yet what is key to the two letters cited above and to the opening section of *Sodom and Gomorrah* is the assertive posture Proust assumed toward basically natural impulses that were depicted under a distorting light by the mores of contemporary society. It was thus in the sexual realm that Proust first experienced his "difference" with the kind of self-confidence and intellectual acuity that were to mark other controversial aspects of his life as a writer and thinker. It is fair to say that he discovered his literary vocation at the same time that he fully acknowledged his sexual sensibilities and identity.

But the notion of identity needs to be clarified, since the term has connotations of separateness and difference that, while pertinent to Proust's sense of himself as an artist and as a sexual being, do not define his essential feelings about himself in relation to the socioliterary world in which he moved. The fact that, as noted by Anthony Everman, he regarded his "marginality" as a necessary precondition of his creative life does not mean that he experienced his life in society as someone alienated and cut off from his fellow writers and intellectuals. Even in the sexual sphere he was not tormented by a feeling of constant estrangement. To cite Rivers once again, "in order to grasp the complexity of Proust's sexuality, we need only to discard the burdensome and misleading idea that heterosexuality and homosexuality are antagonistic and mutually exclusive" (53). In answer to two of the questions put to him when he was nineteen years old by a friend, Antoinette Faure, "What is the quality that I desire in a man?" and "What is the quality that I prefer in a woman?" Proust replied to the first, "feminine charms," and to the second, "manly virtues and sincerity in friendship" (*CSB* 336).

Proust's natural tendency was to disregard or transgress outright many of the conventional boundaries and distinctions that one associates, for example, with literary genres. He had an unruly imagination. Beneath his externally elegant and refined manner, there were the mind and vision of an eccentric, of someone who was bent on finding his own singular path through life. Rigid antinomies never had any place in his scheme of things. It was this lack of discriminatory boundaries between ideas and literary genres that gave him the freedom to move, within one and the same work, on many different thematic and stylistic levels. Just as "manliness" did not preclude feminine charms, so a designated literary genre did not rule out long meandering digressions from the formal requirements of that genre.

What this means from a broadly ideological point of view is that Proust's early response to the privileged social and intellectual milieu he frequented was marked, on the one hand by acceptance of established models, and on the other hand by a defiance of boundaries and by the courage to be different. The educational and social "ideological apparatuses" of which Louis Althusser speaks (in *Lenin and Philosophy*) steered him toward an acceptance of authority, a willing submission to established norms, yet his personal proclivities and preferences impelled him in other directions, toward uncharted territories. Breaking free of certain of the strictures of his society gave Proust the crucial critical perspective he needed to find his own voice and his own vision. It is no accident that he was among the very first of his group to come to the support of Alfred Dreyfus, even if it cost him, as it did, some valuable connections in Parisian high society. Proust lent a sympathetic ear to the arguments put forward by the advocates of French national honor, yet he was even more responsive to the cause of a man to whom the French Army had done grievous harm. One can say also that it was Proust's ready acceptance of ambiguity and his refusal to make blanket categorical judgments of this or that social class that allowed him to be simultaneously appreciative and deeply critical of the aristocratic and bourgeois classes.

Chapter 2

Three Parisian Literary Reviews in the 1890s: *Le Mensuel, Le Banquet,* and *La Revue Blanche*

Upon his return in the fall of 1890 from a year's tour of duty in the Army, Proust had to give serious attention for the first time in his life to the issue of earning a living. However, rather than deal immediately with this problem, and with his parents' support, he embarked on five years of professional study at the end of which, in March 1895, after obtaining a degree in law, he completed another course leading to a degree in philosophy at the Sorbonne. Proust touched on his state of mind during this period in a much cited letter he wrote to his father in September 1893, where he declared himself unfit for anything in life other than literature and philosophy (*Corr. avec sa mère* 52–54). This declaration did not save him from subsequent anguished if desultory efforts to situate himself in a practical way, in order to satisfy his parents' wish that he apply himself to remunerative work of some sort. Despite good intentions, however, Proust apparently convinced his family that he was born to think and to write. He continued to live with his parents at 8, boulevard Malesherbes and, after 1900, at 45, rue de Courcelles, until the inheritance left by his father, who died in 1903, and his mother's death two years later freed him from immediate concerns about supporting himself.

Enough is known about Proust's intellectual experiences at the Faculties of Law and Political Science in the early 1890s and, in 1895, at the Sorbonne, to warrant two observations. One is that his study of philosophy led him to the teachings of Emile Boutroux, for whom the moral and spiritual sides of human nature, while rooted in the same physical realities that govern the natural world, were also what endowed each individual person with his or her subjective identity and unity. This was a notion that Proust integrated into his own way of thinking about art and the creative life. The other is that the years of study he devoted at the Faculty of Political Science to politics, sociology, history, and diplomacy strengthened a tendency he had probably assimilated from his father and in general from the scientific spirit of the times, namely that of seeking the objective "laws" of human behavior that lay behind the apparent chaos of history. During these years he became interested in what Tadié calls "the collective and hereditary impulses" that drive the historical process (139). He developed the habit of comparing different periods and civilizations, and of noting their characteristic features. He acquired at least the rudiments of a philosophy of history that subsequently expressed itself in the tableaux of the *Recherche*. As evidenced by some of the notes he took in a sociology course (UI ms. "Proust 101"), Proust was exposed, possibly for the first time, to the idea that society could be studied scientifically, in terms of its informal and formal networks and relationships and not only in terms of its great personalities. The role of "genius" was always to be given its due importance in the course of human affairs, yet from time immemorial human beings had organized themselves into families, groups, and eventually into national communities by virtue of a collectively applied intelligence. Language itself was the product of an entire society not the invention of exceptional individuals.

Nevertheless, while he became receptive to certain of the social scientific methods underlying the teaching of history, sociology, and law at the time, young Proust remained, philosophically speaking, in the idealist camp. This becomes clear when we begin to evaluate his critical and fictional writings during these still formative years in relation to some of the leading literary and artistic movements of the time, as well as to trends in musical composition, where composers such as Fauré, Debussy, Saint-Saëns, and Wagner were eliciting an almost cultish enthusiasm.

Symbolism, still enjoying considerable reknown in the early 1890s, needs to be looked at not only as a literary movement but, more broadly, as an idealist reaction to the prevalent scientism that had characterized the mentality of the previous several generations. Two of the apostles of modern scientific realism, Hippolyte Taine (1828–1893) and Emile Zola (1840–1902), were by the early 1890s entering the last years of their productive lives. Zola was still active, completing the last of the twenty volumes comprising the *Rougon-Macquart* cycle in June 1893, but despite (or perhaps because of) his fame and immense popularity, his rough canvases were viewed by the coteries to which young Proust belonged as somehow alien to the essential aims of literary expression, one of which was to adapt French prose to the suggestive harmonies and metaphorical correspondences of symbolist poetry. That Zola was also, in his own way, a "poet" who favored the use of highly charged symbolic imagery to convey the ruinous effects and relentless energy of the new machine age (as in *L'Assommoir* and *Germinal*, for example) was perhaps not sufficiently appreciated by Proust and his literary friends.

Proust shared his friends' distaste for Zola's documentary realism, a distaste that was common in French literary circles of the 1880s and 1890s. It grew in part out of a hunger for spiritual redemption in a moment marked by vast alienating changes in the realms of industry, technology, and commerce, of which Zola's cycle of novels was felt to be the literary counterpart. It also grew out of a desire to explore areas of life that naturalism had either rejected or been unable to confront: everything that was allusive and elusive in life, everything that suggested the presence of a mystery at the core of human existence. Huysmans put it well when, in 1903, thinking back to his 1884 novel *À Rebours*, he recalled his feeling in the mid-1880s that naturalism "was out of breath, its heroes deprived of soul, ruled by impulses and instincts," and his equally strong opinion that a new novel of "artifice and illusion" should replace the "vulgar reality" of Zola's fictions. The fact that Huysmans had chosen a wealthy aristocrat as protagonist of *À Rebours*, whom he named Jean de Floressas des Esseintes, signaled an urgent desire to remove himself as much as possible from workaday existence as depicted by Zolian naturalism. One wonders whether Proust's choice of world-weary blue bloods as the protagonists of most of his stories in the 1890s might have reflected the influence of such novelists as Huysmans and his Italian counterpart, Gabriele D'Annunzio.

In Proust's own immmediate literary circle, both of his older mentors, Count Robert de Montesquiou-Fezensac (1855–1921), the principal real-life model for Des Esseintes, and Anatole France (1844–1924), looked askance at naturalism as a ruling philosophy and literary school. Montesquiou was the classic fin-de-siècle aesthete, enamored of beauty, a believer in realms of the spirit inaccessible to ordinary mortals, a man who epitomized the rarefied and exotic atmosphere pervading the work of one of his favorite painters, Gustave Moreau. But even more than Montesquiou, it was Anatole France who, for young Proust, established a standard of literary excellence that excluded naturalistic indulgence in scenes of physical and spiritual degradation. France's reaction to Zola's great novel of rural life, *La Terre*, published in 1887, was typical of a generation educated along classical lines who believed in good taste, skeptical restraint, a carefully controlled irony, and avoidance of descriptive detail about subjects such as sex and violence that might offend readers looking for spiritual sustenance from their reading matter. He accused Zola of having created "a heap of filth. That is his monument, the greatness of which no one can contest. Never has a man made such an effort to vilify humanity, to insult every aspect of beauty and love, to deny all that is good and decent" (Schom 117).

Proust was eventually to reject France's strictures against depictions of degraded sexuality, but in the 1890s he shared his mentor's classical ideals and penchant for ironic commentary on the follies and foibles of contemporary well-born society.

A curious coincidence highlights the gap between the literary worlds of Zola and young Proust, namely that the village whose life Zola recreated in *La Terre* was in the same region of France, the Beauce—along the river Loir, which runs through Illiers via Cloyes and Vendôme—that Proust was to immortalize in the first volume of the *Recherche*, but from a completely different point of view and with other literary purposes. This coincidence points up the difference in sensibility and outlook between two generations of French writers and artists. Zola was a man driven by the cause of social justice, which he pursued with painstaking attention to detail and zealous commitment to telling the truth of human misery and exploitation. He was a crusader bent on removing, or at least diminishing, some of the social ills of his country. Proust, although not indifferent to Zola's concerns, conceived of writing as a much more intimate and personal task, one that depended for its lasting significance on the writer's investigation of himself and on the ability to evoke a mood, a tone of voice, a moment of spiritual crisis, a physical place where revelations can happen that have more to do with the revisitations of memory than with the confrontation of immediate present realities. Zola's novels were "studies" of various social, psychological, and political problems; for Proust, the word "study" had an entirely different connotation, one somewhere between a composition designed as an "exercise" and a musical or visual impression.

Another way to think about Proust's literary values in the early 1890s is to consider the importance that Charles Baudelaire (1821–1867) and Stéphane Mallarmé (1842–1898) had in the artistic life of his generation. Proust's early writings are filled with Baudelairian tropes and images: the sea, sunlight, clouds, urban scenes of beauty and desolation. What Proust and many others of his generation admired in Baudelaire was the mastery of poetic structure and form that allowed him to be at once a profoundly original lyrical poet and a remarkable critical intelligence who had grasped all of the essential features of modernity. Unlike Zola's outcasts and misfits, the human beings who people Baudelaire's poetic universe experience evil primarily as a metaphysical rather than as a social reality. This way of thinking left its mark on Mallarmé, whose elevation of poetry to supreme status in the hierarchy of human expression gave to the literary life that character of religious transcendence that Proust was seeking in a moment of European history dominated by material progress, by technological and industrial innovation, and by market-driven forces. Mallarmé's notion of poetry as a means of expressing humanity's yearning for the infinite even while remaining anchored in an earthbound creaturely existence formed part of a conception of art and literature for which Proust had a strong affinity. The fact that Proust was later to take a position against the "obscurity" of Mallarmean symbolism does not mean that he moved completely outside the symbolist orbit in the late 1890s, merely that he was sometimes impatient with language whose hermeticism risked removing it from a potentially universal intelligibility.

Mallarmé's obsession with essences as opposed to contingent appearances, and his effort to make the poetic word a vehicle with which to strive for magical moments of communion with the Absolute sprang from a metaphysical anguish that Proust did not share, at least not with the same all-consuming intensity that characterized his older contemporary. Yet at the same time, Mallarmé's belief that poetry (in Proust's view, literary creation in all of its genres) was the sole means of redeeming the monotony, the banality, the ugliness of daily life took up residence in Proust's mind in a permanent and profound way. Although Proust was at times somewhat perplexed by Mallarmé, his scattered references to the author of "*Herodiade*" and "*L'Après-midi d'un faune*" indicate also that Mallarmé's total dedication to poetic creation transcended the reservations that Proust had about him (*CSB* 412–413).

Aestheticism and idealism were for young Proust ways of overcoming the flux and dispersion of daily existence, of giving permanence to ephemeral phenomena in a manner comparable to what the still new and vivifying impressionist painters were trying to achieve in their realm. The impressionists inhabited a Heraclitean universe in which everything stable and coherent was dissolved into ceaseless metamorphosis, but their outlook on this universe and their ecstatic visions of light, sea, and air, gave to these transitory and evanescent phenomena an enduring charm. If to this world of artistic and literary expression we add the influence of writer-philosophers such as Rémy de Gourmont (1858–1915) and Gustave Kahn

(1859–1936), both of whom called for a new lyrical novel situated between narrative and poetic modes of discourse, we begin to see the outlines of young Proust's literary value system emerge more or less distinctly.

The relations between writers, painters and composers were never closer than during the 1880s and 1890s, and Proust was no exception to this trend. In this he and Zola would have had a meeting of minds: the founder and major theorist of naturalism and the rising star of literary psychologism and impressionism shared a lifelong devotion to the new painting. Zola's *L'Œuvre* (1886) was much appreciated by Claude Monet, and Zola and the Goncourt brothers were important for Van Gogh. Debussy set Mallarmé's *L'Après-midi d'un faune* to music, while Gauguin enjoyed a fruitful relationship with Paul Verlaine. Nor were these interactions limited to the European continent. Baudelaire's admiration for Edgar Allan Poe is well known. The 1890s was a time of cosmopolitan cross-fertilization of the arts, a notable example of which was Van Gogh's affinity for the poetry of Walt Whitman. The Dutch painter was attracted by what one scholar of the French symbolist movement in the 1880, Sven Loevgren, calls "the American poet's rugged, inspired conception of nature, and by his gospel of universal love and brotherhood." Loevgren considers Van Gogh's "*Le Rhône: Nuit étoilée*," with its lyrical overtones, a "pure Whitman illustration" (180).

In the light of these various connections between young Proust and the literary, artistic, and intellectual currents of his time, the difficult question arises of where exactly to place him in the history of nineteenth- and twentieth-century literature, especially in relation to modernism. Edmund Wilson was among the first to place Proust securely in the history of modernism, together with such figures as Thomas Mann, William Butler Yeats, James Joyce, Gertrude Stein, and Virginia Woolf. In his chapter on Proust in *Axel's Castle* , while showing his appreciation of other facets of Proust's personality—his cosmopolitanism and, at the same time, his "Jewish piety, idealism and moral severity"—Wilson historicised Proust's worshipful attitude toward art and artistic creation, which he, Wilson, saw as part of a widespread reaction to the destabilizing effects of new technology and to the ceaseless flux of a civilization dominated by capitalism. Proust's typically modernist reverence for art, Wilson thought, "was a kind of compensation for the anarchy, the perversity, the sterility and the frustrations of the world" (159).

A work that sheds light from a different point of view on Proust's place in the history of modernist fiction is Nathalie Sarraute's *L'Ere du soupçon*

(1956). Sarraute was a practitioner of "the new novel" in which all of the conventional "objectivist" premises of narrative fiction were vigorously challenged. Her critical perspective on Proust reflects her commitment to a view of reality as marked constantly by disjunctures and discontinuities in all realms of experience, and as dominated by an indeterminate series of subjective perceptions on the part of both author and his/her created characters.

Sarraute saw Proust, with Gide, Sartre, Céline, and several others, as "precursors" of the new novel in that they had already glimpsed a truth concerning techniques of characterization she deigned suitable for an era in which "the novelist no longer believes in the solidity of his creations." Today's heroes, she said, are merely "a reflection of the author himself. They are no longer anything but visions, dreams, nightmares, illusions, reflections, modalities of this omnipotent 'I'." In this sense, she said, "we have entered the age of suspicion" (62–63). We no longer believe in the oldfashioned protagonists of fiction, because they have "the soft consistency and the tastelessness of food that has already been chewed" (65). The reader of today, she continued, "mistrusts the type of plot which, encircling a character like a little band, gives it, at the same time as an appearance of cohesion, a mummy-like rigidity" (67).

Sarraute credits Proust with having anticipated a key insight of the new novel, namely that fictional characters should be pried loose from the constrictive claim made by traditional novelists to reproduce something called objective truth. This was the only way that they could become part of "the infinite complexity of life" that, at the very most, can be revealed only through the evocation of "little true facts" of ordinary life. Proust had understood that fictional characters are believable only when created on the assumption that life means perpetual change, constant metamorphosis. There can be no assurance that a given literary character is or is not the same today as s/he was the day before, nor can objects be reliably described as if they were necessarily part of a single reality, fixed and stabilized forever.

Nevertheless, in an essay of 1956, "*Conversation et sous-conversation*" (Conversation and Underground Conversation), Sarraute judged Proust, Joyce, and other avatars of modernism to be "witnesses of a bygone era." Despite Proust's effort to "separate the impalpable substance of his characters into minute particles, no sooner does one close his books than these particles stick to each other and become amalgamated into a coherent whole by an irresistible movement of attraction." Sarraute praises Proust for the profundity of his writing, but notes at the same time that he never "contents himself so to speak with simple descriptions and only rarely abandons dialogue to the free interpretation of readers." What this amounts to is Sarraute's opinion that, in the final analysis, Proust observed his world from "a great distance" in the manner of the omniscient narrator of earlier times whose account of experience was designed to give readers the feeling that they have been part of an impersonal and "objective" narration of events. In Sarraute's view, dialogue, not description or action as conventionally understood, is the repository of "those subterranean movements at once impatient and fearful" that lie beneath the spoken words of characters and chiefly constitute the basic reality for the new novelists. Proust, she thought, had only partially glimpsed this core element of the new novel (83–122).

Let's look now at the character of the literary reviews in which Proust published his first fictions and critical commentaries, limiting ourselves to some of his early writings that did not appear in *PJ*, which will be discussed in part 2.

The first of the reviews under consideration here is *Le Mensuel*, a typically shortlived literary enterprise that managed to appear twelve times, from October 1890 to September 1891, in issues of ten pages. Its editorial and administrative office was at 45, rue de Lisbonne, the home of the review's editor, Otto Bouwens Van der Boijin (Tadié 144–145).

The review offered a sort of hodgepodge of news summaries, amusing lists of chronologically topsy-turvy historical events and birthdates, special features devoted to fashion, theatre, and the arts, as well as short stories, essays, and prose poems. Occasionally, the review published appreciative notes on artists and philosophers such as that in issue 4 on Schopenhauer, by an anonymous writer (Jan. 1891, 4–5). The essay propounds an interpretation of Schopenhauer's philosophy of music, which attracted the young generation of aesthetes, Proust among them, who conceptualized music as the only muse that existed in an absolutely pure state of her own, free of all worldly contaminations and therefore supremely independent. Music was a universal language in no need of vulgar accompaniments drawn from the other arts: dance, verbal text, elaborate stagecraft, and so on. This conflicted with the new Wagnerian concept of a "total work of art" culminating in modern opera, yet young Proust and others like him were able to accommodate these diverse aesthetic judgments by reason of their intellectual flexibility and rigorous search for new forms of artistic expression. Thus, as an expression of Schopenhauer's notion of "will," music expressed only the primal emotions of joy or pain; it did not express "facts" of any kind and had nothing to say to the mind, as descriptive music is supposed to have. It was because of popular inability to accept music in all its purity that this sovereign of the arts had been compelled to join forces with written texts in the form of Wagnerian "musical drama," where a fusion of the arts took place that constituted the creation of a new art. Such a viewpoint was consonant with Proust's evolving conception of music as superior to all other forms of creative expression. Whether he agreed with the author of this essay that "modern music" was misguided because of its lack of melodic line and its susceptibility to nonmusical interventions, cannot be ascertained. But it is fair to say that he was already, at age nineteen, very susceptible to the appeals of Schopenhauerian aestheticism.

Three pieces in *Le Mensuel*, an essay on contemporary criticism, "*Pendant le carême*" (During Lent), a prose poem entitled "*Choses normandes*" (Some things in Normandy), and a short story, "*Souvenir*" (Remembrance), which prefigures certain themes of "*Avant la nuit*," can be positively identified as written by Proust. "Pierre De Touche," the author of "*Souvenir*," was one of Proust's pseudonyms, while the other two pieces are signed "M.P." and "Marcel Proust."

In "*Pendant le carême*" (Feb. 1891, 5: 4–5) Proust displayed the ability to mix humorous commentary on current trends in criticism with a highly spiritualized attitude toward art, which he distinguished radically from science. He took advantage of, or more probably chose somewhat arbitrarily to accentuate, a recent shift of serious critical writing in France toward light fare such as vaudeville and music hall performances. He cited as an example of this trend a series of five lectures given a few weeks earlier by Hugues Le Roux in the Théâtre d'Application. Like Jules Lemaître, who had become increasingly tentative and cautious in his judgments of literary masterpieces yet quite "dogmatic" and sure of himself in what he had to say about café style music, Le Roux had worked out complex sociological theories to account for the phenomenon of the music hall. Proust attributed this tendency to a neonaturalistic, social scientific predilection for aspects of art that could be classified with "law-like" precision, which fit very well for music-hall comedy and song but which was lamentably inadequate to deal with art's "highest creations." Things that could be reduced to formulas, to objective "laws," he said, because they were "the most physical, the most material manifestations of art," had nothing to do with true art, which "escapes absolutely, through its quasi divine essence, scientific invesigation." Proust borrowed from Pascal to express his own conviction that "The Heart and aesthetic Thought have reasons that Reason does not know at all." This little essay is but one of many places in Proust's early writings where we can detect a fluctuation of attitude toward the relations between art and science. Here he excludes things that can be accounted for by scientific study from the province of art, yet at other times he asserts not only their compatibility but their interdependence. Proust had had an excellent education in chemistry, physics and biology at the Lycée Condorcet, whose impact often manifested itself in his support for scientific methods as a reliable path to knowledge of life's basic laws of existence. At the same time he mistrusted the incursions of science into the realms of aesthetics and philosophy, where he remained staunchly in the idealist camp.

"*Pendant le carême*" was dedicated to Horace Finaly, a future director of the Bank of France who was to become Proust's personal investment advisor, while "*Choses normandes*" was dedicated to Paul Grünebaum-Ballin, whom Proust had known at the Lycée Condorcet and met again at the University of Paris's Free School of Political Science. Such dedications, which characterize almost all of the many short pieces Proust published in reviews during the first part of the 1890s, were more than mere perfunctory acknowledgments. They reflected a need for intellectual community on young Proust's part, a desire to belong to a world where his idealism would be understood and appreciated. There was nothing in Proust's early writing that suggested a wish to reach a large popular audience. He remained focused on himself, on his sensations and impressions, on his memories, which formed a mosaic of lyrical fragments, precious moments rescued from the maw of time that he hoped would be appreciated by his peers.

In "*Choses normandes*" (Sept. 1891, 12: 5–7) Proust lyrically expressed his delight as he contemplated or recalled the seashore and the countryside of Normandy. He invoked its many moods, pausing to consider, in a manner reminiscent of the impressionist painters, the interpenetration of sky and sea.

More significant than "*Choses normandes*" is the story "*Souvenir*" (Sept. 1891, 12: 7–9) in its sad and tender recollection of a journey back to a friend's home in the Normandy countryside where the first-person narrator tells us that he had once spent the happiest days of his life. In the opening paragraphs, Proust drew a contrast between the physical features and natural setting of the home, which had remained unchanged, and the people in it, who had changed profoundly: the story's protagonist, Odette, who has suffered a terrible emotional crisis; her mother, who has died; her father, who does not recognize the narrator when he presents himself; and Odette's younger brother and sister, who live in their own worlds and who are unresponsive to the narrator's arrival.

Seated on the terrace with Odette, the narrator comments (to the reader) on how much the young woman had changed in just a few years as a result of the illness that now threatens her life. Indeed, he says, he would not have recognized her had he seen her elsewhere. Her once vibrant beauty has faded, her once lithe, athletic body has been reduced to contemplating the sea. Reading has replaced the vigorous tennis games she once played with her visitor and other friends. In sum, everything evoked in this scene reminds one of Dante's Francesca da Rimini, who tells the visiting pilgrim through the netherworld that "*Nessun maggior dolore/che ricordarsi del tempo felice/nella miseria*" (There is no greater sorrow than remembering a happy time in present misery (*Inferno* 5, vv. 121–123). The type of reading Odette now prefers is lyrical poetry, for "it is the music of the verses that evokes in me the sweetest memories and makes my entire being vibrate." As she speaks of these readings, and of her memories, the narrator notes that for an instant the young woman becomes animated, losing her "cadaverous color" and becoming pretty again. The story closes with the narrator's departure, his eyes filled with tears, his heart made heavy by his impossible wish to take the young woman in his arms. He walks along the seashore, thinking of Odette. The sea is "indifferent and calm," the sun has disappeared behind the horizon, but is still "splashing the sky with its purple rays."

"*Souvenir*" is an early example of Proustian memory designed to convey the mutability and fragmentariness of human experience amidst the permanence of nature, whose enduring beauty highlights what is charming but also what is transitory in friendship and love. Memories are filtered by a vision that tries to conjoin change and permanence through a prose-poetic transfiguration of ordinary experience into something mysterious and strange. Nowhere in Proust's early writing is the impact of impressionism on his mind and imagination more vivid than in this story of what had once been and could be no more. What is missing from his use of memory in "*Souvenir*" is the involuntary, epiphanic quality that was to crystallize definitively in the *Recherche*.

More is known about the review *Le Banquet* than about *Le Mensuel*, because the former was a genuinely collective enterprise launched by Proust and his friends who had attended the Lycée Condorcet together and because it eventually merged with the prestigious *La Revue Blanche* in 1893. *Le Banquet* appeared only eight times, from March 1892 to March 1893. It included among its contributors two major figures in the history of French socialism and communism, Léon Blum and Henri Barbusse, as well as the core group of the Condorcet, Jacques Bizet, Robert Dreyfus, Robert de Flers, Horace Finaly, Fernand Gregh, Daniel Halévy, Louis de

La Salle, Henri Rabaud, and Proust. Bizet, the group's secretary, issued a membership card to Proust in 1892 identifying him as an editor of *Le Banquet* (UI ms. "Proust 101").

The new review's editors made sure in their opening number that readers would not identify it with any of the current intellectual fashions, and that in literary matters they professed "the most subversive anarchist doctrines." (March 1892: 1: 5). This meant essentially that they preferred to be rigorously eclectic. Intellectual eclecticism, like political liberalism, were ways to distinguish *Le Banquet* from other widely known and established reviews, such as *La Plume*, *Le Mercure de France*, and *La Revue des Deux Mondes*, which were generally associated with one or two individual writers and with more or less distinct political and cultural identities. Proust and his group also intended to inform their readers in France about foreign art and literature. Hence the critical essays they published on Nietzsche, Rossetti, Swinburne, Tennyson, Tolstoy, and others.

The name of the review was borrowed from Plato, an already nostalgic allusion, perhaps, to Alphonse Darlu's lectures on the Greek philosopher. That the name was also intended to recall Plato's famous discussion of Greek homosexuality is probable, at least as far as Proust was concerned. Roger Shattuck associates the name with *la belle époque*, which explains the title of Shattuck's 1961 study *The Banquet Years*, although he was focusing more on some of the avant-garde writers and composers who came on the scene somewhat later than Proust.

The decision to launch the new review was taken at the home of Mme. Geneviève Straus (*Marcel Proust*, Usuels de la Réserve, 57), but the principal meeting place of the new review's editorial group was one made famous by Ferdinand Céline's *Mort à crédit* (Death on the installment plan), the Passage Choiseul, around the corner from the Paris National Library. On the first floor of Number 71, in the Librairie Rouquette, obtained through the good graces and with the financial help of Jacques Bizet's friend Henri de Rothschild, the group could gather in a room "magnificently surrounded by green and crimson rows of rare books in glass-fronted bookcases" (Painter 1: 141). Proust was accompanied to the first meetings by Jacques Bizet, but it was Fernand Gregh who remembered twenty-year old Proust most vividly, as "a very pretty young man, with a regular oval-shaped face, cheeks in bloom, eyelids lowered on black eyes that seemed to see from the side. He coquettishly lamented a slight bump in the middle of his nose" (*Mon Amitié* 32–33). Vanity was among the traits that Gregh disliked in Proust, but he describes himself as one of Proust's most loyal friends.

An annual subscription to *Le Banquet* cost the rather steep price of 10 francs, and mass distribution was out of the question. On the other hand, for a review founded and managed by neophytes, the printing run of four hundred copies per issue was respectable. Gregh recalls affectionately that "the literary public went to the great church of the *Mercure de France* and neglected our little chapel" (*L'Âge d'or* 153). But of course such elitism is implicit in an enterprise of this sort, and one gets the impression that Proust and his friends accepted their elite status as inherent in the mission of literary intellectuals.

Many of Proust's fictional pieces in *Le Banquet* were later published in *PJ* and will be discussed in Part 2. His critical writings in the new review, on the other hand, were not anthologized until 1971 when they were included in the Pléiade volume *Contre Sainte-Beuve*, and merit attention here. They reveal certain aspects of his "liberal conservative" political views and his continuing struggle against what he felt were the ravages of positivist materialism in France.

One of Proust's articles in *Le Banquet* on contemporary politics was entitled "*L'Irréligion d'Etat*" (The irreligion of the state). If looked at together with another essay, on Tolstoy's "*L'Esprit chrétien et le patriotisme*" (The Christian spirit and patriotism), written sometime in 1894 but not published until after Proust's death, a fairly consistent pattern of thought is revealed. Proust was troubled by the assault against Christianity that took the form of a secularized politics and culture in France, beginning with the series of reforms enacted by radical-democratic governments from 1881 to 1886 that made primary education (meaning children between ages six and twelve) free and mandatory and effectively forbade religious teaching in the schools.

Proust's point in "*L'Irréligion d'Etat*" (May 1892, 3: 91–92; *CSB* 348–349)[1] was that, like Robert Greslou, the young protagonist of Paul Bourget's novel *Le Disciple* (1889), who had borne the full deadly weight of his materialist professor's teachings, the French people as a national community was now being undermined in its most intimate beliefs by a government of radicals and socialists as guilty of fanaticism and intolerance as their religiously inspired predecessors. What had occurred, Proust said, was a substitution of state irreligion for the previous state-authorized religion. But the spiritual beliefs that had always formed the substratum of thought within both the Christian and the idealist philosophical traditions were in themselves living testimony to the need for a transcendence of materialist conceptions of reality. Proust credited Christianity with having inspired through the centuries all of the country's literary masterpieces, as well as its noblest expressions in the realm of speculative philosophy. He concluded by blaming the socialists for disseminating a philosophy of "destruction and death," which he illustrated with another literary reference, to Flaubert's radically minded pharmacist, M. Homais, whom educated readers would readily associate with a simplistic ideological adherence to "materialism."

Proust wrote in this article as a defender of tradition, as a writer and thinker loath to cast away the beliefs and values that had sustained the French people since the early emergence of a distinct national culture. It is evident that his one-sidedly idealist education did not equip him to separate himself from radicals and socialists in any way other than to spring to the defense of established religious and moral practices. Not that Proust had suddenly converted to orthodox Catholicism. Rather, what inspired him was the tradition of Christian thought embodied in the writings of such figures as Pascal, one of the thinkers who provided young Proust with some of the ideological concepts that underlay many of the fictional writings he included in *PJ*. Proust does not seem to have been especially interested in the church as an institution. He cared about its basic princples, however, as seen in several of the other short essays he published in *Le Banquet*.

Another side of Proust's personality, a cool skepticism regarding people who liked to present themselves as political pundits without however accepting full responsibility for their ideas, is quite prominent in his report on a make-believe "parliamentary assembly" organized by a group of university professors and students (Feb.1893, 7: 220–222; *CSB* 355–357). He offered some light satirical commentary not on the honesty of the organizers of this mock assembly but rather on their "ability [to harbor] illusions" which they expressed with a "slightly comical and very touching phraseology." Here again, Proust was critiquing the behavior, the language, and the "pretensions" of France's left-leaning and radical democratic adepts.

Proust's belief in the natural origins of patriotism characterizes his short comment on Tolstoy's treatise *Patriotism and the Christian Spirit*, in which the Russian novelist and philosopher had assumed a completely negative attitude toward intense love of country, blaming it for the narrowness and self-interested zeal with which nations pursued their respective goals. Tolstoy also spoke admiringly of the fact that, despite governmental repression, socialism was attracting the same masses of workers and peasants who remained indifferent to "the patriotism artificially excited by their governments." But Proust disagreed with this assessment, saying that workers and peasants were attracted to socialism not by ideal or altruistic motives but instead by naked self-interest, while people of the upper classes who supported socialism were the ones moved by genuine concern for their fellow human beings, since socialism was materially inimical to their interests. It was in this regard that Proust made the claim for patriotism that informs his essay, namely, that like the feeling of family solidarity, patriotism was what gave to a nation its sense of togetherness; it was what inspired the people in war, whose successful prosecution depended not on selfish aims but on commitment to a cause larger than that of particular individuals and groups. The concluding paragraph is worth citing in its entirety, since it articulates an ideological position that, implicitly, was to undergird much of what Proust expressed in fictional form throughout the 1890s, especially in *JS*:

> In the world of matter and of force one can destroy in order to create, use evil [tactics], avail oneself of contrary ideas, subordinate means to end. That isn't the case in the world of Justice and Love. The anarchists who imagine that after they have conquered the world by injustice they will make Justice reign, who think that they can make Charity triumph through violence, misunderstand the meaning of the words justice and charity and the nature of these virtues. All [personal] wealth could be equally distributed by force. In that event never will Justice be further from ruling in the world. Anti-Semites by being violent, slanderous, intolerant will be able to convert the world to Catholicism by force. On that day the world will be deChristianized, since Christianity means an interior God, truth desired by the heart, and approved by conscience. Let us never subordinate a precise and immediate duty of justice and charity to a duty that is obscure, remote and uncertain. (*CSB* 366)

At the same moment in which some of his coeditors and friends were showing interest in the thought of Nietzsche, in socialism, in anarchism, in the labor movement, Proust stood firm—with such thinkers as Pascal as his reference point—on behalf of the spiritual values to which he had been exposed by some of his professors at the Lycée Condorcet, values that necessarily colored his writings in the literary and philosophical domains.

For Proust, the word "thought" had a deeply personal significance. It did not mean a set of organized ideas or concepts deriving from study alone but, rather, perceptions or insights gained as a result of experience, meditation, and self-scrutiny. Thought was what gave literature its energy; it was the spiritual source and foundation of all genuine artistic endeavor. As such, it was closely related for Proust to the notion of vision (Deleuze 115–124). That is why it is important to be aware of what he had to say in writings that fall under the category of cultural and sociopolitical criticism, which cannot, in his case, be detached from the values embodied in his fictional and poetic writings. They are part of one and the same world view, of one and the same "ideology" as understood in a Gramscian sense, as a conception of the world.

In March 1893 the eighth and final issue of *Le Banquet* marked the end of a financially strapped enterprise. But only two months later, most of its writers agreed to merge their forces with a much more solidly financed and widely distributed literary review, *La Revue Blanche*, which in its first two years or so of activity was published in Lièges, Belgium (where it continued to maintain an office managed by Auguste Jeunhomme) but which in October 1891, because of the preponderance of French writers among its regular contributors, decided to move to Paris. The original editorial office was located at 49, Champs Elysées, the home of Paul Leclercq, then at 19, rue des Martyrs; in January 1893 the review moved again to somewhat larger quarters next door, at 15–17, rue des Martyrs. The review appeared regularly until April, 1903, when it ceased publication. Several of its writers affiliated a few years later with *La Nouvelle Revue Française (NRF)* attracted by the quality of *NRF*'s founders, one of whom was André Gide, who had served as *La Revue Blanche*'s prose fiction editor from 1900 to 1903 (Jackson 1960).

The three Natanson brothers, Louis-Alfred, Thadée, and Alexandre, the sons of a wealthy Polish Jew who had emigrated to France, helped to finance the new review and to pay its rent. They established the price of a single issue at sixty centimes, and decided on two types of annual subscriptions, one in deluxe paper and format costing twenty francs a year, the other an ordinary edition at seven francs a year. The Natanson brothers also had a strong interest in the figurative arts, which accounts in part for the review's many articles on contemporary painting, and Alexandre Natanson, who had literary ability as well as business acumen, became the review's director in October 1891, when it began to appear monthly in issues of forty-eight pages (Nattier-Natanson 1959). In January 1894 it increased to one hundred pages. Its average printing run in the first few years was one thousand three hundred copies, but at the end of 1891 it jumped to two thousand five hundred copies. It had many retail outlets all over Paris, in other French cities, and in Belgium. Through Thadée Natanson, *La Revue Blanche* attracted the painters Pierre Bonnard, Edouard Vuillard, Henri de Toulouse-Lautrec, Ker-Roussel, and many others, some of whom created drawings, prints and engravings that appeared frequently in the new review. Another artistic boon for the review was provided by Louis-Alfred Natanson, who was the owner of an important art gallery, the Durand-Ruel, on rue Royale, where innovative and experimental painting was welcomed and encouraged.

Several features of *La Revue Blanche* stand out as one scans the review during its first four to five years of activity, features that had a natural appeal for a young writer such as Proust. Its main pool of writers had cosmopolitan tastes and interests, and the review opened its pages to writings by and about novelists, poets, composers, essayists, and painters from various countries, such as Chekhov, Gorky, Knut Hamsun, Alexander Herzen, Nietzsche, Max Nordau, Strindberg, Tolstoy, Mark Twain, and Oscar Wilde. From the mid-1890s to 1903, the French and Belgian contingents included such innovative figures as Apollinaire, Gide, Jammes, Mallarmé, Maeterlinck, Moréas, Verhaeren, and Verlaine. Unlike *Le Banquet*, which was an all-male affair, *La Revue Blanche* included two women in its editorial group, Marthe Mellot and Misia Godebska. It stayed abreast of work undertaken by other literary and cultural reviews—*Le Mercure de France*, *Ecrits pour l'Art*, *La Revue Indépendante*, *Ermitage*, *La Plume*, *La Revue Moderne*, and so on—magnanimously publishing their names and addresses for the convenience of its readers. It took a lively interest in the intellectual foundations of movements such as symbolism and naturalism, and tried to avoid being identified with any one school or trend, although most people seem to have thought of it as being symbolist in orientation.

Two other noteworthy aspects of *La Revue Blanche* are its responsiveness to new trends in music and painting as well as in literature, and its commitment to an extreme form of philosophical as well as aesthetic individualism, what Anne B. Jackson has called its "cult of the individual personality" (23, 141). There were ample literary sources for such a concept in the culture of the time. Maurice Barrès's trilogy, *Le Culte du moi* (1888–1891) and, later in the decade, Gide's *Nourritures terrestres* (1897) come to mind. But while Gide was an exponent of individual difference (sexual, political, literary) and the cultivation of one's own spiritual resources, Barrès was soon to become a leading theorist of political culture rooted in a people's "blood and soil" and an advocate of the sort of traditionalism that was to characterize the right-wing movement *L'Action Française* founded soon after the turn of the century by Charles Maurras. An essay in *La Revue Blanche* titled "*Lettre à un lecteur facile*" (Letter to an easy-going reader) by Barrès expounded a form of individualism so solipsistic in character that one wonders whether he was writing tongue in cheek or whether the review's editors had somehow hoped to expose the author to ridicule. Speaking as a confirmed "subjectivist" against all believers in "objective knowledge" and in the reality of the external world, Barrès asserted that "action is to want to act on the external world, and if that world does not exist, then we can only act on our selves." Any other conception of reality was false and illusory. He recommended the third novel of his cycle, *Le Jardin de Bérénice*, to his readers because, he said, in that work, he felt he had moved much closer than in the preceding volumes towards attaining a "unity, making possible a potential resolution of the contradictions of the Universe and of the Self that creates it" (Feb. 1892, 5: 65–69).

Lucien Muhlfeld, the review's editor-in-chief, was not a solipsist in the Barresian mold but rather an avowed elitist, arguing that the present "crisis in the relationship between writers and readers" made unavoidable a "public art" for the masses and an art for the select few able to breathe in the effluvia of superior creative minds, whom he called the "mandarins" charged with the responsibility of "safeguarding the disinterested artistic tradition" (Jan. 1892, 4: 53–61). One suspects a Schopenhauerian influence in Muhlfeld's emphasis on the "disinterested" nature of artists and their creations. Rémy de Gourmont seconded Muhlfeld in claiming for the contemporary symbolist movement a poetic practice based on the poet's own singular conceptualization of a symbolic universe (as in Maeterlinck's work) very different in nature from the "universal symbolic systems" of earlier historical periods.

As for the overall tendencies of the writers who published in *La Revue Blanche*, one is struck by their sadness and pessimism, their fondness for withdrawal into dream and fantasy, their preference for the imagery of dawn and twilight (the crepuscular atmosphere of the poetry is pervasive), their stress on "interiority" as the distinguishing mark of great creative personalities, and by their contemplative attitude toward nature and artistic beauty.

As far as I can determine, of the writings Proust published in *La Revue Blanche*, only two, the short story "*Avant la nuit* " (Before the night) and a controversial essay on the language of symbolism called "*Contre l'obscurité*" (Against obscurity), did not appear in *PJ*. The essay will be discussed in chapter 9. The story, Proust's first published work dealing with homosexuality and lesbianism, calls for immediate commentary.

"*Avant la nuit* " (Dec. 1893, 26: 381–385; Laget 247–252) is reminiscent in some respects of "*Souvenir*" in that it concerns a relationship between a young man and a young woman who have been close friends but not lovers. The woman, Françoise, is dangerously weak physically, while the young man, Leslie, the narrator, does his best to comfort and reassure her as she undergoes a painful crisis. As in "*Souvenir,*" the two friends are seated on a terrace overlooking the sea. The time of day, habitually favored by the writers of *La Revue Blanche,* is twilight; the setting sun casts its last rays through the branches of nearby apple and poplar trees. Proust once again treats us to a serene but melancholy Normandy landscape that forms a backdrop to the guilt-wracked confessional impulses of the young woman.

The confessional mode plays an important part in several of Proust's early short stories; in this case Françoise feels an overwhelming need to tell Leslie that it had been his sage opinion expressed some years ago concerning lesbian sexuality that had precipitated her engaging in sexual relations with another woman. This revelation accompanies another, that she had tried to kill herself, unsuccessfully, but that because the bullet could not be safely extracted, causing other complications, she would soon die.

The story's emotional content derives from the retrospective revelation of mutual esteem and love that the two young people had always felt for each other. On Leslie's part, he had always looked upon their chaste relationship as superior to any conceivable sexual liaison with her; indeed, he had always thought of her "as supernatural as a madonna, as sweet as a wet-nurse, I adored you and you cradled me." He speaks of her "maternal hands," reassuring her over and over again that her sense that she had given him very little of herself was untrue. Françoise is tormented by a lapse in her normal heterosexual behavior that had taken place not long after she lost her husband at age twenty. She reveals that it had been precisely Leslie's nonjudgmental attitude toward homosexuality and lesbianism that had pushed her over the edge into the act or acts the memory of which is now tormenting her. Thus by reliving what they had shared in the past and comforting each other in the present, the two young people undergo a sort of cleansing process.

The story has three significant features: the painterly imagery with which Proust evokes the natural surroundings; the delicacy of his psychological analysis as Leslie follows the ebb and flow of Françoise's feelings; and the little disquisition on homosexuality that Proust provides by having Françoise repeat what Leslie had once said to her in defense of a form of love caused by "a nervous disorder that is too exclusively present to warrant a moral content." As I have already noted, it was the persuasiveness of his argument that had caused her to risk her sexual adventure with another woman. Ironically, therefore, her best friend led her to do something for which she later was to feel so guilt-ridden that she had tried to take her own life.

The little disquisition begins with an allusion to the practices permitted by Socrates, then stops briefly to consider the medical side of homosexuality, and concludes with an aesthetically based argument that "in truly artistic natures physical attraction or repulsion is modified by the contemplation of the beautiful." The beautiful can assume both masculine and feminine forms, and there is no reason, Leslie had argued, why some people should not find someone of their own sex as beautiful as someone of the opposite sex.

The passage in which Françoise repeats verbatim what Leslie had said to her is typical of Proust's writing almost from the beginning of his literary activity. One could argue that these little treatises vitiate the lyrical and narrative force of the story, but Proust was of another opinion. He felt that the "thought" encapsulated in such passages enriched the narrative by heightening and elucidating its principal conflicts. It is true that this and countless other similar passages in Proust's fictions could virtually stand on their own, outside the framework of the story, as learned commentaries on various questions. Proust had a much broader view of the relationship between descriptive and analytical writing, between dramatic action and critical reflection. He did not feel bound by the usual constraints of genre and stylistic consistency. This openness to what Raymond Williams calls "the multiplicity of writing" (145-150) is, I would argue, one of the most intriguing aspects of Proust's stories and of his great novel.

It is the Christian concept of moral and physical purity, and possible redemption through confession, that one finds at the heart of "*Avant la nuit*," literally meaning before nightfall and symbolically before death. Both Leslie and Françoise see their friendship as untainted by the "normal" vicissitudes of human relationships in which sexual impulses play a central role. Leslie tells us that he worships and adores Françoise, and Françoise fears that his admiration will be affected by her confession. Resolution at the end comes through their sharing a common emotional and philosophical attitude. Proust focuses on this process of illumination through which the two characters move from ignorance and misperception to some sort of personal truth. It is a truth gained at the price of many tears and with the feeling that never before this twilight enounter had their friendship been marked "by so much bad and so much good."

La Revue Blanche generally preferred not to become embroiled in political issues. One important exception to this was the reaction of many of its writers to the first explosive accusations made against Alfred Dreyfus in October 1894 that led in December to his conviction and imprisonment on Devils Island. Like many others in France, Proust may have accepted the guilty verdict, although Claude Francis and Fernande Gontier claim that Proust and his brother, Robert, were both Dreyfusards since 1894 (87). In any event, two years later, when stories of trumped-up charges began to leak in the press, Proust too had doubts about Dreyfus's guilt, doubts that were strengthened by the campaign to retry Dreyfus begnning in 1897 in which he was among the leaders of the revisionists. Proust was also among the approximately fifty signers (together with most of his friends from the Lycée Condorcet) of the "Protest" against "the violation of juridical forms at the trial of 1894" that appeared on the first page of the newspaper *L'Aurore* on January 14, 1898, the day after the same newspaper published Zola's *"J'accuse!"* Anne Jackson describes *La Revue Blanche*, supported by the salon of Mme Straus, as "a rallying point of writers, artists, intellectuals convinced of Dreyfus's innocence and against the 1894 sentence" (88). To that extent, Proust was part of a struggle that split French society into two warring camps, the one intent on defending the honor of the French Army at any cost, and ready to use whatever popular prejudices were available, especially anti-Semitism, the other those who, with Georges Clemenceau, believed that "there can be no patriotism without justice. The true patriots are we who fight to obtain justice and to liberate France from the yoke of gold-braided infallibilty" (Tuchman 189).

Chapter 3

With Reynaldo Hahn in Town and Country

Eros and friendship were both important in the relationship between Proust and Reynaldo Hahn (1875–1947). Their sexual intimacy lasted for approximately a year, from June 1894, when they met at the Paris residence of Madeleine Lemaire,[1] to the summer of 1895, when mutual jealousy and resentment led to their breakup as lovers. Hahn's place was quickly taken by seventeen-year-old Lucien Daudet.[2] However, the friendship between Proust and Hahn endured until the former's death in 1922. The two men shared many interests, collaborated artistically in various ways, stimulated each other intellectually, enjoyed touring the countryside and the seaside together, and had a whole social world in common, the world of the Parisian salons, cafés, concert halls, museums, art galleries, theatres, and opera houses. They also complemented each other in an artistically productive way. In a letter of May 1895 to Suzette Lemaire, Madeleine's daughter, Proust spoke of this aspect of his relationship with Hahn. While he, primarily a man of letters, believed that music was in essence "infinite" in its ability to touch the soul, and that it existed in an autonomous and superior realm of its own, Hahn conceived of music as an adjunct to the word, to thought; for him music was the handmaiden to poetry, or more generally to feelings and thoughts as articulated by the human voice. In other words, Proust concluded, Hahn was a "literary musician," while he, Proust, tried to infuse something of the "infinite" power of music into literary expression (*Corr.* 1: 388–391). It was because of this complementarity that Proust gladly entrusted Hahn with the task of writing piano accompaniments to poems he wrote on four composers and four painters, the scores of which were published, along with the poems, in the original 1896 edition of *PJ*.

Hahn was four years younger than Proust, having been born in Caracas, Venezuela, on August 9, 1875. His father, Carlos, of Dutch Jewish origin, decided for political reasons to return to his native Europe in 1878 with his wife, Elena Maria Echnagucia, with whom he had twelve children. They settled in Paris, at 6, rue du Cirque. Already fluent in Spanish, Reynaldo quickly mastered French and, more remarkably, was so precociously gifted in music that at age six he made his piano début at the Princesse Mathilde Bonaparte's home on the rue de Berri, where he played and sang melodies from several of Offenbach's *opéras bouffes*. At age ten he began attending the Paris Conservatory of Music, and at age thirteen, while studying composition under Jules Massenet, he wrote the song based on Victor Hugo's poem "*Si mes vers avaient des ailes*" (If my poems had wings) for which he is perhaps most affectionately remembered. One of his competitors in the field of musical composition inspired by poetry, and as a much sought after figure at musical soirées and fancy dress parties, was Léon Delafosse, with whom Proust also collaborated in 1895. Proust's poem "*Mensonges* " (Lies) was one of six poems set to music by Delafosse that appeared in a folio of sheet music published in 1895, containing one poem each by Paul Bourget, Proust, Pierre Quillard, Marceline Desbordes-Valmore, and two by Robert de Montesquiou.[3] Such partnerships were very much in fashion in the 1890s, due to a widespread feeling that all of the arts benefited from close interaction with their sister muses, as well as to the influence of Richard Wagner's concept of the *Gesamtkunstwerk*, the total work of art embracing all forms of artistic expression.[4] A partial list of writers whose poems Hahn either set to music or for which he wrote piano accompaniments includes Théodore de Banville, François Coppée, Alphonse Daudet, Théophile Gautier, Heinrich Heine, Victor Hugo, Jean Lahor, Leconte de Lisle, Pierre Loti, Alfred Musset, Jean Racine, and Paul Verlaine.[5] His melodies inspired by some of Verlaine's lyrical poems of 1891–1892 brought Hahn considerable notoreity. His tastes were therefore in harmony with the poetic sensibilities of the nineteenth century, Racine being the only poet belonging to another era.

In addition to his reputation as a talented composer of art songs, young Hahn also achieved a place for himself in the field of light opera, with such works as *L'Ile du rêve* (Island of dreams), based on a story by Pierre Loti, which was produced in 1898 at the Opéra Comique to favorable reviews. Yet he never attained the renown of a Fauré, a Bizet, a Debussy, a Gounod, a Franck, a Saint-Saëns, or even a Meyerbeer. The reason may lie in the fact that Hahn's music was perceived as intimate and conversational, appropriate for the drawing room, melodic and charming, but rather facile, lacking depth and strong originality. His great accomplishment, by consensus, were his songs, written for the most part when he was a conservatory student, before he was twenty-one.

Hahn was known as a capitvating performer in the fashionable salons of the day, where he used his attractive baritone voice and accompanied himself at the piano with a casual finesse that always won over his audiences (Delage). His concert style was a highly artificial and studied one that made free use of mezza voce and falsetto (Barker 55). He sang "conversationally," almost always with a cigarette dangling from his lips, and a glass of wine at his side, which he sipped judiciously and elegantly between numbers. He wore a flower in his lapel, but he did not come to his recitals thus adorned; the flower was always one that he picked from his host or hostess's vase as he approached the piano. In sum, he had the cool demeanor and aplomb of a polished performer, even at an extremely young age. He had the ability to make a difficult task seem effortless, thus putting his audiences at their ease and virtually guaranteeing himself several encores and repeat performances.

A caricature of Hahn drawn many years later by Jean Cocteau shows him at the piano, a cane on his left arm, dresssed in formal attire and top hat, smoking a cigarette and looking quite dandyish. Henri de Régnier began a little poem on Hahn (Huas 104) with the words "*Reynaldo, vous chantez, cigarette à la bouche, / Des airs vénitiens langoureux et troublants*" (Reynaldo, you sing, with a cigarette in your mouth, languorous and disquieting Venetian airs) and Mallarmé composed the following skillfully rhymed quatrain, no doubt inspired by one of Hahn's engaging recitals (Gavoty 159): *Le pleur qui chante au langage/Du poète, Reynaldo/Hahn tendrement le dégage/Comme en l'allée un jet d'eau.* An unrhymed translation: The tears that sing in poetic mode / Reynaldo Hahn tenderly releases / like a fresh stream of water on a back street.

Hahn's writings, apart from his music criticism, include a diary, *Notes: Journal d'un musicien*, and several volumes of lectures he gave at various points in his career, one of the most interesting of which was on the art and science of singing. The published parts of the diary, from which Hahn readily admitted he had excised many pages that were "too intimate" for public scrutiny, show him to be highly literate, conversant with current trends in the arts, widely traveled, and sensitive to many of the same images and motifs as Proust. Like Proust, he was obsessed by sunlight, and by shades and nuances of light, which made him responsive to the paintings of Monet. His observations about Jean Chardin recall Proust's views on the eighteenth-century painter, in that he preferred Chardin's humble stilllifes and domestic interiors to the grandly classical paintings of a Poussin, which he had seen at the Louvre and at London's National Gallery. One tires of the allegories and poetic episodes depicted by a Poussin or a Philippe de Champaigne, he wrote, "while one takes pleasure and even feels exalted looking at a piece of bread and a carafe by Chardin: there is more poetry in these images than in all the fantasies of his contemporaries (I except certain of the charming visions of Watteau)" (*Notes* 72). There are several entries in the diary referring to his visits to the Louvre with Proust and other friends. A long appreciative entry on the universality and profundity of Leonardo da Vinci also reminds us of Proust's reaction to the Italian painter and scientist.

Two features of the diary that recall analogous elements of Proust's world view are Hahn's cynicism about love ("The pleasure that love gives isn't really worth the happiness it destroys" (*Notes* 18), and his belief in the virtue of work, which he tried to integrate into a rather pessimistic conception of life:

> One must remain free, nothing is good but work, no matter how much pain it gives. Love very little, make oneself useful if one can, resign oneself to sadness, which is inevitably the daily bread of every intelligent being and, finally, "look higher in order not to lose patience," as Mme de Sévigné says. (*Notes* 25)

Literary references are sprinkled throughout the diary, as are comments on the dinners he shared with writers of the ilk of Mallarmé, Rodenbach, and Léon Daudet.

The lectures on singing, *Du chant*, expound Hahn's credo that the beauty and reason for being of song "is the combination, the mixture, the indissoluble union of sound and thought" (17). This beauty depended on "the mysterious alliance of the voice that sings and that speaks, of melody and word." But in this alliance, the dominant partner, in Hahn's view, was the word, involving a necessary "submission" of music to the word. The failure to understand the way in which music supports and enhances thought was what kept many aspiring vocal artists from attaining the excellence they vainly pursued.

The relationship between Proust and Hahn was so close for several years, and intermingled so many different facets of their lives that it is difficult to determine where the thought and feelings of one leave off and those of the other begin. The centrality of Hahn in Proust's life, at least during the 1890s, is evidenced in the humorous tribute Proust paid to Hahn in *PJ*, where Hahn earns a distinguished place among contemporary French composers simply by provoking the displeasure of the two pretentious imbeciles, Bouvard and Pécuchet,[6] for reasons that have to do with his modernity and his admiration for Verlaine. It can be seen more significantly in the fact that the protagonist's inseparable friend in the novel *Jean Santeuil*, Henri de Réveillon, is in very large measure modeled on Hahn. Proust began writing *JS* in the summer of 1895, when he was vacationing with Hahn in Brittany, after spending ten days with him at one of Madeleine Lemaire's summer residences, this one on the Normandy coast near Dieppe. One notes the reversal of the letters *R* and *H* in the given and surnames of Reynaldo Hahn and Henri de Réveillon. Proust enjoyed such reversals of letters and anagrammatic rearrangements to highlight the relationships between his characters.

There are traces of Hahn's influence in various aspects of Proust's personality and outlook on life. The original title that Proust had decided upon for the book that was eventually titled *Les Plaisirs et les jours* was *Le Château de Réveillon*, in honor of the name Madeleine Lemaire gave to her estate in the department of Seine-et-Marne, east of Paris, where Proust and Hahn spent a month in August of 1894, at the height of their passion for each other. In a letter to his cousin Marie Nordlinger written during that memorable month (Gavoty 89) Hahn was delighted to observe that Proust responded to music like an "Aeolian harp," while Proust began fully to appreciate Hahn's acute literary intelligence. It was a time of mutual discovery, which subsequent travels together and "interminable conversations about free verse, metaphors, symbolism and Gothic cathedrals" confirmed and strengthened (Gavoty 108). Proust felt very free at Madeleine Lemaire's country estate, which may explain the nickname that Hahn gave to him that month, "Poney," one of many affectionate sobriquets (Binibuls, Bibuls, Bichnibuls) the two men used with each other in person and especially in their written correspondence. The habit of using such bizarre neologisms was Hahn's, to which Proust adapted himself—always with the fear, however, that if their letters were to fall into the hands of a third party, even the most benevolent friend, nothing would save them from ridicule (Proust, *Lettres à Reynaldo Hahn* 20).

Rivers speaks of Hahn as "a presiding genius of [Proust's] art" not only during the years of their sexual relationship but throughout Proust's career (71). The strongly autobiographical cast of *JS*, revealed in its epigraph[7] owes much to the relationship with Hahn, toward whom Proust experienced emotions ranging from extreme devotion to jealous torment bordering on hatred. Of his affair with Hahn, Proust once wrote in a manner that recalls the oscillation of Swann's emotions during his tragi-comic courtship of Odette: "To wait for the little one, to lose him, to find him again, to love him twice as much in seeing that he has come back with Flavie[8] to pick me up, to hope for his arrival for two minutes or to make him wait five minutes, that is for me the real tragedy, a palpitating and profound one, which I shall write one day perhaps" (Huas 102–103).

A perusal of the letters Proust wrote to Hahn during the early part of their affair provides some clues as to the nature of their relationship. In September 1894, Hahn was the person to whom Proust first communicated his excitement about a short story he was in the process of writing, "*La Mort de Baldassare Silvande, Vicomte de Sylvanie*" (The death of Baldassare Silvande, Viscount of Sylvania) whose protagonist Proust made a musician, possibly thinking of Hahn.[9] In this same letter Proust expresses his love for Hahn, hoping with trepidation that he would accept Proust's invitation to spend some time with him at the Hôtel des Roches Noires, in Trouville, where Proust was staying at the time.

In a letter to Hahn written three days later Proust alludes to a contretemps that, he felt, might have aroused suspicions in the Straus family—who were staying in Trouville—concerning their sexual relationship. Proust had left for Paris before a telegram from Hahn arrived, and Mme Straus, having been given it by the hotel management, forwarded it to Proust in Paris without opening it. Somehow, Proust feared that not opening the telegram was a sign that Mme Straus understood the nature of their relationship. "For the first time in my life since I've been playing the comedy I did not succeed and that will serve as a good lesson," whose moral, he said, was "*Turpe est mentiri*" (It is wicked to lie) (*Corr.* 1: 337). Proust was referring of course to the furtive and sometimes hazardous schemes the two young men, like most homosexual couples, had to devise in order to hide what, in effect, most people who knew them were aware of or suspected anyhow. But the taboo against frank acknowledgment of homosexual attachments was so strong that it was necessary to keep up a front of normalcy and hence to playact for the sake of allowing others as well as themselves to pretend not to know the truth.

One wonders whether it was this aspect of their relationship that led rather quickly to Proust's growing impatience and disillusionment concerning the purity of their feeling for each other. The fact is that in their reflections on love both men were prone to a deep pessimism. The extent to which this pessimism is attributable to the ups and downs of their affair is impossible to determine, but certainly the contrast between devotion and resentment that marked their interaction throughout 1895 must have had its effect. Writing sometime in 1895 to Hahn, Proust expressed a wish "to be master of everything that you desire on the earth in order to be able to bring it to you—the author of everything you admire in art in order to dedicate it to you" (*Corr.* 1: 442).[10] Yet at more or less the same time, Proust was angered by Hahn's apparent indifference to him at a recent dinner party at a friend's home, when Hahn apparently preferred to remain at the party rather than leave with Proust at an hour agreed upon beforehand. Such independence was incompatible with Proust's concept of love as total devotion to the happiness of the beloved person. The upshot of this and other misunderstandings was the surprisingly abrasive tone of a letter from Proust to Hahn that seems to have marked the definitive end to their relationship as lovers in July 1896:

> The history of our friendship gives me the duty to make you touch with your finger the errors of your pride. You do not understand that by inspiring in me the image of a Reynaldo who no longer fears causing me pain, you remove the obstacles which oppose themselves to my desires. Therefore, nothing can stop me any longer. Dare I say that I am worth more than you? (Gavoty 108)

Lest one conclude that this letter is all that Proust had to say to Hahn at that moment, another letter written at more or less the same time, on July 3 or 4, 1896, should put that thought to rest. Proust was inconstant and unpredictable, forever making statements about his undying affection or love for someone, only to turn cool and detached whenever things did not work out exactly as he had planned. Thus he could say to Hahn, at the same time he was beginning another love affair, that "you are truly the person who with Mother I love the most in the world" (Delage 231). Moreover, the letters Proust wrote to Hahn later on that same year show no lessening of affection and esteem for him.

Hahn also had a strong penchant for pessimism in matters of the heart, which spilled over at times into other areas of his life, such as his attitude toward the arts, the very source of his lifeblood yet one he readily dismissed—in accord with the perversely puristic aesthetics of the time—as magnificently useless. Regarding this idea, he made the following observation in a letter to the pianist Edouard Risler:

> We have to say one thing to ourselves: art is not *necessary* in this life. What is beautiful in art is that it is totally useless and that we fasten ourselves–you, me, him, them–with ardor and despair to the croup of a dazzling chimera, the mastery of which has no useful purpose to anyone. (Gavoty 61) [11]

In a similar vein, Hahn wrote:

> The artist, like Icarus, climbs to the heaven of his dream and returns to earth, crushed. I am no exception to the rule. Let's take consolation from a forthcoming flight. But I see quite well, right now, that it is the same with art as with love. One soars, joyously, towards the conquest of the good: sometimes, one is wounded, one is always disappointed. (Gavoty 63)

With the help of several scholars who have studied the relationship between Proust and Hahn, mainly Roger Delage, and with the additional evidence of a little essay that Proust wrote on Hahn many years after their love affair had ended, let me attempt here to summarize or slightly expand several of the things said in this chapter with a view to clarifying with reasonable certainty the nature of Hahn's impact on Proust's aesthetic and sexual sensibilities.

Hahn's influence can be felt chiefly in Proust's evolving aesthetic philosophy, and specifically in the part that both music and painting played in its formation. Several hints point to the rising importance of music in Proust's life. First, at Le Réveillon in the summer of 1894, one of the first projects the new lovers decided on together was a biography of Chopin, which did not materialize but whose significance is nonetheless considerable, since it belongs to a period in Proust's life when he was beginning to strive consciously for a blending of the arts[12] that was to become one of the most characteristic thematic and stylistic features of the *Recherche* and that had already manifested itself in the preface, written in July 1894, to *PJ*. At the end of his dedicatory preface to that volume, Proust alluded to "his true friend" (Hahn) and "to the Master" (Anatole France) who, with the philosopher Alphonse Darlu, made up the triumvirate of individuals in his life who had contributed most to his conception of literature and art; Hahn, because he had inspired him with "the poetry of his music," France, who had offered him "the music of his incomparable poetry," and Darlu, who had initiated him into the serious study of philosophy.

A second example of this new emphasis on the role of music in literary creation shows itself in the project Proust and Hahn brought to successful completion in the important middle section of the 1896 first edition of *PJ* where, as I have already noted, Proust's poems on four composers and four painters appear together with the piano music Hahn composed as musical background for the first four poems. The four composers, Chopin, Gluck, Schumann, and Mozart, were favorites of both Proust and Hahn, as were the four painters whom they commemorated in *PJ*: Albert Cuyp, Paulus Potter, Antoine Watteau, and Anton Van Dyck.[13] Again, one notes the centrality of music in the conceptual framework of *PJ*, due at least in part, I think, to Hahn's influence. I should also point out that several of the little essays, prose poems and meditations included in the section "*Les Regrets, rêveries couleur du temps*" (Regrets, reveries, changing skies) are musical in their titles and evocations: "*Famille écoutant la musique*" (Family listening to music), "*Sonate clair de lune*" (Moonlight sonata), and "*Eloge de la mauvaise musique*" (In praise of bad music). Even more essentially musical in its inspiration is the prose poem "*La mer*" (The sea), at the end of which Proust compares the sea to music in that "it enchants us like music, which, unlike language, bears no trace of material things, which never speaks to us of men but imitates the movements of our soul" (Dupee 139).

Another expression of music in Proust's creative life is the story "*La mort de Baldassare Silvande*," which, when it first appeared separately in *La Revue Hebdomadaire* on October 29, 1895, Proust dedicated "to Reynaldo Hahn poet, singer and musician."[14] Proust had no difficulty in attributing the qualities of a poet to Hahn, just as he liked to think of himself as a writer attuned to the sonorities and evocative expressiveness of music.

Delage argues convincingly, I believe, that it is not only because Baldassare is a musician that one can speak of this story as a "transposition of real elements" but also "because in it one hears the distinct rustling of memories tied to Reynaldo, one finds barely transposed in it the ocean views and landscapes which are those of Trouville and Normandy where Proust wrote it, and that insinuated in it is the theme of remorse which the lovers experience, the lovers who, to love each other, are obliged to hide—like Marcel and Reynaldo—to betray the trust of a dear person, Marcel's mother, a theme that will be expanded until it becomes that of the 'cursed race' [in section 1 of the *Sodom and Gomorrah* part of the *Recherche*]" (229). There is ample evidence of the guilt that his homosexuality sometimes stirred up in Proust because he felt that it was a side of his personality that his mother did not and could not understand. Proust never liked to formulate his identity in homosexual terms. For him, it was a preference, a taste, not a defining behavior. Yet it played an enormous role in the development of his vision of life, and contributed to his understanding of what made human beings so protean, fascinating, and complex. It helps to explain why so many of his characters of both genders, from *PJ* to the *Recherche*, are either bisexual or homosexual. In any case, Delage's point here is that many features of this story, to which Proust attached considerable importance, reflect the presence of Reynaldo Hahn in Proust's life during these years. Both men enjoyed friendships with many women, for whom they expressed strong affections.

Nevertheless, on the basis of available evidence, one is entitled to believe that these friendships were Platonic, not amorous and romantic.[15]

A short essay Proust wrote about Hahn that was not published during Proust's lifetime and that the editors of his critical writings place between the years 1909 and 1914, when Hahn was music critic for the *Journal*, provides an additional piece of evidence in support of the view that the composer was an active force in the writer's creative life.

Proust began this short but deeply felt piece[16] by recalling the tributes paid to Hahn's musical genius during the 1890s, when Hahn composed the music for his mentor Alphonse Daudet's play *L'Obstacle*, and attracted the serious scholarly attention of such figures as Mallarmé and Pierre Loti. Despite the nitpicking of several detractors, it was during those years, Proust said, that Hahn made his theatrical début and wrote the vocal and instrumental works that excited "the great admiration that the most refined artists of our time will always feel for his music."

Proust then pointed out "the errors of judgment" issuing from the minds of certain "amateurs" who evaluated avant-garde art in accordance with the degree of its adherence to whatever was believed to be the latest technical and formal innovations of the day. This notion of an avant-garde, Proust said, had nothing to do with what was genuinely new and revolutionary in works of art. He then moved to his conclusion where we discover a viewpoint that looms up very large in Proust's aesthetic philosophy and ideology as he had conceptualized it in the 1890s and reaffirmed some fifteen years later. It hinges on the notion of interiority, of "truth" as something "intimate and psychological" rather than objective and "veristic," as exponents of "neo-Italianism" thought of it. He was referring here to the operas of Leoncavallo, Mascagni, and Puccini, towards whom Hahn, and apparently Proust as well, felt a rather strong antipathy. Hahn's music, Proust said, "is not that song of which Hugo speaks 'where nothing human remains.' It is the life itself of the soul, the internal substance of language, liberated, raising itself, taking flight, that has become music" (*CSB* 556).[17]

Whatever bitterness may have remained in Proust concerning his relationship with Hahn, it is clear from this essay that Hahn had a place in his personal pantheon of artists who penetrated the veil of appearances to the inner core of psychological and spiritual truth.

Chapter 4

Young Proust, Robert de Montesquiou-Fezensac, and the Society of the Parisian Salons

As a center of upper-class fashion and taste in the Paris of the late nineteenth century, the salon[1] provided a site for writers and artists to meet with their peers and with prominent representatives of the business, diplomatic, and professional intelligentsia. Even more than other institutions such as literary and political journals, academies, and learned societies, the salons offered an ambience where like-minded people with common intellectual and cultural interests could mix freely within the social guidelines established by their hostesses, and in accordance with established canons of etiquette and rank.

Almost every salon had its leading personality, usually a man, whose weekly or biweekly presence would guarantee to the hostess a certain tone and cachet capable of attracting the people she wished to cultivate. Almost every salon also had its favorite activity: some were devoted to music and theatre, some to intellectual discussion, and some merely to socializing and refined gastronomic pleasures.

As far as social class was concerned, like their predecessors in the eighteenth century, when the salons initiated by such distingushed women as Mme de Lambert, an aristocrat, and Mme Du Deffand, a bourgeoise, tended (together with the new cafés and clubs) to replace the court as the main fulcrum of cultural life, most of the Parisian salons in the second half of the nineteenth century accepted guests from diverse social backgrounds, as long as they met other criteria for inclusion such as intellectual or literary accomplishments, conversational brilliance, and influential connections. There were, however, some aristocratic salons that did exclude, or at least made extremely difficult, access to people of lower social station. This was true of the salons in the Faubourg Saint-Germain, which remained closed to young Proust until his blueblooded friend and sponsor, Count Robert de Montesquiou-Fezensac, made it possible for him to gain entry to them. But even with Montesquiou's assistance, most people who have looked into this aspect of Proust's life seem to think that he was never fully accepted by the aristocratic families who reigned in the Faubourg Saint-Germain during the years with which we are dealing in this study. At least one scholar, Bernadette Morand, has concluded that, despite his successful conquest of both aristocratic and upper bourgeois salons, Proust was never recognized and valued by them for what he was; that far from being a place of refuge, the salons were for him really "places of exile."[2] Nevertheless, he was able to penetrate these alien places sufficiently to make them a favorite setting for his prose narratives. Moreover, there is ample evidence pointing to young Proust's need to define himself in terms of the values that certain of the most illustrious literary and social salons embodied. He hungered for acceptance by and was deeply attached to salon hostesses such as Mme Arman de Caillavet, Countess Laure de Chevigné, Duchess Elizabeth de Clermont-Tonnerre, Mme Alphonse Daudet, Countess Elizabeth Greffulhe, Mme Madeleine Lemaire, Countess Anna de Noailles, and Mme Geneviève Straus. He acquired the manners associated with graciousness and generosity: he gave expensive gifts to his hostesses, excelled in charming repartee, and dressed in fashionable attire.[3] He became known in the early to mid-1890s as a *soiriste*, a writer who specialized in describing the soirées, fêtes and parties that featured well-known personalities in the arts and high society.

Proust's exquisitely refined manners, his *politesse*, were proverbial among the cognoscenti. He was known affectionately as "little Proust" or "little Marcel," (Clermont-Tonnerre 9; Ferré 205), but the diminutive was not meant to be condescending, since his company was eagerly sought after by reason of his effulgent wit, his talent for mimicry, his knowledge of literature and the arts, and his prodigious memory. He could cite page upon page of verse by his favorite poets and long passages from beloved playwrights. Yet at the same time many people did regard him as an amateur, a drawing-room dilettante. He had the misfortune of being seen by some, even among his close friends, as the embodiment of the very foibles and vices he wrote about in the early short stories collected in *PJ* and that he later integrated into his great novel: snobbery, vanity, dandyism, social climbing, sycophancy, hypocrisy. Some of these attributions were unfair, yet the image was not entirely undeserved. We are entitled to think that the face of the profoundly serious writer behind the social mask was not always visible even to his peers in the Parisian intelligentsia.

According to Emilien Carassus and Laure Rièse, both diligent researchers in late nineteenth-century French social history, the three salons that were most important in shaping young Proust's moral and intellectual sensibilities from about 1888 to 1893 were all governed by bourgeois not aristocratic hostesses: Mme Geneviève Straus, to whose residence Proust gained access through his friendship with her son by her first marriage, Jacques Bizet; Madeleine Lemaire, whose passion for music attracted Reynaldo Hahn and other composers and performers; and Mme Arman de Caillavet, the long-time mistress of Anatole France. All three women had talents in their own right (as writers, linguists, and painters) and offered to the aspiring writer and socialite a rich assortment of cultural refinements and personal graces. Two were Jewish: Straus was the daughter of the composer Fromental Halévy; Caillavet's maiden name was Léontine Lippmann. At the same time, Carassus and Rièse credit Proust's rapid rise in the aristocratic salons to Lemaire, who introduced him to Robert de Montesquiou in March 1893, a meeting that, as previously mentioned, facilitated his acceptance by other blue-blooded salons, such as those of Princess Mathilde Bonaparte, the marquise Julie de Roccagiovine, the countesses de Luynes and de Noailles, and the countess de Beaulincourt. Proust's ability to move easily and simultaneously in aristocratic and bourgeois circles was symbolized by the fact that the countess de Beaulincourt and Mme Straus both lived on rue de Miromesmil, the former at number 12, the latter at number 104, so that "to go from one salon to the other, Proust had only to walk up the block" (Rièse 43).

But these details of Proust's social existence in the 1890s need to be considered in a broader historical context. There is the issue of young Proust's attitude toward the three classes that were contending for power and authority in France (and in Europe generally) in the last decades of the century: the aristocracy, the bourgeoisie, and the working class (including the peasantry), the last of which was taking shape under the leadership of socialist and mainly Marxist-inspired political parties in close collaboration with a burgeoning labor movement. We need to consider what his letters and journalistic writings of the time tell us about how he saw the world. These help to define the fundamental ideological choices and class-based affiliations that he made at the time he was writing the portraits, sketches, short stories, and prose poems gathered in *PJ*.

As a young man (and probably throughout his life) Proust was unaware of or uninterested in Marxism, and his knowledge of the natural sciences did not suffice to consolidate in him a lasting intellectual bond with the principles of modern materialist thought.[4] This is surprising in that the late 1880s and 1890s was a moment in which modern European civilization was passing through processes of vast practical and theoretical significance stemming from changes in the mode and relations of material production, and from the corresponding rise of the socialist and labor movements. But as we try to shed some light on these issues it will be necessary at the same time to look at aspects of young Proust's personality and way of comporting himself in society that make whatever we might say about him at the very least somewhat problematic. One of these has to do with the concept of "entre-deux" as expounded by Antoine Compagnon, the other concerns several caveats that must be heeded by anyone trying to make sense of Proust's ideological orientation at this juncture of his career.

To use Arno J. Mayer's phrase, Proust exemplified "the persistence of the old regime" in France well beyond the decade of the 1870s when, most historians think, the bourgeoisie finally ascended to a preeminent place in French political and economic life, while at the same time he stood on the threshold, and was himself a representative, of a new culture. It is impossible to connect Proust unqualifiedly with a class or with a way of life, for he remained resolutely independent and was not at all uncomfortable with the need to straddle two worlds, to belong and yet not to belong, to fit in and not to fit in, according to the circumstances and requirements of the moment. He was *in* the social world of the aristocratic salons, but was he *of* it? Like Thomas Mann, while sharing the middle class's commitment to work and to a vocation, he also rejected middle-class values, and the form that this rejection took was mainly aesthetic, or artistic; the supreme vocation of the individual who wanted to transcend the narrow views and perspectives of the bourgeoisie was that of writer, of poet, of artistic creator. It was through art and literature that Proust registered his idealist critique of both the aristocracy and the bourgeoisie, not through political or philosophical opposition to the existing order of things (except for the Dreyfus Affair).

Proust was at one in spirit with the "revolutionaries" in the arts, especially painting, and he stood with the republicans in defense of Dreyfus; but in the depths of his soul, he was also with prerevolutionary France, including some of its aristocratic values and its classically based humanism. Because of this attitude, he identified himself with the French aristocracy and aspired to incorporate its code of honor, its generosity, even its naive devotion to ancestor worship, into his own value system. He recognized that the ceaseless flux that characterized bourgeois society under an ever expanding capitalist system could not be reversed, yet he yearned for the stability of a precapitalist, preindustrial social order, when the wheel of fortune did not spin as chaotically as it did in modern times. When he looked at and studied the faces of his aristocratic friends, he had the feeling that he was quite literally contemplating a bygone era that still lived in the present.

It is important to remember that the French nobility had its own distinctive way of life that lasted until and beyond the post–World War I period, and that this class continued to supply the Army, the diplomatic corps, and even the Church hierarchy with some of their top personnel. In other words, while it is true that the struggle for hegemony in France, that is to say, with Gramsci, the struggle for "political and moral leadership" in French society, was being decisively won by the bourgeoisie, the old legitimist aristocracy retained its prestige and its luster to a considerable degree at the time Proust was entering salon society.

If Proust was looking for an alternative scheme of things to that of his own bourgeois class, he could find it either in the nascent working-class movement or in the aristocracy. His choice was never in doubt. His only contact with people of the working class was with representatives of its service sector: waiters and hotel personnel, carriage drivers, domestic servants, and the like. He enjoyed his contacts with the humble people whose labor allowed the privileged milieus he frequented to maintain their charm: for example, he spoke at length with Alphonse Daudet's Italian valet about Dante, and often engaged in lively exchanges with his own servants. But this did not amount to a personal identification with the working class per se. The truth seems to be that young Proust sympathized with the problems of ordinary working people and appreciated their virtues and skills as individuals, but this had nothing to do with the kind of spiritual identification that marked his relations with the aristocrats. Proust's workers and peasants are almost always "embodiments of folk wisdom. They are a living link with feudalism" (Bowie 1998, 148) not the harbingers of an emancipated humanity.

Proust distinguished between the old prerevolutionary legitimist nobility and the Bonapartist nobility, the latter of which had risen to the pinnacle of social rank during the Second Empire. But when the Second Empire came to an ignominious end in 1871, the nobility of the ancien régime regained its social and cultural primacy and was once again lionized by the fashionable circles that Proust frequented (Carassus 49).

The person who perhaps best epitomized the qualities and flaws of the legitimist aristocracy in France was Count Robert de Montesquiou-Fezensac, a man whose lineage on his father's side (his mother, Marie du

Roux, was a bourgeois Genevan Protestant) was virtually as old as the French nation itself[5] and whose unusual talents and personal traits made him, for almost four decades, the very incarnation of what was most alluring in the ancien régime. Poet, collector of antique furniture and modern paintings, specialist in interior decoration, extravagant host of innumerable parties, dinners, and fêtes, flamboyant, contentious, arrogant friend and mentor to numerous younger men, to whom he was drawn either by their sexual appeal or by their intellectual abilities, Montesquiou lived in an openly homosexual partnership with his personal secretary, Gabriel de Yturri, a relationship that, in his case, was more or less accepted as part of his idiosyncratic life style. If young Proust was dazzled by the nobility and treasured his friendship with a group of aristocrats he called "the young dukes," whom he invited regularly to his home simply because they charmed him with their titles and relaxed acceptance of their social prestige, it was largely because of Montesquiou's seductive influence on his world view. Montesquiou gave Proust the chance to see and feel at first hand what it was like to carry within oneself the bloodline and the cultural heritage of France's most distinguished and oldest noble families. Proust counted many other aristocrats among his friends—the princes Antoine and Emmanuel Bibesco, Count Robert de Billy, Prince Constantin de Brancovan, Pierre de Chevilly, Bertrand de Fénelon, Marquis Robert de Flers, Gabriel de La Rochefoucauld, Georges de Lauris, Count Henri de Saussine, above all Viscount Clément de Maugny—but it was Montesquiou who set the tone and established the standards by which Proust learned to appreciate the unusual qualities—and to assess the notable deficiencies—of the French aristocracy.

The relationship between Proust and Montesquiou, who was sixteen years his senior, was not always a smooth one. Madeleine Lemaire seems to have anticipated the friction that was to characterize their relationship when she introduced Proust to Montesquiou with the words, "This is my delicious page, Monsieur Marcel Proust, promise me that you will be kind to him" (Chaleyssin 148). Proust's talent for mimicry was most advantageously on display in his imitations of the gestures and speech mannerisms of Montesquiou and Anatole France. France seems to have accepted it good-naturedly, but Montesquiou resented this playful persiflage and let Proust know more than once how he felt about it. He was the first to point out Proust's social gaffes, and during the height of controversy that surrounded the Dreyfus case, Montesquiou made fun of Proust's Jewish loyalties, refusing to credit him with motives that transcended mere "racial" defensiveness. Proust replied quite honorably to these jibes, and on one occasion, in a letter sent shortly after a dinner at which Montesquiou and other guests had indulged in some anti-Semitic innuendos, Proust reminded his mentor that, as the son of a Jewish mother, he had not been able that evening to take part in or enjoy the cutting remarks of his fellow guests (*Corr.* 2: 66). Tadié attributes Montesquiou's "verbal sadism" to his need to find a "compensation" for the lack of "carnal relations" with various young men in his entourage (Tadié 226). There is no evidence that Proust was among Montesquiou's sexual conquests. He might well have been repelled by the count's blackish teeth, which Montesquiou always covered with his hand when he smiled.

Montesquiou's qualities as a poet, although widely appreciated in his own time, have lost much of their original appeal,[6]—an appeal due to his erudition, his gift for word play, his floral imagery (the rage in the 1890s), his mixing of pagan and Christian symbolism in his nature poems, and his frequent evocation of rural customs and fêtes, which conveyed to jaded urban readers the simplicity of a revered peasant way of life. Also attractive to many readers was his credo, as expounded in a sonnet titled "Ordinaire" that recalled Théophile Gautier, which he included in his 1896 book *Les Hortensias bleus* (Blue Hydranges 11–12): "*Le singulier me touche et l'étrange me charme; / J'excuse le bizarre et me sens fort épris/ Du rare*" (I am touched by the singular and charmed by the strange / I excuse the bizarre and feel smitten / By the rare.) As a poet, he brought into play a curious blending of classicism, hedonism, and symbolism. One of his poetic traits that no doubt influenced Proust's inclusion of four poems on painters in *PJ* that he, Proust, had written was Montesquiou's flair for verbal descriptions of paintings, such as his "*Pinacothèque*" (Picture gallery) of November 1887, which describes works by Moreau, Burne-Jones, Degas, Manet, and others (172–174); his quatrains devoted to Pierre Puvis de Chavannes, whom he called "the modern Orcagna"; his description of the Dutch interiors of Van Dyck and Quentin Metsys (159–160); and his poem (inspired by Manet's famous painting) "*La belle Olympia*," which he dedicated to Mallarmé (181–183). Montesquiou was not only in fashion, he actually helped to form the tastes and topics of his time. It was no wonder that Proust, despite the blackish teeth, called Montesquiou "the professor of beauty."

Two of Proust's many letters to Montesquiou, one written in June 1893 several months after the two men met for the first time at a musical recital hosted by Madeleine Lemaire at her home on rue de Monceau, the other dated October 2, 1894, illustrate the nature of their literary relationship and the feeling of mystical ardor that seems to have descended on young Proust whenever he addressed himself to this representative of France's oldest nobility.

The letter of June 1893 mainly concerned Montesquiou's second published collection of poems, *Le Chef des odeurs suaves* (The best of sweet odors), which followed by a year his first collection, *Les Chauves-souris* (The bats). The letter was written from somewhere in the countryside, at nighttime, while looking at the starlit sky, which may account for the fact that Proust seems to have been engulfed by feelings of reverence as he read the recently published book of poems. "I am too troubled to be able to compare this book with *Les Chauves-souris*," he said,

> but for what is not the object of a reasoning process—because the divine reason that takes hold of it is freed from time, space and relations—for what is purely mysterious like music or faith, I think that there are more verses here [than in *Les Chauves-souris*] that give a presentiment of it, and that reveal it, in embodying it. (*Corr.* 1: 214–215)

After citing some of the verses that he felt exemplified this "presentiment" of what was beyond mere human reason to comprehend, Proust expressed his feeling that such poetry "makes the heart swoon, one doesn't know why." These were the kind of words that, thus far in his life, Proust had reserved for figures such as Racine and Baudelaire, but now Montesquiou joined the elect group of poets to whom one owed a priceless debt. In this same letter he compared the effect of Montesquiou's poems to those that "certain phrases of Wagner" and "certain expressions" of da Vinci paintings had on the listener or viewer: a strange "sweetness." "Your verses," he said, "are this mysterious honey whose rays have the sweetness of those of heaven." Then, after referring to a reading given the previous day by Montesquiou of some of his new poems, Proust closed what was in essence a kind of spiritual love letter by first telling his friend, in a postscript, how impatiently he was waiting for his photograph and then by saying that if he were to send Montesquiou a literary review containing one of his own writings (probably in *La Revue Blanche*), Montesquiou should not dwell on the ridiculous side of such an exchange, a ridicule that would befall Proust if there were "the absurd thought of an exchange of my earthworm with this starry firmament."

One might attribute such smarmy words to a brief extreme infatuation, if it were not for the fact that Proust's passionate admiration for Montesquiou lasted not just a few weeks or months, as was his wont, but many years.

The letter of October 2, 1894, is one of many heaping fulsome praise on Montesquiou, partly in tribute to his poetic "genius" and partly to convey the fascination that Montesquiou's name, lineage, and breeding held for Proust. Like the previous letter, it mixes literary concerns with considerations of social rank and prestige. Basically, Proust wanted Montesquiou to accept a dedication to him of one of the short stories destined for inclusion in *PJ*, "*La Confession d'une jeune fille*" (A young girl's confession). But such a request was not a simple matter, it had to be couched in terms that would please and flatter the great man. It is likely that Proust really meant what he said to Montesquiou in this letter (but see the caveats discussed below). Evidently Montesquiou had some reservations about lending his name to this story and about the other names that would appear with his in the preface, to which Proust responded in the following manner:

> As for [your reservations], I shall respond to your hesitations by removing for a few days (from my publisher when he will be able to release it, I think before a month) the manuscript or the proofs of the obscure short story to which you will be entreated to add the prestige of your name (the only one it will have), whose syllables, for every well-born ear and well educated imagination, are so rich in the past, the present and the future. You will judge whether this road is not too poorly constructed or too little frequented to inscribe on the wall a name that is so glorious and so dear to the world of letters. (*Corr.* 1: 343–344)

The mixture of self-deprecation and boundless esteem for the man Proust was soon to address as "Mon Maître" or "Mon cher Maître"[7] was typical of young Proust's way of relating to people high up in society or in the literary establishment. To a late twentieth-century ear at least, his letters have a sycophantic ring to them. But Proust would not have accepted such an epithet, because he felt that his words were a necessary tribute to a social class, or better a caste, to which the French nation owed a great debt of gratitude. It was precisely for this reason that he reacted to the deficiencies of this class, as seen in both *PJ* and later in the *Recherche*, not by proposing or suggesting the possibility of an alternative to the existing sociopolitical order but, rather, by feeling deep disappointment that the class to which he looked for inspiration, the aristocracy, had compromised itself irrevocably by ceding an authority based on breeding and education to another class, the bourgeoisie, which owed its authority more often to material wealth than to creative and intellectual accomplishments.

Proust's was a politics of disappointment, not of rebellion; and disappointment, when not accompanied by an impulse to remove its causes, can only lead to the kind of spiritual protest that one finds in several of the stories in *PJ*. Proust was simply incapable of envisioning a society fundamentally different from the one he knew. Unlike some of the philosophical reformers of the eighteenth century, and unlike some of the late nineteenth-century ideologues who spoke for the popular and proletarian classes, Proust thought and wrote from within the existing order, hoping to amend its most serious defects but not to replace it with something new. On this level of analysis, then, we can say with some confidence that the comparison he made between his story as an "earthworm" and Montesquiou's new book as a "starry firmament," between his "obscure" short story and the exalted writings of his "teacher," really reflected a historical judgment on Proust's part and was not the expression of an exclusively personal and self-interested flattery.

There is another possible reason why Proust was so enamored of Montesquiou, and that is his physical appearance (apart from the black teeth), if we can take two portraits of him—one painted by Elie Delaunay in 1878, when he was twenty-three, the other by Jean Boldini,[8] when he was in his forties—as faithful likenesses. They are both profiles, the younger one affording almost a three-quarters view of his face, the other more of a side view, where Montesquiou sports a handlebar moustache missing in the earlier portrait. Thick wavy hair over a high forehead, a thin angular face dominated by a prominent aquiline nose, a slightly recessive but firm chin, and attire featuring a clasped ribbon tie and long flowing frock coat with vest are the quite striking features of the twenty-three-year-old man. The portrait by Boldini shows Montesquiou at about age forty-five in a somewhat more dramatic pose, with gloves and an expensive-looking, exceedingly long tapered cane in his right hand, and an unidentifiable object in his left, which draws one's attention to very long fingers and a general air of disdainful hauteur. Despite various illnesses that plagued him all his life, Montesquiou appears in both portraits as a man exuding poise and self-confidence.

At this point we need to take under consideration a few caveats concerning Proust's relationship with Montesquiou and others of his type, caveats that cast a rather long shadow of doubt on the precise nature of his attitude toward the rich and well born, and of course toward himself.

Put plainly, the question is: Can we take Proust at his word?[9] Was he being entirely true to his real feelings when he addressed his "teacher" or "lord and master," as the case may be, with words of such extreme praise?

We know that the enjoyment of humor was not merely an occasional tendency in Proust but, rather, a permanent trait, which expressed itself in several different ways: mimicry was one, which in literary terms became the delicious parodies and pastiches that appear in *PJ* and that characterized every phase of Proust's literary life. Painter considers Proust's parodies to be "the funniest and most profound in the French language" (2: 99). They are the equal, I think, of Joyce's superb parodies of various English writers in *Ulysses*. In fact, the comic spirit is never far from Proust's writing; it hovers around even the most tender moments in his fictions. Ironic jibes at his own foibles and those of friends and enemies were another aspect of his sense of humor; his infectious giggling and laughter at dinner parties, which could be set off by almost any revelation of gaucherie or pretense that struck him as funny, was legendary in the world of the Parisian salons. One is therefore entitled to entertain the possibility that the above-cited letters to Montesquiou were predominantly humorous in intent, that they were imitations of the grandiloquent style associated with Montesquiou and others of his social world.

Another question that presents itself is: Why was Proust so dogged in his pursuit of friendships among the aristocrats? Was it because he had a genuine admiration for them, or did he need to gain their confidence in order to use what he learned in his writing? One wonders to what extent Proust, like many other writers, approached the society of his time—whether consciously or unconsciously is hard to say—as so much grist for his mill, as raw material for future literary projects. One of Proust's biographers, Alain Buisine, sees humor as but one manifestation of a "fundamental ambiguity" in everything he did and everything he wrote, whether fiction, letters, or socioliterary criticism. What was most characteristic of Proust, Buisine thinks, is that in all spheres of life and in all of his interpersonal relations, he was "at one and the same time the farthest from and the nearest to" whomever he was with (25).

Two of young Proust's friends, Jacques-Emile Blanche and Fernand Gregh, add further complicating observations to the question of Proust's "sincerity" when mixing with his social superiors. Concerning the small group of aristocrats whom Proust liked to call "the young dukes," Blanche believes, on the one hand, that he invited them to "his famous literary dinners" because he liked to rub shoulders with these avatars of the legitimist French aristocracy, but on the other hand that he "pretended" to be dazzled by them (Blanche 103), in other words, that he was playing a rather elaborate social game for reasons having to do with his "enigmatic" and "polymorphous" personality, terms used respectively by Daniel Halévy and Jacques Rivière in their recollections of Proust in the 1890s. For his part, Gregh was severely critical of Proust for his fawning behavior when in the presence of the nobility, yet he insists that Proust only "pretended" to be on his knees before the genius of Montesquiou. Basically, Gregh maintained, Proust's attitude was one of "admiration spiced with irony" toward titled people (*Mon Amitié* 10).[10] The admiration was genuine, but not unalloyed, and not really servile as some of Proust's critics claimed.

Tadié contributes two other observations that make one take a circumspect approach to Proust's social behavior in the 1890s. He stresses Proust's relentless questioning of everyone he spent time with, irrrespective of their social class or position. This kind of curiosity, together with the gimlet eye through which Proust observed the world around him, are not fully compatible with the behavior of someone whose only or primary goal is to impress his superiors and gain access to their drawing rooms.

On the basis of this and other aspects of Proust's attitude toward the social milieus he frequented in the 1890s, Carassus insists on his difference from such satirical novelists of high society at the time as Paul Bourget, Abel Hermant, Paul Hervieu, and Henri Lavedan. He insists also on Proust's moral superiority to these writers, whom he resembled only "superficially." We can grant the difference between the typical "worldly" social novels of the 1890s and the *Recherche*, where the doings and pastimes of salon society are subjected to a thoroughgoing critique from a variety of perspectives, but to make such claims for Proust's writing in the 1890s is much harder to justify. I would, however, agree with Carassus when he speaks of the many instances in which Proust partook in and exemplified the manners and mores of the time, and when he remarks that Proust's work "must assuredly be put back into that time of refinements and aesthetic crazes" (536). As we shall see, in *PJ* Proust probes the psyches of his aristocratic characters more deftly and sensitively than do his contemporaries, but he cannot really be detached from his fellow writers as if he belonged to an entirely different literary universe. The relationship between a writer or artist of genius, such as Proust, and the surrounding socioliterary world is not one of incommensurable differences. As Eagleton reminds us in *Criticism and Ideology*, writers, even geniuses such as Proust, do not make the materials with which they work; rather, forms, values, myths, symbols, ideologies come to them already worked upon. Writers effect significant interpretations and modifications of these received materials, but their innovations cannot be separated from the pre-existing or from the socioliterary world around them; the new is not autonomous, something created ex nihilo. Mallarmé said this as well as anyone: "*Le génie se sert de la langue, et des idées en cours, avant d'y mettre le sceau.*" (Genius uses language, and current ideas, before placing its [distinctive] mark on them, *Œuvres complètes* 640).

Two of Proust's writings published in *Le Gaulois*, the snobbish, semi-official organ of Parisian high society, offer a glimpse into how he viewed this glittery world in the mid-1890s. One is a piece he wrote on the extraordinary *fête* that Robert de Montesquiou hosted at his estate in Versailles on May 30, 1894; the other is a short article on how the banal remarks of concertgoers managed to spoil the otherwise exquisite pleasure he had had in listening to Beethoven's Fifth Symphony and several other orchestral works at the Conservatory of Music in early January 1895.

Painter thinks that the *fête* of May 1894 was a crucial event in Proust's life, because it was there that he met for the first time many of the aristocratic salon hostesses of the faubourg Saint-Germain (1: 179). Montesquiou's biographer, Philippe Jullian, makes similar claims concerning the importance of this event to its host: "The great fête of 1894 at Versailles," Jullian writes, "seemed to Montesquiou the best of his lessons in Beauty; its success proved to him that he had a genius for parties" (188). Thus mentor and disciple were quite probably at one in perceiving this particular party as not just another in a series of social events but as a unique occasion that showed off the wealth, finery, and culture of Paris's upper crust to best advantage.

Proust's tone of voice throughout his description of the *fête*[11] is one of ardent admiration, for here were gathered many of the most brilliant names among the Parisian nobility, and not just for the pleasures of witty conversation and delectable dining.[12] The main attraction was its musical and literary fare, which featured the pianist Léon Delafosse playing Bach and Chopin, and Sarah Bernhardt, who shared a reading with two other actresses of the 1792 "Ode to Versailles" by André Chénier, written two years before the poet was guillotined on July 25, 1794. It is possible that Montesquiou chose this particular poem not only to celebrate Versailles but also to remind his guests that the *fête* was taking place almost exactly one hundred years after Chénier's death. Proust reminded his readers of Chénier's last years of life with his beloved "Fanny," and cited the first stanza of the poem read by the three actresses.

Among the artists and poets present were Maurice Barrès, Jean Béraud, Alphonse Daudet, Henri de Régnier, and Georges Rodenbach. Several of the host's favorite poems by François Coppée and Verlaine, and of course a few of his own poems, were read by Julia Bartet and Suzanne Reichenberg

(1853–1924), who for thirty years was the leading ingénue of the Comédie Française. In the long list of invitees that Proust dutifully included in his piece, only five or six (apart from the poets and artists present) belonged to bourgeois families, among whom were the ubiquitous Madeleine Lemaire and her daughter, Suzette, at whose château in Seine-et-Marne Proust and Reynaldo Hann were to spend some happy days three months later. The two women's presence was no doubt due in part to their work as specialists in floral painting, which Montesquiou adored. Proust took pleasure in noting the flowers that were strewn with studied nonchalance on both sides of the path leading to the tent where the main events of the day were held. He described as well the Venetian lace and embroidery of the gowns and hats worn by the most prestigious female guests who arrived on the arms of their husbands, friends, and lovers. "The hall is full. And what a hall! The social elite of Paris!," Proust exclaimed, but not before paying tribute to the owner of the Versailles mansion, who had provided the residence, the floral décor, the Japanese hothouse with its rare flowers and birds, the manicured garden, the "sweet music" produced by an orchestral ensemble discreetly hidden in a nearby wooded area, and the "marvelous" improvised theatre above which, on a frieze, was the word "*éphémère*," whose three syllables were Montesquiou's initials, but in reverse order (*ef/em/err*), FMR, in the aesthetisizing motto "Isn't everything beautiful and good ephemeral?" Proust delighted in such playful rearrangements of letters and words, as did his host. After citing verses from three of Montesquiou's poems read by Sarah Bernhardt, and mentioning Delafosse's performance of a rhapsody by Liszt, Proust closed his piece with an almost nostalgic allusion to the reign of Louis XIV:

> It's over. The dream has ended. We have to return to Paris, where there is talk of a ministerial declaration, of interpellations and other such things. With what a lovely memory and with what regret do we leave Versailles, the royal city, where, for several hours, we felt that we were living in the century of Louis the Great! (*CSB* 364–365)

Proust customarily wrote in these years as both an "aristocratizing aesthete," to use Arno Mayer's phrase, and as an austere moralist who condemned the very pleasures that gave him such exquisite delight. In this piece, we have only the aesthete.

The article "*Un dimanche au Conservatoire*" (A Sunday at the conservatory, *CSB* 367–372) appeared in *Le Gaulois* on January 14, 1895. It is of a different order than the piece on the fête, since in this case powerfully evocative music, Beethoven's Fifth Symphony, provided an occasion to comment on how such creations briefly united people who otherwise had no connection with each other. In other words, art transforms mere juxtaposed existences into a cohesive collective spirit. For a short while, everyone in the audience was able to feel the inseparable bond between truth and beauty. But no sooner had the music ended than Proust's ears were offended by a woman seated near to him who asked her friend: "Do you want some candy?" The heroic enchantment of Beethoven's music was thus rudely dispelled, just as the party carefully arranged by Montesquiou had to end with an obligatory return to the city. Heading home from the concert with his brother and a friend, he noted that both men had already cast off the spell of the music, and were already thinking of their next apppointments.

In his 1930s essay "The Image of Proust," Walter Benjamin maintained that Proust's attitude toward the Parisian upper crust, especially the aristocratic caste, was not only that of a "disillusioned, merciless deglamorizer of the ego, of love, of morals" but also that of a writer who cast his "merciless" gaze on a whole way of life he judged to be ruined by pernicious social and moral compromises. According to Benjamin, Proust looked upon the society, indeed the entire civilization he depicted in his narratives, as being on the brink of collapse, an attitude he conveyed through his portrait of a "consumerist" ruling class that expected its privileges to be supported eternally by the producing classes. But Benjamin was probably too deeply influenced by the anticapitalist catastrophism of the 1930s to appreciate the much more ambivalent nature of Proust's stance vis-à-vis the aristocracy. One of the reasons why Benjamin hammered so hard, and so brilliantly, on the character of Proust's critique of contemporary society was that he wanted to minimize Proust's dependency on idealist thought and move him much closer to the materialist camp. I do not think that such a *démarche* is warranted by a thorough review of Proust's critical and fictional writings. It seems to me that Proust's ambivalence toward the elegant but morally flawed society he had come to know in his late teens and early twenties is a prominent feature of *Les Plaisirs et les jours*, the work that I discuss in the following four chapters.

Part Two

LITERARY AND IDEOLOGICAL CROSSCURRENTS IN *PLEASURES AND DAYS*

Chapter 5

The Vicissitudes of a Text

My review in this chapter of French, English, and German editions of *PJ* should be read in relation to the larger aim of part 2, which is to determine as precisely as possible what Proust's "little things," as he often called the close to sixty separate pieces that comprise *PJ*, can tell us about his conception of the world in the 1890s, what they offer that is relevant to the ideological and sociohistorical interests of this study.

In general, it is safe to say that the prodigious technological innovations of the mid to late nineteenth century, the rise of a powerful labor and socialist movement, the reforms enacted by sucessive liberal and radical governments, the expanding ambitions of French colonialism, and the definitive shift of real power from the old landed aristocracy to the new urban bourgeois class, all leave rather faint traces in Proust's fictional and poetic writings of the years 1890 to 1896. The absence of these events and trends is a telling symptom of the times and of the extent to which young Proust retreated from the great public questions of the day. However, he *was* keenly sensitive to change and to the clash of opposing viewpoints and strategies in the intellectual and cultural spheres, where the underlying material forces competing for dominance were articulated in literary and philosophical terms.

The interactive relationship that exists between all literary texts and specific social groups is particularly important in the case of a work such as *PJ*, since before it appeared in book form many of its stories, prose poems, portraits, and sketches had either already been published or had circulated among writers and intellectuals associated with various Parisian literary periodicals. There is no doubt that *PJ* reflects and responds to many of the prevalent tastes and tendencies of its particular moment in historical time. In my perusal of the reviews *Le Mercure de France*, *La Plume*, *La Revue Blanche*, *La Gazette des Beaux Arts*, and *La Revue*

Hebdomadaire, I have found striking similarities between Proust's ideas and those of his fellow writers and intellectuals in the Paris of the 1890s. It would be strange not to find them since we are talking about a relatively cohesive socioliterary world.

But some of this interaction between Proust and his readers is hidden from view in the transition from one type of publishing framework (in peridodicals) to another (in book form) and from one edition to the other. Proust's exchanges of ideas over a three-year period (1893–1896) with many of his friends and colleagues concerning the practical as well as formal and aesthetic problems posed by a book such as *PJ* can only be appreciated by looking at materials such as inscriptions, dedications, and letters. It is in these types of documents, as well as in the interstices of the work itself, that one can find the lines of connection between fictional or poetic writing and the social world of which it is a part.

The 1896 Deluxe Edition[1]

The "text" referred to in the title of this chapter is the first deluxe edition of *PJ* published on June 12, 1896, by Calmann-Lévy in Paris. This is the base text inasmuch as it is the only one corrected and authorized by Proust himself, together with the editorial staff of the publisher, and in close collaboration with Madeleine Lemaire, the book's illustrator, and Reynaldo Hahn, whose scores composed originally as musical settings for the four poems called "*Portraits de peintres* " (Portraits of painters) were printed from photoengravings for the 1896 edition.[2] This first edition has never been reproduced. On the other hand, some of the post–1896 editions have the merit of providing explanatory footnotes to numerous recondite textual allusions. In the 1971 Pléiade edition and the 1993 Laget edition, the reader will find some examples of variants that occurred when certain of the pieces were transferred from their first home in periodicals to their new abode in book form, as well as a smattering of the changes from the 1896 to the 1924 French editions.

The 1896 edition is characterized by its pictorial features due entirely to the hand of Madeleine Lemaire. It consists mainly of rather insipid pen and ink drawings that serve the purpose of illustrating characters, places, and things mentioned in the stories and prose poems. The book is oversized, eleven and a half inches high and eight inches wide, and has a pale green cover adorned with barely visible irises on the left and right sides. The lettering of Proust's name and the title on the cover, separated only by a small floral colophon, are framed within a rectangular background that itself suggests a painting set inside a frame.

More significant in terms of the initial inspiration for the book and the identity of the illustrator is the drawing on the inside title page of a château, no doubt Lemaire's Château de Réveillon, which appears on the frontispiece surrounded by stately pine trees. Another drawing of the château, but seen from a greater distance, and with a large iron gate topped by a crown and coat of arms, appears at the end of the book. The fact that the book opens and closes with drawings of the château has led some Proust scholars—notably Bernard Gicquel and Pierre Daum—to divine a symbolic design in them, signifying a comprehensive "circular" order that Proust wanted to give to this collection of what had originally been scattered writings.

The fine paper and the drawings suggest that the book itself was conceived as a work of art in its own right; that it was a typically 1890s testimonial to the three sister muses of literature, painting, and music, a relationship especially dear to the hearts of Proust and Reynaldo Hahn. But to these three muses we should add a fourth, Thalia, the muse of comedy, present in a subterranean way throughout the fourteen mainly satirical portraits of Parisian sophisticates, the last of which is titled "*Personnages de la comédie mondaine*" (Actors in the comedy of society, or Characters in the comedy of society), a faint echo of Balzac's "Human Comedy." A drawing of the figure of Harlequin holding a sign that says "Fragments de comédie italienne," (Fragments from Italian comedy) and a drawing of the famed commedia dell'arte character Pantalone at the end of "*Fragments*," are additional signs of how important Thalia was to young Proust.

Following a three-page preface by Anatole France is Proust's five-page dedication to his recently deceased English friend Willie Heath, which is set off from the rest of the text by its italics font. The dedication is headed by a drawing of books and manuscripts interspersed with pansies that recalls the same motif on the written text's last page, again pointing to the idea of symbolic and unifying "correspondences." A drawing of a dove with olive branch marks the end of the dedication. One wonders whether Proust thought of his book as a gesture on behalf of world peace and harmony. The final paragraph of the last piece in the collection, a short story titled "*La fin de la jalousie*" (The end of jealousy), is a Tolstoyan appeal for human fellowship and reconciliation. The story's protagonist, Honoré de Lenvres, lies on his deathbed. The imminence of death has at last delivered him from years of tormenting jealousy. The young woman who has been the object of his jealousy, Françoise, speaks to him:

> Weeping at the foot of his bed, she murmured the loveliest of their former words: "My country, my brother." But having neither the desire nor the force to undeceive her, he only smiled and thought that his "country" was no longer in Françoise but in the sky and throughout the entire earth. In his heart he whispered, "My brothers," and if he looked at her more than at the others it was only out of pity, because of the flood of tears she shed before his eyes; his eyes that soon would close and that could no longer weep. But he did not love her more than he loved the doctor, the old relatives, the servants, and not differently. And this was the end of his jealousy. (Dupee 161–162)

The fact that the opening story of *PJ*, "*La Mort de Baldassare Silvande, vicomte de Sylvanie*" also ends with an epiphanic death scene in the manner of Tolstoy, supports the conjecture that Proust arranged his book in such a way as to give the reader a feeling of completeness and of a unifying principle of order governing otherwise disparate materials.

The writings of *PJ* are presented in the following order: two short stories, "*La Mort de Baldassare Silvande, Vicomte de Sylvanie*" and "*Violante ou la mondanité*" (Violante, or worldly vanities); twelve society portraits dealing mainly with snobbery which form the "*Fragments de Comédie italienne*" (Fragments from Italian comedy); a dialogue between the two Flaubertian characters Bouvard and Pécuchet about society and music; a short story called "*Mélancolique villégiature de Mme de Breyves*" (The melancholy summer of Madame de Breyves); eight "*Portraits de peintres et de musiciens*" (Portraits of painters and musicians) in rhymed alexandrine verses; two short stories, "*Un Dîner en ville*" (A dinner in society) and "*La Confession d'une jeune fille*" (A young girls's confession); a miscellany of thirty short narratives, sketches, and impressionistic prose-poetic descriptions titled "*Les Regrets, rêveries couleur du temps*" (Regrets, Reveries, changing skies); and a concluding short story, "*La Fin de la jalousie*" (The end of jealousy).

All of these sixty-odd pieces were written between 1891 and 1895, but they are not presented in chronological order. For example, the opening short story, "*La Mort de Baldassare Silvande,*" was written in the latter part of 1894 and published in *La Revue Hebdomadaire* on October 31, 1895, while some of the pieces in "*Regrets*" in the penultimate section of the volume, such as "*Une famille écoutant la musique*" (A family listening to music) and "*La Mer*" (The sea) were written in 1892. It is clear that Proust was interested in criteria of placement other than chronology.

Calmann-Lévy did what it could to launch the book, prompted not only by its desire to recoup at least what it had spent on producing it but also by Proust's repeated prodding.³ On June 9, 1896, *Le Gaulois* announced the imminent publication of *PJ*, stressing the Lemaire drawings as an added enticement to its readers, and *Le Figaro* published Anatole France's preface to the book. On June 13 another newspaper, *Le Temps*, highlighted precisely those aspects of *PJ* that amused some of Proust's friends and offended others: the *grand luxe* appearance of the book, its "charming" drawings, its cachet of literary elegance.⁴ Indeed, the book was placed on sale at 13.5 francs per copy, four to five times as much as the price of an ordinary book, thereby assuring that only a tiny elite of potential readers could afford to purchase it. In December 1896, after six months of failed efforts to interest the reading public, the publisher tried another tack and offered it in the December 15th issue of *La Revue de Paris* as "a lovely Christmas gift." But the book was destined to remain a collector's item for almost thirty years. In 1918, of the original print run of 1500 copies, only 329 had been sold. It took Proust's posthumous fame as author of the *Recherche* and the publication of a new inexpensive edition in 1924, to begin to move *PJ* out of the publisher's warehouse. By 1927, Gallimard, which had acquired the rights from Calmann-Lévy, was putting on sale the thirty-fifth reprinting of *PJ*. Laget estimates that about eighteen thousand copies were sold in three years.

French Editions from 1924 to 1993

The second 1924 edition of *PJ*, published by Gallimard, was presented to the reader as a "reprint" of the first 1896 edition and as having been "decided upon and prepared during the author's lifetime." But as I have already mentioned, the supplementary "framing" items were not included in this or in any of the subsequent editions. Larkin Price is inclined to think that Proust did not supervise the editorial process in the early 1920s, since the changes made from the 1896 edition were all minor and insignificant (Price 1965, 156–157).

The 1935 and 1950 editions of *PJ* were both perfunctory reprints, without editorial or critical distinction. But the 1971 Pléiade edition prepared by Pierre Clarac and Yves Sandre and the 1993 paperback edited by Thierry Laget are milestones in the history of Proust studies. Both volumes benefited from the discovery and recovery of Proust materials unavailable to scholars before the mid-1950s, and from the considerable amount of illuminating scholarship and criticism done after the late 1950s by Bernard Gicquel (1960), Larkin Price (1965), Emilien Carassus (1966), Ninette Bailey (1966), J. Theodore Johnson (1967), Anne Henry (1973 and 1983), Paola Placella (1976), Luzius Keller (1987 and 1988), Renée A. Kingcaid (1992), and Pierre Daum (1993), not to speak of the host of scholars whose work on other aspects of Proust's life and writings throw light on *PJ*. The more deeply Proust scholars probed the origins, form, and purposes of his major work, the more it became possible to look at his earlier writings with an appreciation for the essential continuity linking the period from the 1880s to the great turning point in Proust's life, the year 1908, when he began to compose the *Recherche*.

Both volumes provide wide-ranging introductory essays and the kind of critical apparatus that is necessary for an adequate understanding of a book as saturated in literary history and as filled with obscure but often significant allusions as *PJ*.

In the Pléiade edition, *PJ* appears together with *JS*, the unfinished novel that Proust worked on intermittently for about five years, from 1895 to 1900. As far as the text is concerned, Sandre explains in a brief note that he and his colleagues had examined the voluminous Proust materials at the Bibliothèque Nationale to check on the degree of correspondence between the first typewritten manuscripts and slip-proofs and the definitive edition of 1896. The only discrepancy they found was in the order in which a few of the pieces appeared in 1896 compared with the place they occupied in the proof pages. Otherwise, they did not find a single correction in Proust's hand on either the typescripts or the proofs. However, Sandre took the liberty of "modifying the punctuation and the spelling" of the original edition, mindful of the need for "prudence and coherence" in such an editorial intervention.[5] They also corrected some "obvious typographical errors" in the 1896 edition. But Laget notes that the 1971 edition repeats some of the many errors in the 1924 edition, while correcting others. In at least one instance, he observes, the Pléiade editors did not catch a rather important error stemming from a misreading or misinterpretation of what Proust was trying to convey in his dedicatory remarks: the Pléiade version reads, "I have never depicted immortality except among human beings with a delicate conscience" whereas what Proust was talking about was "immorality."

The two features of the 1971 Pléiade edition worthy of comment are the introductory "Notice" and the notes and variants furnished at the end of the volume. These are so detailed and lengthy that it would have been impossible to place them on the same page as the passages to which they refer.

After saying in the "Notice" that it is no longer possible to consider *PJ* as an insignificant work of Proust's youth, Sandre discusses the features joining *PJ* to the *Recherche*. He alludes to Proust's penchant for symbolizations and poetic stylization; his predilection for certain "impressionist" themes like flowers, boats, clouds, and the sea; his deep interest in the mores of uppercrust society; and his concern with "the counterpoint of death and time." Sandre is favorable to the structural approach taken to *PJ* by Bernard Gicquel in his influential 1960 essay. I think that *PJ* does have a structural coherence and unity, but that this is a less important unifying element than the philosophical vantage point from which Proust wrote the miscellany of pieces that comprise *PJ*. The book's real unity, I would argue, lies in its point of view, its network of ideas and its psychological insights into the problems of human existence.

Thierry Laget's introduction to the 1993 paperback is more critically astute than its counterpart in the 1971 edition. Laget's account of Proust's early years and his associations with a variety of literary groups is excellent, and his summary of the stages through which the planning and publication of *PJ* had to go takes advantage of recent scholarship to good effect. He connects the book to several contemporary trends and offers his own views on the structuralist readings popular since the 1960s. He does, however, tend to sound a little vague when he attempts to gather a miscellany of texts into a more or less solid thematic framework.

English and German Editions

The two English editions of *PJ*, the first published in 1948 (and reissued in 1986), the second in 1957, have no critical apparatus whatever, but both do have informative and perceptive introductions by D. J. Enright and F.W. Dupee. Enright picks up on the theme of "decadence" sounded by Anatole France in his preface, where Dupee speaks of the "hothouse atmosphere" that permeates *PJ*. This is an aspect of the book that an American Proust scholar, Renée A. Kingcaid, has done most to highlight in recent years. But Enright also points out the original and distinctive features of *PJ*, maintaining that "it is wrong to suppose that *Pleasures and Regrets* is interesting only for its prefigurations of *Remembrance of Things Past*, or as the otherwise negligible juvenilia of someone who later achieved fame."

Dupee offers a more thoroughgoing review of the book's literary characteristics, among which, anticipating the *Recherche*, is its remarkable array of genres. He suggests that one of Proust's aims in this early work was to answer Mallarmé's call for a comprehensive "Book of Life" that would "embrace all experience and all literary forms." Another fertile theme touched upon by Dupee concerns the "abstract" nature of Proust's stories, their tendency to take on the colors of "symbolist fables." He also comments suggestively on the reasons why Proust borrowed the title of his collection from the Greek poet Hesiod's *Works and Days*.

Important parts of the original 1896 French edition were excised from both English- language editions. Not only are the drawings and musical scores absent, for obvious reasons, but both lack the vitally important dedication to Willie Heath, as well as the eight poems on painters and composers. These defects are tantamount to a misrepresentation of Proust's artistic intentions. As for the translations, they are competent, although they sometimes miss the musical qualities of Proust's prose.

The first German edition of *PJ*, translated by Ernst Weiß and titled *Tage der Freuden* (Days of pleasures), appeared in 1926 and was reprinted with the same title in 1965 and 1985. Like the two English editions, it lacked the dedication and the poems. The other German translation, edited and translated by Luzius Keller with great diligence and attention to detail in both the introduction and in the notes, appeared in 1988 with the title *Freuden und Tage*, an exact translation of the French original.

Keller places *PJ* in the context of "the literary and ideological currents" of the late nineteenth century. He insists on his belief that the single pieces in their original form underwent a fundamental change when they appeared together in the 1896 edition, that they acquired thereby "a new shape and meaning." Whether he is correct in assuming that Proust already had a book in mind when he wrote his first youthful pieces is difficult to say. We know only that he began to plan for their publication in a single volume in the summer of 1893, and that he spent the next three years looking for a publisher and revising some of the writings he planned to include in the collection.

The notes in the Keller edition are especially useful for what they tell us about the epigraphs and about the names of Proust's characters. His edition also has the distinction of having restored the dedication and the poems to their rightful place in the volume.[6]

The question of the book's original French title and its English and German translations is more complicated than one might think. As I have already indicated, the title that Proust had originally chosen for the book was *Le Château de Réveillon*, which from an autobiographical point of view, as a reminder of Proust's close relationships with both Madeleine Lemaire and Reynaldo Hahn, is much more revealing than the one he eventually chose by mid-April 1896, *Les Plaisirs et les jours*. Laget claims that it was Lemaire herself who persuaded Proust to use the name of her château. In any event, a preliminary set of proofs dated March 20, 1896, still has the château title. Proust's resolution of the problem, coming only two months before the book's publication, suggests the possibility that he gave up his first choice reluctantly, shifting from a title that conveyed a strong sense of place and an already nostalgic recollection of golden days to one drawn from a classical source, Hesiod's *Works and Days* (written in the eighth century B.C.), which he used as a form of ironic contrast (for readers with a classical education) to the shallow pleasures and fruitless obsessions depicted in his own work. Anatole France (or as some think Mme Arman de Caillavet, née Léontine Lippmann) was the first to allude to the classical source of Proust's title in his (or her) preface to the volume. Since France signed and dated the preface, I shall credit it to him.

The replacement of "works" with "pleasures" is noteworthy in view of the fact that none of the protagonists of Proust's fictions in *PJ* live by any visible form of work. They make love, go to parties, stay up late at night, worry obsessively about the meaning of their lives, suffer torments of jealousy, and die, sometimes quite dramatically, but they do not work.[7] The only people who work for their bread in *PJ* are a few coachmen and domestic servants, a musician in "*Mélancolique villégiature de Mme de Breyves*," and young Honoré in "*Violante ou la mondanité* " who abandons Violante to sign on to a merchant ship for a long tour of duty. But *PJ* has something else in common with Hesiod's poem: its awareness of the decline and decadence of the contemporary world, and its implicit belief that drastic measures would have to be taken to rectify an appalling moral laxity among the citizenry. In this regard, Walter Benjamin was accurate in his reading of Proust, even though, as I have said, he probably went too far with it. There is no doubt that much of Proust's writing in *PJ*, like Hesiod's, has a didactic aim.[8] I agree with Germaine Brée, who argues that Proust retained Hesiod's moral intent but that onto the Greek's classical didacticism he superimposed Judeo-Christian values and ways of looking at the moral life. If looked at from this perspective, several of the stories in *PJ* might be read fruitfully as allegories (Brée, *The World of Marcel Proust*, 41).[9]

In view of this link with Hesiod's epic, although we might tend to favor the title *Pleasures and Regrets* of the 1948 English edition as being closer to the prevalent state of mind of Proust's characters and more in harmony with Proust's own attitude toward love, jealousy, and regret, the fact remains that any title other than *Pleasures and Days* strays too far from the author's intention. "Days" are seen in relation to "Pleasures" by Proust, while they were seen by Hesiod in relation to "Works." The differences and the similarities are crucial for understanding how the title connects with the main characteristcs of the Proustian vision in *PJ*.

As for the two German editions, I think that Weiß's translation *Tage der Freuden*, although hinting at something of what Proust intended—namely days given over to the pursuit of pleasure—loses the force of the *relational* emphasis in Proust's title, so that the "Days" or the passing of time are obscured by locking days and pleasures in such a tight embrace. Therefore Keller's choice of *Freuden und Tage* was a necessary one.

There is a feeling of world-weariness in Proust's title, of time passing in endless repetitive gestures, which Samuel Beckett caught nicely in his 1931 essay on Proust. "Proust's creatures," Beckett wrote, "are victims of this predominating condition and circumstance—Time. There is no escape from the hours and the days. Neither from tomorrow nor from yesterday" (2). Proust shows us that the escape into pleasures[10] does not cure the *taedium vitae* of his upper class characters, it only exacerbates their despair. This is why he turned to Thomas à Kempis's *Imitation of Christ* for several of the epigraphs in *PJ*.

Chapter 6

Problems of Structure, Unity and Aesthetic Philosophy

Much of the critical debate about *PJ* has centered around the question of whether it can be considered a structured, unified whole rather than a mere patchwork of miscellaneous pieces. This is an important question inasmuch as the way a writer organizes and arranges the material of a fictional work often reflects the point of view from which s/he has embarked on the task of writing.

Proust always paid careful attention to how the parts of his writings related to the whole and the whole to the parts. Bernard Gicquel picks up on precisely this aspect of Proust's mind in pointing out the book's "circular" form, and others have noted its many "correspondences," to which I shall return later in this chapter. With respect to the *Recherche*, Proust often felt misunderstood by those who failed to grasp the degree to which he had molded and shaped his material in accordance with well-established principles of architectural design, on the one hand, and musical composition on the other. It would be odd if this trait were not to manifest itself at all in his earlier work, from the time in the summer of 1893 when he decided to gather his scattered writings into a single volume.

Another consideration of a general nature has to do with the philosophy and aesthetics of symbolism, which exerted a strong influence on young Proust, despite his critical distance from it as a school of literary theory and practice. Symbolism's concept of correspondences between the material and the spiritual worlds is a powerful current in Proust's writing. He was an eager disciple of the idea that there is a hidden cosmic order to which the affairs of the earthly human domain are somehow organically connected. His conception of nature as animated by mysterious forces to which the artist is compelled to respond is evident in many of the prose poems of *PJ*. Proust was also sensitive to the ability of metaphorical language to provide access to the deepest layers of the human psyche. Such language opened up a pathway to truth that was independent and autonomous vis-à-vis traditional logic. As I have previously noted, the techniques of musical composition were also important to Proust. Pierre Costil makes reference to this in his analysis of how "musical construction" became an active force in Proust's evolving "aesthetic of [literary] composition" (Costil 1958, 489).

Important personal concerns and values were at stake for Proust in the publication and critical reputation of *PJ*. On February 3, 1897, Jean Lorrain published an article on *PJ* in *Le Journal* to supplement a review he had written the previous year making fun of the book's "precious and pretentious" style. This time he broadened his attack by alluding to Proust's personal relationships. Anatole France's preface to the book amused him, and he predicted that "Proust's next preface would come from another eminent novelist, Alphonse Daudet, who was quite incapable of resisting the solicitations of his son" (Barker 71). The son Lorrain referred to was Lucien Daudet, Proust's lover at the time. Offended by these insinuations, Proust immediately challenged Lorrain to a duel. The ritual armed encounter took place in the Bois de Meudon, at the Ermitage de Villebon, on February 6, 1897. Seconded by Gustave de Borda and the painter Jean Béraud, a close friend, Proust acquitted himself with a bravery and sang-froid that Reynaldo Hahn, noting Proust's accomplishment in his diary, said "do not surprise me at all" (*Notes* 54).

Proust had probably had some experience handling guns during his year of service in the Army, and Lorrain may also have had some knowledge of firearms. Despite this, it is possible that the two men did not really intend to duel at all, just pretend to do so. The fact is, however, that Proust faced an opponent who was positioned at close range, and who could easily have killed him without suffering any legal repercussions. Moreover, in a letter to Lucien Daudet written on the same day as the duel, Proust was uncustomarily direct and laconic: "My dear little one, I wasn't touched nor was Lorrain although my bullet landed almost at his right foot" (*Mon cher petit: lettres à Lucien Daudet* 130). This leads me to believe that he was prepared to die to protect his honor and to defend the integrity of his literary efforts. I would think that his motives were not dissimilar from those that led him to come to the defense of Alfred Dreyfus. In certain circumstances, he could feel as offended by insults to another person as he was to those directed against himself. The duel was among the experiences of his life in which Proust appropriated "the heroic ideal" he had discovered in his student days in the tragedies of Pierre Corneille.

That it was also an act which could earn him the respect of a socioliterary milieu he valued highly cannot be discounted. This is how he spoke of the incident about ten years later, as recalled by his housekeeper, Céleste Albaret:

> Poor mother! She didn't want me to go. Nor did many other ladies either. But this man had offended me and no one encouraged me to do it; it was I alone who wanted this duel. Jean Lorrain was jealous of the preface that Anatole France had written for my book *Les Plaisirs et les jours*; he claimed that it was nothing but a salon-like favor to a young socialite suffering the pains of literary ambitions. We exchanged two bullets in the forest of Meudon. (Albaret 195–196)

This recollection, if accurate, bespeaks an impulse to distinguish himself as a man of courage and honor who resisted the counsel of several women in his life, mainly his mother, who advised him to avoid the confrontation. He seems to have been anxious to disprove once and for all the gossip that categorized him as "effeminate."[1]

On the lighter side, but no less significant for what it tells us about Proust's literary intentions and ambitions in the 1890s, was his reaction to a skit titled "*Les Lauriers sont coupés*" (The laurel trees are cut down). The little play was part of an amateur theatrical performance in which a friend of Proust, Léon Yeatman, imitated his voice and mannerisms with great precision.

The play[2] was performed on three evenings, from March 18 to 20, 1897, at the home of Jacques Bizet on the Quai Bourbon. Bizet was co-author with Robert Dreyfus. Larkin Price says that it attracted an "upper crust" audience. The play concerned the literary activities of several members of the Lycée Condorcet circle during the preceding year. Proust was not the only one to be roasted. Bizet, Dreyfus, and Fernand Gregh had often twitted Proust about the cost of *PJ*, and it was this aspect of the book which they accented in their skit. One part of it, which features Proust, played by Yeatman, a young man, played by Ernest La Jeunesse, and Fernand Gregh, playing himself, reads as follows:

Proust: Have you read my book?
A youth: No, sir. It is too expensive.
Proust: Alas! That is what everyone says. And you, Gregh, have you read it?
Gregh: I cut it in pieces in order to review it.
Proust: And did you find it too expensive as well?
Gregh: Not at all. There is a lot for the money.

Proust: Isn't there? A preface by M. France, 4 francs. Pictures by Madeleine Lemaire, 4 francs. Music by Reynaldo Hahn, 4 francs. Prose by me, 1 franc. Verse by me, 50 centimes. Total, 13 francs 50.
Surely not too much?
Youth: But, sir, there is much more than that in the *Hachette Almanac*, and that costs only 25 sous.

Instead of being amused by the skit, which he heard about from friends since he did not attend the performance, Proust was pained and indignant, according to almost all of his biographers. Why was this the case? Renée Kingcaid provides a possible explanation.

Kingcaid sees the publication of *PJ* as "an important first gamble" on the part of young Proust to convince his parents, especially his father, that his pursuit of a literary career was a feasibile option for him (1992, 36). Her main point is that what Proust feared most of all was literary impotence and premature death. Since the age of nine, he had suffered debilitating asthma attacks, to which he refers frequently in his letters. He was haunted by the thought that this illness would prevent him from realizing his literary aspirations, an especially burdensome fear for a person who saw the creation of a work of art as the summit of human endeavor. Since 1891 he had submitted to his parents' will by following a course in law, which led to a degree in 1895, but the practice of law or of an associated profession was never a realistic life choice for him. Yet what other prospects were there, if a career in literature and philosophy, the two fields which he felt he was born to cultivate, turned out to be illusory? Some of this anxiety may explain why he made such an intense effort to mobilize a wide network of friends and colleagues to stimulate interest in *PJ*. What all of this amounts to in practical terms is that the close to three years Proust spent finding a publisher, working with Madeleine Lemaire and Reynaldo Hahn, inducing Anatole France to write a preface to the book and recommend it to publishers, and giving advanced notice of his writings by publishing them in Parisian journals, were years of travail, of anxiety over his future that the publication of *PJ* somewhat allayed.

Proust referred several times to *PJ* as a book of "little pieces" without serious claims on the reader's attention. But this typically self-effacing remark, like his calling the contents of his new book "things of the imagination and sensibility, the two ignorant Muses that one does not cultivate,"[3] are offset by two other letters, one to Mme Sauvage de Brantes (née Louise de Cessac) on June 12, 1896, the book's date of publication, the other three years later, to his friend Viscount Clément de Maugny.

The letter to Mme de Brantes continues the self-deprecating tone, but it does so in a manner that lets us understand how different his various writings appeared to him in book form from how they appeared when they were first published separately in periodicals. The intervening effort he had put into the task of gathering them up in a single volume is what stands out, implicitly, in his homage to Mme de Brantes:

> To Madame de Brantes:
> so that she will deign to accept the respectful homage of this book whose only value will remain that of having pleased her when it was scattered and formless, and to which the benevolence of her sympathy—*in this circumstance alone* I will not say the clear-sightedness of her intellect and her taste—has given distinction and elect status. (*Corr.* 2: 74)

Gathered in a single volume, the many "little pieces" were no longer "scattered and formless." They had assumed an order, a new reason for being, which he, the author, had given to them.

Clément de Maugny was probably Proust's most intimate friend among the French aristocracy during the 1890s; intimate in the sense that they related to each other as equals and shared many interests in common. Now and then Proust was de Maugny's guest at the family's fourteenth-century château, and he refers to his friend's kindnesses and generosity during the preceding three years, from 1896 to 1899, when Proust was prey to many disappointments. In a letter written on July 13, 1899, acknowledging de Maugny's sympathetic attention to his problems after the publication of *PJ*, he spoke of the emotional pain he had experienced years earlier, during a period in his life when de Maugny did not know him. It was in this context that he presented his book to his friend. Here is the relevant part of the letter:

> Often we show a friend who only got to know us much later a photograph of when we were a child. The same holds true for this book which introduces you to a Marcel whom you did not know. May I say it? You who have seen me in pain, without ever having made me suffer from a mistake in tact, from a lack of compassion, which is also quite rare, you have seen the birth and dissipation of sadnesses that will not seem very different to you from those depicted in this book. What makes us cry changes but our tears resemble each other. It seems to me that, involved so closely with my pains during these years when you were my confidant and friend, you will feel more than others what these pages still retain of storms that will not return ever again. (*Corr.* 2: 291–292)

This letter expresses something of the personal suffering that Proust associated with his first literary efforts. *PJ* marked a beginning and an end for him; it documented his emotional life in disguised and fictional form, a stage in his life when he was still unsure of the direction that his future writing would take. But at the same time the letter is indicative of a certain detachment from early experiences that allowed him to place them in a different framework than would have been possible in earlier years.

A question needing brief commentary concerns the book's disparate genres. My point of view on this characteristic of the book is simply that the organic connection between these writings is not essentially generic but philosophical and symbolic; it is to be found in the vision of life that inheres in them. By this I do not mean that a short sketch or prose poem may not have originated in a side of Proust's personality and experience that was substantially different, say, from the one revealed in his short stories. Yet the links between the shorter items and the longer ones are, in several instances, noteworthy. For example, the painterly prose of "*Les Regrets, rêveries couleur du temps*" alludes to the same sense of fleeting time and of the "derisory" nature of certain illusions that permeates several of the short stories. The idea that beauty, like all spiritually inspired values, is not in things themselves but in the mind of the artist in "*Promenade*" (A walk) is what—in perverted and illusory form, to be sure—gives the fantasies of "*Violante*" and "*Mélancolique villégiature*" their interest as travesties of idealism in which "the omnipotence of thought"[4] leads to misery and loneliness in contrast to the fulfillment experienced by the artist. Throughout the collection, in almost all of its parts large and small, one senses Proust's passionate attachment to a conception of art that does not refuse but, rather, delights and finds inspiration in the most ordinary and humble aspects of life. Human passions, ideals, hopes, illusions, memories—all combine with a reverential attitude toward natural beauty to endow this collection with its own particular charm and cohesiveness.

An example of the book's unity despite the generic diversity of its "little pieces" can be seen in the "*Fragments de comédie italienne*," where Italian comedy serves as a metaphor for contemporary society in the stylized form of masked faces, affectation, foolishness, self-delusion, pretention, assumed identities, sudden changes of character and fortune—a whole array of situations in which individuals play strange roles and display unpredictable, often contemptible, behavior toward themselves and toward others. This is the lot, or threatened fate, of Proust's lovers in the short stories (as it will be for many characters of the *Recherche*), the only remedies for which are either the epiphanic moments that precede death or the liberating effects of artistic creation. For Proust, there are no others.

Bernard Gicquel was the first to devote systematic study to features of *PJ* that made it a "composed work." He argued that themes, images, and situations in the book "respond to each other, reflect each other, evoke each other" even at some distance, and in this respect convey a sense of organicity. They suggest "an underlying order" far more significant than mere chronology, an "intentional placement" that substitutes for chronology "an aesthetic order desired by [Proust's] mind." Gicquel made much of the centrality of the *Portraits*, situated in the exact middle of the collection, surrounded on both sides by four stories or cycles of short pieces. This order manifested a "geometric arrangement" of its parts. He concluded from the position of the château drawings at the beginning and end that this was Proust's way of giving the book "a circular order" not dissimilar, he noted, from the "cyclical" collections of poems that were popular in the Middle Ages. Originally a symbol of the return of the seasons, the circle becomes in *PJ* the very image of time, of those "days" alluded to in the title. Furthermore, Gicquel maintained, the story "*La Mort de Baldassare Silvande*," with its five chapters, contains the essential five themes of *PJ*: worldly vanity, sensuality, imagination, will, and death.

Luzius Keller's commentary in the 1988 German edition of *PJ* (*Freuden und Tage* 277–287) is the other critical work that, joining Gicquel's essay, has gone furthest in arguing that *PJ* is constructed according to a compositional principle that gives Proust's youthful writings a "new shape and meaning." He stresses the centrality of art as a theme and as a unifying principle of the book, and the "symmetrical" arrangement of its various materials. Like Kingcaid, he points out the prevalence of "decadent" themes (forbidden loves, confessions, matricide, suicide, illness and so on) seen against a "broad intertextual horizon" including such names as St. Augustine and Thomas à Kempis.

Keller considers "*La Mort de Baldassare Silvande*," written in 1894 and revised in 1895, as a summary or recapitulation of Proust's writing up to that point, a sort of prefiguration of the book as a whole. This story, he believes, mirrors Proust's entire aesthetic experience, from Augustine to the French moralists, from Anatole France to Tolstoy, from Montesquiou to Hahn. Montesquiou's presence can be seen in the decadent aestheticism and elaborate finery of Baldassare's existence (exotic animals, a collection of musical instruments, the coat of arms), while Hahn's influence in Proust's life is reflected, among other links, in the title of the story inasmuch as the letters of "Reynaldo" are concealed within the name "Baldassare Silvande" except for the o and the y taken from "*Vicomte*" and "*Sylvanie*." However farfetched this may seem, what we know about Proust's fondness for verbal play gives Keller's observation more than speculative value.

Keller's main point is that the book is arranged in such a way as to convey the notion that art and death are the means through which several of Proust's characters become aware of the "factitiousness" of so much of human life and approach the threshold of "truth and essentiality." This idea is certainly present, whether or not the arrangement of the materials in the book is meant to highlight it. Baldassare and Honoré, in the first and last stories, "pay for an instant of authentic life with life itself." At the same time, Keller regards Gicquel's thesis concerning a "negative" and a "positive" valence as very questionable. He prefers, as do I, to see the unity of the book as residing more in its philosophical standpoint, in its tendency to focus on "the fluctuations and forces" of the world, than in its structural features per se.

Keller introduces another possible source of unity by looking at the book's pastiches and at how its many epigraphs play upon a series of interpenetrating themes. Proust used the devices of imitation, parody, and pastiche as forms of commentary on some of his favorite writers; for example, "*Violante*," "*Oranthe*," and "*Bouvard et Pécuchet*" were essentially "stylistic studies" of Anatole France, La Bruyère, and Flaubert. To this Keller adds two other observations. First, he maintains that the shifts in narrative viewpoint that mark "*La mort de Baldassare Silvande*" and "*Mélancolique villégiature*" imply "a critical reflection on literature," that is, a self-conscious manipulation of narrative methods rather than a formal error committed by a novice writer. Second, and more important as far as the work in its entirety is concerned, he argues that in *PJ* Proust strings together forms of expression, fashionable trends, and beloved authors belonging to the latter decades of the nineteenth century. His motive in doing so, Keller believes, was to provide a "panorama of fin-de-siècle literature," a kind of overview of contemporary literary currents. This interpretation runs the risk of overstating a fruitful idea, yet when we look at Proust's subsequent writing, culminating in the *Recherche*, and note that he incorporated into these works theories and views on contemporary painting, music, and literature, it does not seem off the mark to read *PJ* from this panoramic perspective.

The pastiche, remarks Léon Deffoux (187), is a form of satire without malice, a spoofing without ill will, as distinguished from parody, which uses "grosser artifices," and aims at making the ideas and the style of a writer an object of ridicule, usually in a theatrical and burlesque manner. Both pastiche and parody are forms of irreverence, but in the case of pastiche the irreverence can also be an indirect way of paying homage to a writer whom one admires. Jean Milly observes pertinently that pastiche was a "permanent activity" of Proust, a mode of literary appropriation through which he could at one and the same time pay tribute to writers who were important to him and "free himself from influences that were too strong, in order to achieve his independence, his full capacity as an original creator" (1970, 37). In other words, if this general point of view has validity, we would be entitled to add the word "critical" to Keller's characterization and call *PJ* "a critical panorama of fin-de-siècle literature."[5]

In his 1993 study of *PJ*, Pierre Daum approaches the work from a rather rigorously structuralist point of view. But he also identifies some of the book's stylistic traits, its rhythms and sonorities, and its alternating tones of lyricism and moralism. He sees the book as essentially a series of "studies of human souls." According to this view, then, the unity of *PJ* is more psychological than philosophical, more intimate and introspective than ideological, as I have defined this last term.

Daum examines an aspect of Proust's writing in *PJ* about which there has been relatively little commentary. He characterizes several of the stories as having extremely vague temporal and spatial coordinates, as bearing very few traces of historicity, of rootedness in a specific time and place. I strongly agree with this perception. The stories seem to be detached from time, as if they were intended to be fables rather than conventionally realistic accounts of human experiences. The "mythic," otherworldly tales of one of Proust's literary friends and idols, Henri de Régnier (1864–1936), may have been the crucial influence pushing him in this direction. Stories such as "*La Mort de Baldassare Silvande*," "*Violante*," and "*Mélancolique villégiature*," and shorter pieces such as "*Rencontre au bord du lac*" (Encounter by the lake) and "*L'Etranger*" (The stranger) seem suspended in time, despite a few allusions to things and people reminiscent of Parisian society in the 1890s. The often abstract, fabular atmosphere in *PJ* reflects young Proust's desire to retreat into a timeless realm where ideal types could act and ideal situations could unfold free of the real historical determinants of human thought and action. His intention was to highlight the universal significance of his characters' inner lives and relationships. He wanted to suspend his readers' attachment to the world by transporting them to the imaginary domain of abstract elemental forces at work in human destiny. Either he gives his characters names—Baldassare, Violante, Madame de Breyves,

Heldémone, Adelgise, Oranthe, Cardenio, M. de Laléande—that have an exotic or un-French sound, or he gives them no name at all, as in "*Rencontre au bord du lac*" and "*Rêve*" (Dream).

This does not mean that *PJ* lacks critical bite. On the contrary, Proust's critique of a self-indulgent, wasteful, superficial society is evident. What it means, however, is that he wanted his criticism to transcend the moment in which the stories were written, so that the reader would feel free to attach a general human significance to them rather than associate them with a specific social milieu. Too much historical material could spoil the subtler workings of fantasy. Proust was after the general, the universal, the "laws" of human nature as revealed in similar and recurrent situations.

It seems to me that we gain access to Proust's ideology precisely through these attempts to protect a domain of fabular purity from the contaminations of history. He shared this need with many other artists and writers of the late nineteenth and early twentieth century. That he eventually transcended his penchant for the timeless fable in favor of a resolute psychological realism, as seen in the *Recherche*, is one of the things that sets him apart from many other writers of his generation.

PJ reflects Proust's readings of Kant and Schopenhauer, as Anne Henry has demonstrated in her study of Proust's aesthetic theory. The philosophy and implicit ideology of Proust's early writings are testimony to his assimilation of certain notions about the nature of the human mind, about art, and about the relationship between empirical and ideal truth that derive in part from the two German thinkers. If, as I have claimed, the unity of *PJ* consists to a significant extent in its philosophical premises, then German idealist and neo-idealist thought must be taken into account.

Raymond Williams's characterization of the history of modern aesthetics as "in large part a protest against the forcing of all experience into instrumentality ('utility'), and of all things into commodities" (*Marxism and Literature* 151) is pertinent to the reasons why Proust and many of his contemporaries found Kantian thought to be congenial to their aesthetic and moral perspectives.

Kant based much of what he said in *Critique of Pure Reason* on the assumption that human beings possess and exercise a faculty of pure a priori cognition inherent in the mind and not dependent on empirical evidence. The proper tests of such cognition, he argued, were universality and necessity. He applied the term "transcendental" to all knowledge "which is not so much occupied with objects as with the mode of our cognition of these objects, so far as this mode of cognition is possible a priori" (Kant 1934, 38).

In this regard, Kant continued, what was of interest to him philosophically speaking was not the nature of "outward objects" but the properties of the mind, of the subjective knowing entity. "The object of our investigations," he said, was not to be sought without, but altogether within ourselves. Kant did not, however, discard or minimize the role that objective knowledge played in human cognition. There were at bottom two sources of human knowledge, sense and understanding. By the former, objects were *given* to us; by the latter, *thought*. Building on these premises, Kant went on to present the foundational principles of his "transcendental aesthetic" philosophy that required a distinction between empirical intuition, which works on all phenomena given to us through the senses, and pure intuition, which exists a priori in the mind, the preliminary abode of thought.

Both space and time, Kant reasoned at a decisive turning point of Western philosophical thought, were concepts that could be spoken of only from the human point of view. Space, he said, was not a form that belongs as a property to things, but was rather the form of all phenomena as they are perceived by the subjective condition of the sensibility; objects remain quite unknown to us in themselves. What we call outward objects are nothing but "mere representations of our sensibility" (47).

Kant considered time "the formal condition a priori of all phenomena whatsoever." While space was the form of our "external intuition," time was nothing but the form of our "internal intuition." Time inheres not in objects themselves but solely in the subject (or mind) that intuits them. The conclusion he drew from all this was what made his thought exceptionally appealing to the mind and sensibilities of writers such as Proust, who were looking anxiously for a way out of the constraints imposed by various forms of materialist and positivist thought.

The key point to be made here is that, instead of embracing a dialectical and historical materialist approach to problems of knowledge and perception, Proust—following a growing number of writers and artists in the nineteenth century in an ever-expanding movement of thought that culminated in the symbolism and spiritualism of the century's last decades—embraced Kantian idealism as it was expounded in part in the famous "Introduction" to *Critique of Pure Reason*. In his "general remarks on transcendental aesthetic," Kant wrote as follows:

> We have intended to say that all our intuition is nothing but the representation of phenomena; that the things which we intuit, are not in themselves the same as our representations of them in intuition, nor are their relations in themselves so

constituted as they appear to us; and that if we take away the subject, or even only the subjective constitution of our senses in general, then not only the nature and relations of objects in space and time, but even space and time themselves disappear; and that these, as phenomena, cannot exist in themselves, but only in us. What may be the nature of objects considered as things in themselves and without reference to the receptivity of our sensibility is quite unknown to us. We know nothing more than our mode of perceiving them, which is peculiar to us, and which, though not of necessity pertaining to every animated being, is so to the whole human race. With this alone we have to do. Space and time are the pure forms thereof; sensation the matter. The former alone can we cognize a priori, that is, antecedent to all actual perception; and for this reason such cognition is called pure intuition. (54)

This revolutionary affirmation of idealist thought[6] also found expression in the pages of Kant's *Critique of Judgment*, where he presented what he called his "Analytic of the Beautiful" (Kant 1963). In this work, explains Walter Cerf, we find ourselves immersed in a series of "dualisms" and "binary oppositions" that lie—as Jacques Derrida, Barbara Johnson, Joseph Buttigieg and others have told us—at the very core of Western metaphysical discourse. They form the conceptual horizons of the Kantian philosophy of pleasure: the metaphysical concept of the soul-body dualism, the epistemological concept of the subject-object scheme, and the concept of the cause-effect relation. Indeed, everything Proust wrote, from the early stories and prose poems to the later masterpiece, is difficult to imagine without the philosophical underpinnings provided by this essential dualism inherent in Kantian idealist thought. The soul-body dualism goes back many thousands of years, attaining in Christian philosophy a preeminent place of honor, but it was only in its specific elaboration by Kant and his followers that it became fully accessible to and assimilable by writer-philosophers such as Proust, who needed a spiritualist grounding for his theory of art but one that was couched in terms that were free of explicitly religious connotations. This he found in Kant, especially in the way Kant applied his thought to problems of knowledge and aesthetics.

Kant's aesthetics rested on the distinction between impure pleasure and pure pleasure, the latter untainted by the senses. What he envisioned was a theory of the beautiful which, on the one hand, was separate and autonomous vis-à-vis the senses, yet on the other hand could help form a part of the bridge between the analysis of cognition and the analysis of morality. In other words, he accorded autonomy to the aesthetic, but at the same time insisted on its ultimate relation with moral judgment.

What stands out for our purposes is Kant's assertion that the judgment of taste, which is the faculty of judging the beautiful, is not logical but aesthetic, which in turn cannot be other than subjective. This feeling for the beautiful, he argued, was rooted in the human capacity for pure disinterested pleasure, as opposed to the pleasure that rests entirely on sensation. The judgment of taste is merely contemplative; it has no object or rationale beyond a disinterested enjoyment of the beautiful in and for itself. Kant was committed, avers Dieter Henrich, "to the view that beauty and all other elementary and purely aesthetic qualities depend exclusively on the formal arrangement of a perceived manifold" (54–55). If this is the case, we can see why Proust was uncomfortable with some of the implications of Kantian aesthetic purism, since he wanted to reintroduce into aesthetic philosophy the notion of humanity's moral life and destiny, to which the experience of art could add vital elements. He was not prepared to isolate "form" from "content" in writing or in the other arts. But this is an aspect of Proustian thought that remains somewhat unclear. It does not seem to me that he was ever entirely ready to align himself with a formalist aesthetics resting on the presumed Kantian theory that it is design and composition "which are the proper objects of pure judgment" (Kant 1963, 31).

Proust made only a few explicit references to Schopenhauer, yet the German thinker appears to have had a certain appeal for him based on the fact that, even more resolutely perhaps than Kant, he gave to art a distinctive place in human experience, but did so by accenting concerns and considerations that had not played any real part in Kant's scheme of things. Schopenhauer introduced into Western philosophy an Eastern component that gave to the material world a transitory, illusory quality. For Schopenhauer, "the ideality of time and space" was the key to all true metaphysics because "it made way for an order of things quite different from what is found in nature" (20). But he noted in typically pessimistic fashion that most people were incapable of entering this different order; they were victims of foolish illusions about sensual gratifications and so "the very thing they allowed to slip by unappreciated and unenjoyed was just their life, precisely in the expectation of which they lived" (22). Something of this attitude can be detected in Proust's way of analyzing the role of illusion in the general problematic of human existence.

Schopenhauer's reflections on the qualities of "genius," one of whose characteristics was the ability "to see the universal in the particular," led him to another notion that, theoretically, was to play an important part in Proust's aesthetics, namely that "the kind of knowledge of the genius is essentially purified of all willing and of references to the will; [from which it follows] that the works of genius do not result from intention or arbitrary choice, but that genius is here guided by a kind of instinctive necessity"

(87). This idea fascinated Proust as a principle of literary and artistic creation, although it conflicted with another aspect of his world view, which was that "thought" and therefore conscious reflection were what gave true dignity to works of art.

Where Schopenhauer left his mark on Proust was in Schopenhauer's reflections on the relations between history and art, the former seen as displaying "the transient complexities of a human world moving like clouds in the wind, which are entirely transformed by the most trifling accident" (107), the latter a realm in which what was of permanent and universal value could find its fulfillment in lasting works of the creative imagination. In this concept, Schopenhauer felt that he had identified a crucial element of the "philosophy of the moderns," which derived largely from Berkeley and Kant but purified of the tendency to discount the necessary dialectical relationship between the thinking subject and its object of thought.

Much of what Proust had to say both in fictional and in critical form was grounded in the presuppositions and principles of idealist philosophy, even if he tempered some of its more mystical features—as seen especially in Schopenhauer—in favor of what Mieke Bal calls his "visual poetics" resting in turn on a theory of knowledge

> that does not separate the domain of the mind from that of the body, in other words, that does not separate the cognitive, the affective, the aesthetic, and the sexual domains. Rather it explores all avenues, however unusual they may be, that lead to the discovery of new aspects of the real by means of sensations, experiences, and the very pores of one's being. It is for this reason that we can treat Proust as a philosopher and even view him in the same light as the greatest philosophers of this century. (239)

Bal's formulation allows us to see what distinguishes Proust's philosophy of art from that of his idealist forebears. The material world has a palpable presence in Proust's writing that, even if still bound by the constraints of dualistic thinking, adheres to and illuminates sense experience in an admirably realistic manner.

I have referred several times to the work of Anne Henry as a helpful guide to Proust's early intellectual and literary development. This is an appropriate moment in which to say a few words about her contribution to Proust studies.

The singular distinction of her work is that it mixes a thorough analysis of the philosophical foundations of Proust's ideas, especially concerning the nature and purposes of art and literature, with a series of critically acute judgments that effectively demystify much of what had passed up to then for Proust's absolute originality and transcendent genius. In her hands, Proust returns definitively to the fold of French writers at the turn of the century who shared intellectual interests, political and moral concerns, and literary aspirations. In an earlier essay on *PJ*, she discovered "troubling resemblances" between some of Proust's stories and prose-poetic evocations and those of other writers of the time, among whom she singled out Tolstoy to document what she felt amounted to "plagiary" on Proust's part, instances where he had "pillaged" motifs and devices from the great Russian novelist and short-story writer (Henry 1973). I shall discuss these so-called "plagiaries" in chapter 8.

In *Marcel Proust: Théories pour une esthétique*, a massive study only a small part of which will be mentioned here, Henry resumes her inquiry into the armamentarium of philosophical notions on the basis of which, she argues, Proust built his world view and produced his fictional universe. These notions turn out to be those of the entire European Romantic heritage, which drew copiously from German thinkers, especially from aesthetic and moral philosophers such as Schelling and Schopenhauer. Proust was also shaped, philosophically speaking, by Slavic influences (Tolstoy and Dostoievsky) and of course by French philosophers, from his own philosophy instructor Alphonse Darlu to Gabriel Séailles, Jules Lachelier, and Emile Boutroux. It is entirely possible that Darlu, in addition to inculcating into his responsive student a reverence for truthseeking at all costs, was also responsible for sensitizing him to French social questions, as seen from a radical-socialist point of view (Bonnet 1961, 46, 57, 68). It was Darlu as well who exposed the young writer to the thought of Immanuel Kant, which Proust regarded as "the Himalaya" of moral philosophy (Henry 34).

Henry points out that Proust derived his understanding of the "unconscious" not from Freud, whose writings played no direct role whatever in his conception of human personality, but from Karl von Hartmann's *The Philosophy of the Unconscious*, published in 1869. Henry feels that this work was an important source of Proust's pessimism about the ability of human beings to exert rationally motivated control over their behavior. Proust did not take Hartmann's pessimism as far as some others did, yet it may very well be that his view of love as inevitably "illusory" and even pathological in nature, and his recourse to art as the sole means with which to redeem an otherwise empty existence, stemmed in some measure from Hartmann. I would think, however, that in this realm Proust was probably the interpeter of his own life experience, for which he then found confirmation in philosophy and psychology.

Henry makes much, but with rather slight evidence, of a turn or shift toward aesthetics in Proust's thinking in the mid to late years of the 1890s. The evidence for this turn consists of three articles, the first on the liberating power of music, which he regarded as the queen of the muses (*CSB* 367–372), the second on Chardin and Rembrandt (*CSB* 372–382), the third on symbolism, where he challenged the poetic authority of Stéphane Mallarmé and his disciples (*CSB* 390–395). In these articles, especially the last two, Proust was performing an intellectual exercise that paralleled the approach he took in *PJ*, where music, poetry, and painting join forces thematically and even typographically in a tribute to the sisterhood of the muses. What one finds in these three articles is an effort to raise the arts to a spiritual, a sacred level. Henry connects this sudden exaltation of art with the frequently mentioned letter Proust wrote in September of 1893 to his father, where he humbly yet confidently declared himself to be unfit for anything in life except philosophy and literature, and with the lectures given by Emile Boutroux on modern philosophy, which Proust attended at the Sorbonne in 1894–95. It was in this state of mind, Henry maintains, that Proust read and was marked forever by Schelling's *System of Transcendental Idealism* and by the thought of Schelling's French disciple, Gabriel Séailles.

Henry treats Proust's philosophical formation with deep seriousness, and she enlarges our understanding of his emerging world outlook. The only problem in her approach is that her focus on intellectual history is so intense that she loses sight of a broader historical contextualization that would have given her analysis of Proust's ideas more connections with the practical experiential world.

A recent critical study that sheds further light on Proust's aesthetic philosophy is Anthony Albert Everman's *Lilies and Sesame: The Orient, Inversion, and Artistic Creation in* A la recherche du temps perdu (1998). Everman ascribes Proust's way of conceptualizing art to the influence of Kant, Schelling and Schopenhauer, whose thought "posits that the creation of art falls under the domain of *génie*, an interiorized, subjective, irrational yet transcending force with ostensible roots, perceived by certain Europeans, in the ascetic traditions of Hinduism and Buddhism" (157). Flowing from this root assumption is the idea that artistic creation is the fruit of the individual creator's feeling of marginality, of separation and estrangement from the norms of society, for such a condition allows the artist to see beneath appearances, to unearth and reveal what society prefers to conceal out of fear that knowledge of the "truth" of human affairs will subvert the established order of things. One form of estrangement is that of the sexual "invert," who quite literally "overturns" accepted notions about what is and what is not the truth of human sexuality. Sexual difference is a key component of the Proustian vision of the world, Everman argues. It is closely linked to the notion of "Orientalism" in that the Orient, for Proust, is associated with a realm of being where the imagination and aesthetic sensibilities can have free play to express themselves, and where there can be "reconciliation between the components of a fragmented personality" (34). Thus, in Proust's scheme of things, what most members of modern society take to be aberrational turns out to be precisely the key to that crucial "difference" vital to creative life.

Whether, as Everman seems to think, Roland Barthes was correct in seeing "inversion" as not only a dominant structure of the *Recherche* but also as "a source of delightful surprise and *jouissance* on the part of the reader and the protagonist" (70) is difficult to say. But what can be said with some degree of confidence is that at least two of the novel's principal "homosexual" characters, Charlus and Albertine, are, although morally ambiguous, the embodiments of a special fascination and "beauty" that other so-called "normal" characters do not possess. They incorporate an aspect of reality that Proust urgently wished to reveal, one that depended on his need, derived in part from his own "marginal" sexuality, to undertake an "outing" of much of the society represented in his novel (91).

Everman penetrates the psychological and social attitudes that lay behind Proust's depiction of contemporary French society at a time when one way of life and conception of the world with roots in the remote feudal past were being definitively replaced by a new bourgeois *Weltanschauung*. His study allows us to see motifs and character types in Proust's early writing that anticipate the ideology of "Orientalism" in the *Recherche*.

Chapter 7

Elitism and the Primacy of the Spiritual

Proust was essentially an independent thinker who never unqualifiedly identified himself with any school or movement. Literally and figuratively, he stood "between two centuries." He was classically educated and revered the Greco-Roman heritage, yet he was clearly a modernist who derived ideas and inspiration from impressionism and symbolism. He was formed, intellectually, by idealist thought, yet his close attention to physical detail in his writing, his interest in inherited traits, and his constant concern with understanding the laws of human behavior show that he was far from indifferent to the new experimental sciences in the fields of biology and psychology.[1]

Balzac, whose great novel cycle was built on the assumption that everything in life, including the most apparently eccentric and aberrational phenomena, could ultimately be understood and classified, was a probable literary source for the scientific and "positive" side of Proust's world view. Balzac was among the first modern novelists to formulate and put into practice a belief in the necessary alliance between literature and science. In this sense, Proust's search for the laws that govern human psychology and action was an outgrowth and a continuation of Balzac's project.

Proust's ability to reconcile opposing views on many issues in the search for higher and higher levels of philosophical synthesis mark him as basically an eclectic thinker with little if any tolerance for hard-and-fast, absolute positions. Although a nonbeliever, he spoke of art with religious enthusiasm, and used the word "divine" frequently in his commentary on various writers and artists. Nevertheless, despite this characteristic "inbetweenness," I think it is fair to say that Proust shared three interrelated values with many writers and intellectuals coming of age in the 1880s and 1890s. These were elitism, individualism, and spiritualism. It will be the task of the remainder of this chapter to show how these values manifested themselves in *PJ* and in several other writings of the 1890s.

Young Proust's elitism appears most strikingly in his dedicatory preface to *PJ* and in a letter he wrote to a friend, Pierre Lavallée, on or around June 12, 1896, when he used the occasion of his book's publication to comment on his relationship with Lavallée and others belonging to their circle.

The elegaic dedication of *PJ* to his English friend Willie Heath (Laget 39–43)—a sensitive and refined person whose early death was a great personal loss to Proust—was written in July 1894. It is learned and deeply felt, somewhat ornate and precious in style, and comprehensive in its tributes to the people who were most important to Proust at the time. In six pages, it mentions, alludes to, or cites passages from (in the following order) Ernest Renan, Homer, Alexandre Dumas fils, Madeleine Lemaire, Robert de Montesquiou, Anton Van Dyck, Leonardo da Vinci, Proust's mother, the Bible, Virgil, Racine, Count Charles de Grancey (a boyhood friend), Reynaldo Hahn, Anatole France, and Alphonse Darlu. One might be tempted to call this mere name-dropping, a form of pedantry, yet each of these names and the works with which they are associated had an undeniable importance in Proust's development as a writer. He wanted the dedication to Heath to function also as an acknowledgement of his indebtedness to his mother and to a group of esteemed writers, artists, thinkers, and friends.

One feature of the Heath dedication that makes it somewhat typical of its historical moment is its attempt, in the manner of contemporary decadentism, to link illness and the possibility (or reality) of imminent death with artistic creativity, or better, with the psychological detachment from the quotidian affairs of the world that is often a condition of creativity. The link is established through the sequence of images and allusions relating first to Heath, then to the Van Dyck portraits of King Charles I and the Duke of Richmond who, like Heath, were marked for imminent death,[2] and finally to himself, where Proust recalls his feeling of sadness as a boy when his mother read to him about Noah, the "patriarch" who was forced to spend forty long days on his ark cut off from the rest of the world. But this sadness was replaced some years later, Proust tells us, by his growing realization that "Noah was never able to see the world better than from his ark." This insight was made possible by his own illness, followed by a convalescence and eventual recovery of health that, although welcome and joyous, was also accompanied by a certain nostalgia for a period in life when "the special grace of illness brings us closer to certain realities that are beyond death."

The themes of elitism, based on what Proust calls "moral elegance," which Heath had in common with the men depicted by Van Dyck, and of the privileged condition of persons suffering illness who, like lovers and poets, "feel themselves closer [than other men] to their soul," are deftly interwoven into this brief dedication. Immediately after citing in the first paragraph a few of Montesquiou's verses devoted to Madeleine Lemaire, Proust referred to the "elite" among her many admirers who would have recognized Heath's qualities had they been able to know him as he, Proust, had. Thus Proust sees himself here as an intermediary figure, a translator, as it were, charged with the responsibility of interpreting certain feelings and experiences for the benefit of those in his social world who were able to receive them. He tells this elite in particular about the pact he had made with Heath, "the dream, almost the project, of living more and more with each other, in a circle of magnanimous and select women and men, far enough from stupidity, vice and wickedness to feel ourselves protected from their vulgar insults."

Faith, creativity, love, awareness of death and of "certain realities that are beyond death"—these are the ideas and values that Proust exalted in his dedicatory preface to *PJ* and which he shared with writers and artists of his generation and his social background who thought of themselves as an intellectual vanguard charged with a mission to resist the encroachments of vulgar materialism into the realms of art and culture. Proust was among French literary intellectuals in the early 1890s who expounded this point of view in periodicals such as *Le Mercure de France, La Plume*, and *La Revue Blanche*. It will be helpful, therefore, to look briefly at a few of these reviews' representative essays.

The editors of *La Plume* saw as one of their primary purposes that of clarifying what separated them from the "crowd" of soulless worshipers of Mammon and from the "utilitarian" critics and theorists who were concerned (foolishly, in their opinion) with what literature was supposed to be doing for the cause of the weak and the downtrodden. Any such mixing of art with social struggles would lead, ipso facto, to a defilement of its supreme spiritual mission (Bourget 1890). Like *La Plume*, the venerable *Le Mercure de France* was a rallying point for the avant-garde at the time. The review resolutely opposed the rise of "mass" culture, which made of everything that was easily digested, quickly understood, and commercially successful the end-all of the publishing industry. Railing against the "contaminations of commercialism," many of its writers celebrated the "solitary" artist who, disdaining illicit profit and resisting the "stupid cajolery of the plebes," worked in silence for the realization of an ideal. "Innocence" and "purity" were the virtues of Renoir, said G.-Aubert Aurier, making of him the very embodiment of what a true artist ought to represent in the world (Aurier, Aug. 1891). In another essay, devoted to Gauguin, he spoke of "the imbecilic human herd" that would never understand the ideas and ideals of the modern creative spirit (Aurier, March 1891). Rémy de Gourmont recalled Huysmans's defection from naturalism as marking the beginning of a new era in the history of French literature (Gourmont 1891). Saint-Pol-Roux spoke of the poet as a "second creator" inspired directly by God, the first and eternal creator, thus establishing a bond between divinity and art that was dear to the hearts of Proust's generation (Saint-Pol-Roux 1892).

Typical of French bourgeois literary intellectuals in the 1890s was a belief that art and philosophy had few prospects in an age ever more relentlessly subverted by social upheavals and, as we have seen, by the rise of a mass culture that was widening the gap between the creative minority on the one hand, and the oppressed classes on the other. How can we expect to reach such masses, asked Marcel Collière, when the deficiencies of popular education and the demands of daily labor made them impervious to beauty and to the "higher things" embodied in the writings of Homer, Shakespeare, and Mallarmé. Camille Mauclair believed that the essential flaw of naturalism was its interest in "the object in and for itself," whereas it was the subjective apprehension by the poet of "the pure idea" that gave poetry its unique appeal.

The editor-in-chief of *La Revue Blanche* in the 1890s, Lucien Muhlfeld, put his finger on an essential problem of the time in two articles, one devoted to various contemporary writers but with special attention to the Belgian symbolist playwright and poet, Maurice Maeterlinck, the other to what Mulhfeld called "a crisis" in the relationship between writers and readers in "an age of transition." Calling Maeterlinck "the most interior of interior" spirits, the one and only "true mystic" of the age, Muhlfeld connected him to the poetic tradition of Baudelaire and Poe, who were in turn the beneficiaries of a "mystical" purism originating theoretically with Plato, followed then by Plotinus, and reaching the modern era in the poetry of Novalis and Coleridge (Muhlfeld 1892). It was the esoteric, symbolic, "mystical" qualities of Maeterlinck's language that gave it a special appeal to Muhlfeld and others like him who were looking for a way of justifying their feeling of superiority to and difference from a mass civilization they perceived as threatening to art and culture. Not all of the writers associated with *La Revue Blanche* agreed with Muhlfeld, of course, but enough of them did to give the review a pronounced elitist coloring.

Muhlfeld's other article deals with the same problem of art and literature in a time of mass culture in which the popular and working classes were clamoring for a greater role in the political life of the country, usually in the name of programs that were socialist, egalitarian, and often Marxist in their ideological orientation. He spoke of the end of an era in which writers and readers understood each other and could safely assume that they shared the same or compatible values, and the onset of a new era where what he called "public art" for the masses and "mandarin art" for the few could no longer communicate easily if at all. But whatever the regime or social class in power, he said, especially one where popular democracy was the ruling creed, artists must not be obliged to contribute to "national progress." Art had its own unique ends, and the mandarin class had the duty of safeguarding a hoary tradition of "disinterested" cultivation of precisely these ends, and no others.

Muhlfeld was articulating a point of view that separated him from the vision of "national-popular" culture which, in Gramsci's view, distinguished two nations above all others: France and Russia. It was in these two countries, Gramsci believed, that one could find a fertile relationship between artists and people, between intellectuals and the masses, that had allowed for the emergence of a literature that spoke of and to the popular masses in a language that could reach a large audience without sacrificing artistic values. If Gramsci's way of posing this question has any merit, it is clear that Muhlfeld and his colleagues represented a countercurrent in France, one that placed the writer and the intellectual in a category by themselves, apart from and superior to the common life of the people. This raises difficult questions about the history of nineteenth- and twentieth-century avant-garde movements, some of which, like impressionism, surrealism, and, later, existentialism, certainly aspired to a communicative and interactive relationship with the people. But in the 1890s the avant-gardists attached to reviews such as *La Revue Blanche* were not in a frame of mind that made them friendly to, or feel in solidarity with, democratic or socialist struggles. In the main (and there were exceptions), they had very little sympathy with national-popular culture in any of its forms.

It is difficult to know where exactly to place Proust with respect to this widening gulf between a self-proclaimed elite and the people during the 1890s. That there was something in his attitude toward writing and its revelations that made him a familiar figure in the milieu of writers such as Muhlfeld seems to me to be quite evident. Yet at the same time, there are also hints in his early writing of a responsiveness to certain popular complaints and criticisms directed against elitism—whether social or spiritual in nature—that demand, in his case, that we not rush to judgment.

In *Qu'est-ce que la littérature?* (What is literature?), published in 1947 (English translation *Literature and Existentialism*, 1949) Jean-Paul Sartre spoke of Proust's generation with an understandable ambivalence. The essay was a call to arms, a summons to French literary intellectuals to make of writing the most serious and engaged of human occupations. The questions Sartre sought to answer in his treatise were at once old ones yet perennially new: What is writing? Why write? For whom does one write? Unless one asked these questions, Sartre maintained, it was impossible to free oneself from the confinements of formalism and elitism.

Where Proust fit in this scheme was not directly addressed by Sartre. However, on the basis of what we know about Proust's general orientation toward life and letters in the period that primarily concerns us in this study, the late 1880s and 1890s, we can say with virtual certainty that what Sartre observed about the relations between literature and society in France at the end of the nineteenth century was meant to apply to Proust as much as to other writers of the time who found refuge in the idea of literature as a spiritual commitment requiring "solitude" and "withdrawal into one's inner self." While we know, Sartre asserted in the third section of his treatise, "that literature, ordinarily, represents in society an integral and militant function,"

> bourgeois society at the end of the nineteenth century offers the unprecedented spectacle of an industrious society, grouped around the banner of production, from which there issues a literature which, far from reflecting it, never speaks to it about what interests it, runs counter to its ideology, identifies the Beautiful with the unproductive, refuses to allow itself to be integrated, and does not even want to be read [and nevertheless, within the bosom of its revolt, still reflects the ruling classes in its deepest structures and in its "style."] (Sartre, *Literature and Existentialism*, 145–146)[3]

To this characterization of the late nineteenth-century avant-garde, Sartre immediately added a qualifying judgment that revealed his deeply ambivalent attitude toward writers such as Proust: "We must not blame the authors of this period: they did what they could and we find among them some of our greatest and purest writers."

Despite Sartre's implicit rejection of the way Proust and his contemporaries conceived of the literary vocation, Sartre nonetheless articulates a concept of literary "autonomy" in relation to what he called "the temporal powers" of the world that is reminiscent of Proust's views on the issue. Sartre finds common ground with Proust in his bedrock understanding of literature as having its source in the ideas of freedom and "renewal" of the world:

> I say that the literature of a given age is alienated when it has not arrived at the explicit consciousness of its autonomy and when it submits to temporal powers or to an ideology, in short, when it considers itself as a means and not as an unconditioned end. (152)

Before turning to *PJ* for signs of Proust's understanding of elitism, individualism, and spiritualism, we need to look at the letter to Pierre Lavallée that, together with the dedicatory preface, expresses succinctly the nature of Proust's feelings about the social world he wanted to reach and with which he identified himself.[4] It is a subtle letter, one that gives the impression of hiding more than it reveals, of implying a structure of feeling that only the initiated can fully grasp. It exemplifies quite well some of what Foucault is alluding to when he speaks of "fellowships of discourse" whose function is to preserve or to reproduce discourse, but in order that it should circulate within a closed community, according to strict regulations, "without those in possession being dispossessed by this very distribution" (225).

Here is the letter in its entirety:

[Around June 12, 1896]

My Dear Pierre,

> Like someone whose name appears alone on a subscription that several of his friends have helped to pay for, I feel a little ashamed to hear people speak of this book as mine, to inscribe to you a book that could just as well be yours, if you, having like me, better than me, dreamt of it all your life had, instead of me, taken the trouble to write it. Even though I have managed to put into it the things to which I attach the greatest value—a certain feeling about metempsychosis, which I have no need to define more clearly when speaking to you—what is there to love in it that one does not find, and with greater distinction and purity, in you, and that is not the common heritage of our souls, the native ground in which our sympathies have united together, the very foundation, older and more durable than ourselves and than it, of our friendship. But in any case, this particular copy deserved a special dedicatory inscription. A book read by you, especially if it is a copy of my book, could not resemble any other. How many meanings hidden from others, what—relative—depths known to you alone, will come to light, if you are the reader. I say my book as though I were never to write another. You know well enough that that is not true. If I can finish the one I have undertaken and

begin others, I beg you not to hold back from me the inspiration of your affection, the reward of your understanding. Love my faults and help them to grow, for to you they are the best part of me. Our good qualities belong to us less, and there is no need of so warm an affection, so close a resemblance, to enjoy them.

Your grateful friend

Marcel Proust. (*Selected Letters 1880–1903*, 123)

Among other questions, the letter to Lavallée almost compels us to ask this one: At the time that young Proust was assembling his writings for publication in *PJ*, did he effectively feel himself connected only to a small literary and social elite, or did he see himself as being, at least potentially, in touch with a larger popular audience that would understand and appreciate what he had to say despite the predominantly aristocratic social types and subject matter depicted in his writings?

Everything we know about the circumstances of *PJ*'s publication—its cost, its appearance, the type of elite readership Proust hoped to attract by reason of Lemaire's illustrations, the select group of individuals who, like Lavallée, received inscribed copies—conspires in support of an elitist conception of writing.

My reasons for thinking that this is the case are based not only on the letter's explicit statements but on the character of the person to whom it is addressed. Lavallée, like all of the individuals to whom Proust dedicated and sent inscribed copies of his book, belonged to an aristocracy of intellect and culture, if not of birth. But that is precisely the point: young Proust cared considerably more about this ideal or spiritual elite than he did about an aristocracy of birth, although the names, appearance, habits, breeding, and way of life of the aristocracy always fascinated him, as we have seen in his relationship with Robert de Montesquiou and other members of the French nobility. I would say that his elitism was informed by a concept of highborn and upper bourgeois individuals who incorporated in their persons that "common heritage" to which he alludes in the letter. People of the working classes could and did, for Proust, embody aspects of that heritage, for they too drew their identities from a common soil that nourished the French people as a whole. But the intellectual and spiritual components of that common heritage had been transmitted only by and through select individuals who, by reason of their birth, their education, their culture, had appropriated it in its highest form. Therefore, when Proust spoke of what he shared with Lavallée and of what belonged to both of them, such as "a certain feeling about metempsychosis," he was probably not alluding so much to an occult belief system deriving from the Orphic religion, or to the theosophic teachings of Emmanuel Swedenborg, as to the genetically and culturally determined transmission of traits passed down for centuries by families, from one generation to the next. The "transmigration of souls" was rooted primarily, for Proust, in biology and heredity, not in occult practices and beliefs. Yet this "transmigration" was also a "mysterious" force, something that one felt to be true and that did not require elaborate scientific experiments to substantiate. While it must be acknowledged, as Anne Henry observes, that the word "metempsychosis" has a distinctly "exotic and mystical coloration" (Henry 1973, 70), I rather doubt that Proust looked upon it from a religious point of view. When it came to supernatural and mystical beliefs as understood in a literal sense, I think that Proust was, if not a convinced nonbeliever, certainly a skeptic.[5]

But here again we need to proceed with caution. In *Esotérisme et écriture dans l'œuvre de Proust*, Juliette Hassine makes a fairly strong case for Proust's interest in and perhaps partial acceptance of the doctrines of the *Zohar*, the chief work of the Spanish Kabbalah in which the image of light (Zohar means "brightness" in Hebrew) is of central symbolic importance. This is in itself a suggestive idea in relation to Proust inasmuch as the sun and its manifold properties is a pervasive theme in many of his fictional writings, especially in *JS,* as will be seen in chapter 10. Hassine points out that the *Zohar* offers a view of creation "as a writing of signs" supposed to have revealed themselves beginning with a primary light identified with Wisdom. She then refers to the role attributed by this system of thought to Memory and to Music in the creation of the world. Obviously, we need to read no further to catch the fascinating possibilities of a connection between this body of thought and the Proustian vision of things.

Another element of the letter to Lavallée that seems to support the notion of elitism lies in Proust's sense that Lavallée would understand certain of the book's meanings that remained "hidden from others." Proust had met Lavallée at the Lycée Condorcet, where they took a course on rhetoric together in 1887. In 1893, when they met again at the Law Faculty, the two became close friends and remained so until the end of the decade, when Lavallée married and their paths diverged. Lavallée was one of three friends (the others were Reynaldo Hahn and Robert de Billy) with whom Proust enjoyed visiting the Louvre and discussing the fine points of particular paintings such as those mentioned in his "*Portraits de peintres.*" Indeed, Lavallée was to become the chief curator of the library and museum of the School of Fine Arts in Paris, and a specialist in the history of European drawing. His list of scholarly writings is impressive. He belonged to a select group of art connoisseurs, historians, and curators that included the Henraux brothers, Emile Mâle, Emmanuel Bibesco, and Bertrand de Fénelon, from whom, Tadié tells us, Proust learned a great deal, including detailed knowledge about museum holdings and foreign cities he had not been able to visit in his early years because of ill health. In sum, Lavallée had the special qualities that Proust acknowledged by sending him a copy of the rice-paper edition (no. 29 of thirty copies printed) of *PJ* on or close to the day the book was published, along with the letter just discussed (*Selected Letters 1880–1903*, 123 n. 1).

As already noted, Proust rarely ventures outside the social world he depicts; he never stands apart from it in order to provide the reader with a feeling for the conflicts and issues that make his characters the way they are. His is an insider's glimpse into this world, true enough, and as such the book offers a rich array of social types and genealogies. But the conflictual element that is present in *PJ* almost always concerns a character's inner life, or involves a close familial relationship, such as that of mother and daughter.

One might argue that the short stories and prose poems of *PJ* cannot be expected to achieve the depth and dimensions of social analysis we find in a sprawling novel such as the *Recherche*. However plausible such a viewpoint, the fact remains that there is nothing inherent in the short-story form that precludes penetrating sociohistorical analysis. To limit ourselves to the nineteenth and early twentieth centuries, the cases of Tolstoy, de Maupassant, Giovanni Verga, and Thomas Mann are there to confirm that the short story can be powerfully engaged in issues of class struggle, alienation, political and moral differences that define and condition the lives of typical characters ("typical" in the way Georgy Lukàcs used the term, to mean representative of broad currents of historical change and conflict at given moments in time).

Another way to look at what I have just said above is that in *PJ*, truth-seeking, always a fundamental aspect of Proust's conception of the writer's function, is a private, self-scrutinizing act that takes place on the basis of the implicit assumption that truth is a value for the individual alone to discover. The source of this truth lies in some mysterious abstract realm to which the conflicted or sinful individual, as the case may be, gains access solely on his or her own initiative. That truth might be conceived differently, as a socially and historically constructed value involving contending forces in a struggle whose outcome is always in question, is a notion fundamentally alien to young Proust's mindset.[6] His point of departure and point of reference is always the idea of an individual conscience that draws sustenance from its internalization of essentially Christian moral doctrine. Proust's is a form of Christian individualism, which conceives of salvation and damnation in strictly personal terms, by postulating the possibility that a single person, through either adherence to or rejection of "the truth" of righteousness and purity, will either save or condemn himself. It does not matter very much that Proust avoids any explicit reference to heaven or to hell. His characters live their own heavens—or more often their own hells—as a consequence of their actions. One might say that Proust's world view in *PJ* is the spiritual counterpart of bourgeois individualism in the political and social spheres, a notion that disallows collective deliverance from the ills that afflict humankind. Nowhere is there any sign whatever of solidarity between individuals, except within familes and, in a few instances, between master and servant. But then, where would solidarity come from? None of the life forms and activities typical of modern civilization are present in the book, including collective work processes. Young Proust was a shrewd psychologist and insightful moralist, but still a rather poor sociologist.

These ideological preconceptions depend in turn on another idea close to Proust's heart almost from the beginning of his life as a writer, namely the notion that there is something called *le moi intérieur*,[7] the authentic inner self, which the individual can find only by separating him or herself from society and social relations, conceived as the matrices of falseness, superficiality, and inauthenticty. In other words, this inner self lives by reason of a committed renunciation of society and of the corruption that society embodies, with its illusory, merely material rewards. The idea that the individual self could be realized, on the contrary, by understanding how and why the human personality is always formed, for better or for worse, in the course of its "active relationships"[8] with others was not a decisive element of young Proust's consciousness, just as the notion of salvation or redemption was understood by him as a matter for the individual "soul" to deal with, not for humanity as a whole. What this amounts to is that Proust had internalized one of the bedrock dualities of bourgeois civilization—that is, the notion that society does not provide the means by which the individual self can fulfill itself but, rather, constitutes a great barrier to selfhood because of its inevitable corrupting influence on naturally creative and productive human beings. It is the doctrine of Rousseau writ large, but without the moral passion that drove the French thinker to declare, in *The Social Contract*, that "man was born free, and he is everywhere in chains" (Rousseau, 49). Rousseau was condemning a particular sociopolitical order, the one he knew, while young Proust, although deeply critical of certain attitudes and practices prevalent in the society he lived in, was interested basically in revealing the moral gradations within that society, not in challenging its foundational principles, in the manner of Rousseau. He devoted his talents as a writer of fiction to examining the codes and prejudices of a class whose survival was threatened, not by opposing forces but by its indifference or blindness to its own deficiencies.

What young Proust did, he did very well. But because this is a study of ideological questions as they connect to literary representations, my task is to "show the text as it cannot know itself," not "to redouble the text's self-understanding" (Eagleton 1976b, 43). At the same time, I must also acknowledge that, as Eagleton has argued brilliantly apropos of Jane Austen, while young Proust did not confront the issues typically of interest to Marxist or Marxist-influenced thinkers, what he did accomplish was in a sense attributable (as in Austen's works) to the very "exclusion of the real as it is known to historical materialism." This was true, Eagleton avers, because

> without the exclusion of the real as it is known to historical materialism, there could be for Austen nothing of the ethical discourse, rhetoric of character, ritual of relationship or ceremony of convention which she presents—nothing, in short, of those elements for which we find her fiction "valuable." (1976b, 71)

Two pieces in *PJ* that bear upon and illustrate the question of "the inner self" in contradistinction to "the outer or exterior self" in society are "*Olivian*," one of fourteen compositions forming the suite titled "*Fragments de comédie italienne*," and "*L'Etranger*," item sixteen of "*Les Regrets, rêveries couleur du temps*." They encapsulate the book's thematic core, which turns up in a variety of narrative settings and situations.

"*Olivian*" (Dupee 50–51) is a short, morally charged entreaty addressed by the writer to Olivian, evidently a cultured "man of letters" who spends his time mainly going to theatre, traveling, talking, and making love with his "dull mistress." Its message is that time spent in society, talking with even the most brilliant conversationalists, is a waste of time, for it is time spent with people who use only their "bodily eyes" to see, while the truth is that "the voice of the imagination and of the soul is the only voice that can make the whole soul and the imagination echo happily." Instead of making fruitless journeys to far-off places in foreign lands, Olivian is advised by the narrator to remain safely at home cultivating his own garden, and thereby come into touch with his true self, his inner self. Accompanying this "lesson" in moral philosophy is the notion that living in the present, as Olivian does, is a grave error, since the imagination, on which a writer depends for inspiration, thrives only on the past or the future. The present is dead to the man of sensibilities, for it offers only ephemeral pleasures.

In one fell swoop, Proust gives us some of the essential ideas that will, in much more elaborated form, reappear in the *Recherche*. The difference, however, is that the society in which Marcel grows from childhood to maturity in the novel, although depicted as being just as illusory in many ways as the one alluded to in "*Olivian*," is also seen as providing the intersubjective relationships from which the budding writer will derive his understanding of himself and of his artistic mission. The novel lets us see the dynamics of human interaction, spiritual influences, a process of evolution and change from various perspectives. The implication of "*Olivian*," on the other hand, is that solitude, self-scrutiny, withdrawal into oneself, listening to the voice of one's own soul, is the only path to deliverance from the bondage of society. Whereas in the novel, conversation, the exchange of ideas and feelings between the narrator-protagonist and numerous individuals, is of vital importance, the explicit message of "*Olivian*" is that "conversation, even the most exquisite, is only the pleasure of men devoid of imagination."

Of course, a short "study" in the manner of La Bruyère such as "*Olivian*" has an entirely different function than that of a novel, yet I do not think that a comparison between them, from a thematic point of view, is irrelevant. It is the root assumption governing "*Olivian*," its ideology of the inner self as somehow separable and independent from the surrounding society, that calls for scrutiny. Moreover, the idea that the inner self must take precedence over any and all forms of social interaction is not absent from the *Recherche*. It is in those moments when the narrator devotes himself to self-scrutiny, to listening to the "voice" of his imagination and his soul, that he produces the fundamental insights and perceptions on which the novel is based. So it can be said that in this sense too, as André Gide came to believe, *PJ* foreshadows the *Recherche*, that it anticipates the novel's central concerns and themes. In their humble way, "*Olivian*" and "*L'Etranger*" too reflect several of the key values informing the entire history of Western metaphysical thought.

"*L'Etranger*" (Dupee 120–122)[9] is a still more emphatic assertion of spiritual elitism. I regard it as a crucial document in the formation of Proust's theory of the soul as an inner essence that must be nourished and above all protected from the corrupting influences of society. It is a charming parable, designed to illustrate an idea that radiates throughout Proust's writing in a variety of ways and in many different styles and genres.

This modern morality tale, somewhat longer than "*Olivian*" and more trenchant in its depiction of an idle and complacent group of social butterflies, is written in the third person and concerns a young man named Dominique who, unlike Olivian, is aware of the threat to his "soul" posed by his incessant soirées and dinner parties, but is unable to do anything about it because, he admits to himself, he "cannot bear to be alone." This inability to be alone is what makes Dominique reject "the stranger," that is, his own soul, and choose the company of his boisterous and superficial friends. Once again, the idea is that the soul of a human being can grow and expand only in solitude. The crucial point is that "the stranger," who is none other than Dominique himself, since the soul is the essence of a person, tells him that he cannot have it both ways: "if you wish me to stay," the "stranger" tells Dominique, "you must send the other guests away." Here, in stark and decisive terms, Proust gives us the essential kernel of thought that he will develop in all sorts of complex and intriguing ways in his future writing.

But there is more to this little parable. Three points that merit additional comment are, first, that when the "stranger" speaks to him, Dominique is gripped with fear and remorse, for he had never before allowed himself to heed its voice; second, that, very much in accord with earlier periods of storytelling, the abstract figure of Habit interposes itself in the parable when the "stranger" blames it for having so repeatedly and grievously wounded him as to leave him close to death; and third, that when the "stranger" appears to Dominique the storyteller notes that "no crest was inscribed on his signet ring, nor had wit frosted his speech with its sparkling needles." In other words, in the presence of the soul, all of the social privileges and distinctions that characterize the milieu to which Dominique attaches such importance fall away into utter insigificance.

What we have here is a depiction of ordinary social relations as inimical to the happiness and purity of the inner person, the inner self that can live and prosper only apart from society. There can be no compromise between the rigorous demands of spiritual life and the habits of an existence based on conversation and dinner parties. The social and public dimension of life is radically discounted, while the private and intimate side is virtually apotheosised. "*L'Etranger*" is a telling example of how far young Proust had taken the teachings of Thomas à Kempis in *The Imita-*

tion of Christ, which he cites epigraphically several times in *PJ*. Theoretically at least, if not in practice, a virtuous solitude and renunciation of worldly pleasures were for Proust the necessary price that one had to pay to come into touch with the deepest part of oneself, the part from which one drew in the creation of works of art. That this notion conflicted with other aspects of his thought is undeniable. Yet it remained one of the principles on which he grounded his aesthetic and moral philosophy.

In the final analysis, the idea that seems to be circulating through many of the short "studies" as well as longer narratives of *PJ* (a few of the latter will be examined in the next chapter) is the rather unpleasant one that the life most people lead in their normal everyday pursuits is hopelessly degraded from the very outset, and has value only insofar as it provides the source from which are drawn the intoxicating revelations that spiritual purity and artistic expression make possible. Real daily life cannot produce a stable "residence for ideality,"[10] which exists only in the mind of the dreamer, the visionary, the poet. Life as lived by ordinary mortals is a miserable affair, redeemable solely through the gift of memory and the creative transformation of experience in works of art.

The idea that works of art, or more broadly speaking the creation of beauty, are what give artists their liberatory function in society, is omnipresent in *PJ*, and is often associated with high social rank. It will be recalled that Baldassare Silvande is a musician. The orphaned young aristocratic protagonist of *"Violante ou la mondanité"* (Dupee 25–34) inherits from her parents both their titles and their lively interest in the arts, containing in her person a "harmonious" blending of their best traits. Twice abandoned by young men who had aroused her sexual feelings, she decides to leave the duchy of Styria, of which she is now the mistress, to go to the Austrian court, where she marries the Duke of Bohemia and sinks into a morass of "bourgeois" pleasures and ambitions. But on an ideal plane, she represents for young Proust that potential alliance between magnanmity of soul and artistic creativity that can be found in only a few privileged individuals. The fact that she betrays her spiritual inheritance is what gives the story its pathos. Her tutor and servant Augustin responds in this manner to her announcement that she wants to leave Styria:

> "God help us," said Augustin. "What will the poor people here do without your charities while you are living in the midst of all those wicked people? You will no longer play with our children in the woods. Who will play the organ at the church? We shall no longer see you painting in the fields, you will no longer compose your songs for us."

"Don't worry, Augustin," she replies, "just keep my castle beautiful and my peasants of Styria faithful. The world for me is only a means to an end. It gives one vulgar but invincible arms, and if some day I am to be loved I shall have need of them."

But the means become the end, and everything of value in Violante's life is squandered. It is no wonder that Thomas à Kempis provides two epigraphic quotations for this story. It reads like a parable, a fable designed for didactic purposes. The fact that it is dated August 1892, and was therefore written when Proust was only twenty-one, matters much less than that he revised it for inclusion in *PJ* four years later. The story spoke for an important side of his personality and of his evolving vision of life. Central to that vision was the hope that art and nobility might combine to liberate the low-born and lift them to a higher level of culture. This vision was what made Violante's inability to realize her potential so significant and so disappointing to Proust.

A question that presents itself here is whether Violante's life history was truly meant to be a parable of moral and intellectual betrayal by France's elite, or whether it was subtly intended to poke fun at a widespread form of snobbery on the part of sectors of all the French social classes. The question is relevant because of the attention Proust gave in *PJ* to various types of snobbery. For young Proust, writes Emilien Carassus, snobbery was a major symptom of what he thought was ailing French high society, comprising both bourgeois and aristocrats. But as already indicated, while directing his sharpest arrows at a spoiled and self-deluded class, Proust does not really call into question the social conditions and hierarchies on which that class based its still considerable prestige. After all, Proust himself, the scion of a wealthy and privileged family, was not ready in the mid-1890s to challenge the social order that had spawned him and given him the means with which to assert himself as a writer and moralist. He was inclined toward nuances, not to stark confrontations. For this reason, even while noting his dislike of discriminatory social practices and attitudes, we have to grant the possibility that in this as in most other aspects of his life, Proust was ambivalent and thought that certain types of snobbery were compatible with spiritual and intellectual distinction.

We have to ask ourselves: Would a writer who rejected the existing social order and all forms of snobbery have appealed to and relied upon a newspaper such as *Le Gaulois* to publish his writings, advertise his book, and speak enthusiastically about his talents? That seems unlikely. The editor-in-chief of *Le Gaulois*, Arthur Meyer, was among the most reactionary figures in the Paris of the 1890s, yet it was not until the schism caused by the call in January 1898 for a revision of Dreyfus's trial, against which Meyer took an intransigent antirevisionist stand, that Proust became alienated from him. *Le Gaulois* was a newspaper written by and for the social elite. It took an unyielding conservative position on everything that affected French politics and culture. On May 31, 1894, it published Proust's article on the literary *fête* organized by Montesquiou in Versailles; on June 21, 1895, his "*Portraits de peintres*," and on June 12, 1896, the piece on the Tuileries from "*Les Regrets: Rêveries couleur du temps.*" Moreover, Proust asked Madeleine Lemaire to recommend him to Meyer in order to give him the entrée he needed to have various writings from *Le Château de Réveillon* published in *Le Gaulois*. In other words, it was probably not until Meyer turned down these writings that Proust changed the title of his collection to *Les Plaisirs et les jours*, only three months before the book's appearance. The name of a château was much more attractive to the editors of *Le Gaulois* than a (for most readers) obscure reference to a work by Hesiod.

In a section of *The Prison Notebooks* titled "The Modern Prince," Gramsci spoke of "the basic innovation introduced by the philosophy of praxis [that is, Marxism] into the science of politics and history" as being

> the demonstration that there is no abstract 'human nature', fixed and immutable (a concept which certainly derives from religious and transcendentalist thought), but that human nature is the totality of historically determined social relations, hence an historical fact which can, within certain limits, be ascertained with the methods of philology and criticism. (Gramsci 1971, 133)

In the 1890s, but later on as well, even if modified by all sorts of historical and philosophical mediations, Proust's conceptual frame of reference was fundamentally alien to the viewpoint alluded to by Gramsci, in part by choice, in part as a result of the values that he assimilated from teachers and friends and from the general spiritualist emphasis of French literary life at the time. His was essentially a "religious and transcendentalist" outlook, resting not on conventional religious thought but, rather, on its modern secular variant that redirects metaphysical thinking toward art and the life of the mind.

Chapter 8

A Profusion of Intertextuality

> Proust's work is like a lens where all the
> tendencies of our literature converge.
>
> Simone Kadi, *La Peinture chez Proust et Baudelaire*

As a critical approach to various forms of literary appropriation by one writer of another writer's work—images, stylistic mannerisms, epigraphic passages, technical devices, even plagiarism, an example of which, according to Anne Henry, is Proust's use of Tolstoyan death scenes for several of the short stories in *PJ*—the study of intertextuality has become a staple of contemporary literary criticism. Julia Kristeva, who helped to popularize the term, considers it a key component of the poststructuralist view of writing as perpetually open to new readings and interpretations.[1] But its usefulness to ideological criticism is just as important.

Intertextual references are pervasive in *PJ*. In the title itself Proust borrows playfully from a Greek classical work, Hesiod's *Works and Days*. The irreverent nature of the title derives from the fact that it points up a contrast between Hesiod, who conceived of work as a remedy for corruption and evil, and the modern era, where the pursuit of pleasure was not seen as an occasional respite from toil but as the primary purpose of life. In the opening section of his poem, Hesiod recounts the five ages of the world, which parallel the five races or "generations" of human beings created by Zeus, the last of which, forefathers of the generation existing in Hesiod's own time, is in desperate need of redemption. Such redemption, the poet says, can come only from pious respect for the superior power of the gods and from daily labor both in the fields and in the industrious production of useful goods. In short, religion and work were Hesiod's solutions to the ills that afflicted humanity.

The title of *PJ*, therefore, accomplished by insinuation what would have taken many pages to accomplish by persuasive argument, namely to highlight the current moral decline, seen in turn as a possible portent of economic and social decline. In this sense, a rather substantial part of *PJ*, especially the stories and the portraits in "*Fragments de comédie italienne*," can be read as *exempla* illustrating prevalent situations and character types in the Paris of the 1890s. On the one hand, the title serves to connect *PJ* to an ancient tradition of thought about the human condition, and on the other to complicate that connection by inviting the reader to reflect on the similarities and differences between past and present. In *Marxism and Literature*, Raymond Williams notes that tradition is usually "a version of the past which is intended to connect with and ratify the present" (116). But Proust uses literary and cultural tradition in a highly selective manner; he is an arbiter and decision-maker, not a servile imitator. One part of him wanted to ratify the present by appealing to the past, but another equally strong part of him interrogated and critiqued that past, and questioned the present. He no doubt wanted to stimulate his readers to look at the state of their society from a morally critical point of view, not, to be sure, with a view to radically changing it but, rather, to correcting certain of its egregiously harmful habits and vices. Like his mentor Anatole France, and in the spirit of idealist philosophy imparted to him by Alphonse Darlu, Proust was seeking in his own way to restore the conception of literature as a vehicle of thought and worldly enlightenment. By linking himself to the classical world in this way, he was trying to reaffirm the natural, millennial alliance between literature and moral philosophy.

In her 1966 study *The World of Marcel Proust*, Germaine Brée observes that "For Hesiod's round of work, Proust substituted the calendar of social pleasures, but he kept the moral intent. His short stories read like allegories, and the 'Fragments of Italian Comedy' are transparently moral in mood" (41). This is a handy formulation, which Luzius Keller takes one step further when he opines, with reference to the biblical allusion in the dedication, that Proust wanted the story of Noah and the Ark to stand for the imminence of an "apocalyptic" end to modern civilization. Like the apocalypse mentioned in Hesiod's *Works and Days*, Keller proposes, "the flood is the punishment for the decline of morals" (Keller, 291 n. 10). In another remark in his German edition of *PJ*, Keller sees a thematic connection between Hesiod and modern decadence in the portrait "*Olivian*," where the writer, speaking directly to his character, admonishes him to "have the courage to take up rake and hoe. And one of these days you will know the pleasure of sensing a delicious odor rising in your memory as from a garden wheelbarrow filled to the brim" (Dupee 51).

With this allusion to pick and hoe, Keller believes, Proust was alluding to a poet who was among the first to value manual labor as a remedy against destructive pleasures and amusements.

But Keller's ingeniously conceived literary and moral connections between Hesiod and Proust rest on somewhat shaky ground, inasmuch as the allusion to Noah in the dedication was designed to convey a deeply felt personal memory, not primarily an apocalyptic one, while the passage from "*Olivian*" has a distinctly metaphorical character, even if it is possible to see the allusion to "rake and hoe" as a reminder of the agricultural labors recommended by Hesiod. Keller's interpretations of these two passages do have the merit, however, of recalling to mind the "prophetic" side of Proust's personality, which has been appropriately emphasized by several literary scholars, notably by Edmund Wilson in *Axel's Castle* (143–145).

The epigraphs and other literary appropriations in *PJ* are too numerous to be discussed in detail within the framework of this chapter. I shall limit myself therefore to the most significant ones and attempt to give the reader a sense of their purpose in the overall economy of the book by pointing out what I think are the basic attitudes and ideas Proust wished to communicate through them. I am referring specifically here to the epigraphic uses he made in *PJ* of the following writers: Emerson, Thomas à Kempis, Horace, Racine, Baudelaire, La Bruyère, and Tolstoy.

Emerson

An unexpectedly dominant epigraphic presence in *PJ* is that of Ralph Waldo Emerson, two of whose essays, "History" and "The Poet," had a strong impact on Proust. In 1894 or 1895, he read them in a French translation by Emile Montégut. It is possible, however, that his attention was first drawn to the American philosopher by an article in the June 1894 issue of *Le Mercure de France*, where Camille Mauclair reviewed a more recent translation of Emerson's essays prefaced by the Belgian symbolist playwright and poet Maurice Maeterlinck. In his twenty-page preface, Maeterlinck called Emerson "the wise man of ordinary days," meaning that while Emersonian philosophy was transcendental in its inspiration, it was also practical and down-to-earth. Mauclair felt that Maeterlinck's long preface "was one of the rare metaphysical documents of French intellectuality in this century" and that it constituted a crucial link between American transcendentalism and European spiritualism.[2] In any event, in a letter to Reynaldo Hahn, written on January 18, 1895, Proust said that he was reading Emerson *avec ivresse,* in an "enraptured" state (*Corr.* 1: 363). The fact that he was under Emerson's spell at this particular time probably accounts for the four epigraphic citations from his essays in *PJ*, one each at the beginnings of *"La Mort de Baldassare Silvande," "Fragments,"* and *"Regrets,"* and one for part 3 of *"La Fin de la jalousie."*

As Larkin Price has shown (1965, 233–235), the passage from Emerson's "History" that introduces part 1 of the story *"La Mort de Baldassare Silvande"* intrigued Proust; it appears in various guises elsewhere in *PJ* and in several of his letters. What attracted him to this particular passage in "History" appears to have been not only its explicit philosophical content but also its form, which relies on myth to convey its meaning rather than on logical argument. But a problem presents itself here: the French translation (translated in its turn into English) cited by Proust reads as follows: "Apollo kept the flocks of Admetus, say the poets; each man is also a hidden god who apes the fool." The original English is: "Apollo kept the flocks of Admetus, said the poets. When the gods come among men, they are not known. Jesus was not; Socrates and Shakespeare were not" (Emerson 13).

Both passages stress the role of poets in transmitting myths down through the ages, myths that encapsulate basic narratives of birth, death, and rebirth, and signal the eternal duality of the human soul, which is of divine origin but which also assumes a fallible, all-too-human form. But the French passage is more laconic; it stresses the double nature of the human species. The English original honors the poets among us by comparing Socrates and Shakespeare, mere mortals, to Jesus, and it does so by placing them on the same plane as God. The French passage is more pertinent to the story of Baldassare Silvande, because he, although a gifted musician and composer, has "aped the fool" by devoting much of his life to superficial and wasteful pursuits instead of cultivating the deepest part of himself. Yet he is "a hidden god," his genius comes from above, it cannot be attributed solely to chance, or to biological heredity. This hidden god also performs humble tasks, he mixes with ordinary people, and suffers in the same way that all mortal creatures suffer.

The passage introducing *"Les Regrets: Rêveries Couleur du temps"* is taken from the essay "The Poet," where Emerson undertakes "a consideration of the nature and functions of the Poet" in modern times. One of the characteristics of this essay for which Proust felt an affinity was that it gave a primary role to philosophical thought in the process of poetic creation. Proust found in Emerson a kindred spirit, for he was a thinker who understood what Proust felt almost instinctively, namely that it is not meters, but a meter-making argument, that makes a poem,—a thought so passionate and alive, that, like the spirit of a plant or an animal, it has an architecture of its own, and adorns nature with a new thing. The thought and the form are equal in the order of time, but in the order of genesis the thought is prior to the form. The poet has a new thought: he has a whole new experience to unfold; he will tell us how it was with him, and all men will be the richer in his fortune. (Emerson 68)

In Emerson's somewhat overheated prose we recognize some of the cardinal features of Proust's idealist aesthetics: his belief that each new writer or artist renews the world with a fresh vision of things; his belief that thought is generative of beauty; his subordination of form to feeling. But the passage he uses for "*Les Regrets*" is of another order; it concerns the poet's "manner of living," where Emerson's responsiveness to the ordinary aspects of natural life struck another sympathetic chord in Proust. In this case, the French translation is more literally faithful to the English original. It exhorts the poet to live a simple life, and to take delight in the sun, the sky, the air. Proust translated Emerson's advice, for example, into the exquisitely earthy lines that open the prose poem "*Promenade.*" This prose-poetic fragment, written in the first person, begins by describing the colors, the vibrancy, the joyfulness of a cold morning in early spring, where an "intense and ardent" sky and the clear water of a nearby pond form the backdrop of an idyllic scene. But in the second paragraph, Proust shifts our mind's eye to another very different site, a nearby barnyard, which leads then to a moment of reflection and to the use of imagery that express one of the core principles of his aesthetic philosophy:

> The barnyard, where one went for eggs, was a no less pleasing sight. The sun, like an inspired and prolific poet who does not scorn to dispense beauty in the humblest places, which no one had ever dreamed of including in the realm of art before, warmed the salutary vigor of the dunghill, of the rough paved court, and of the pear tree broken and bent like an old serving woman. (Dupee 102)

This short passage suggests that Proust's obsession with sunlight may have had a "mythic" origin in that Apollo was at once the god of light, of poetry and music, and of youth (and therefore of ardent desire). He was also associated with the care of flocks and herds, noted earlier with regard to Baldassare Silvande, which reappears in the final paragraph of "*Promenade.*" After drawing the reader's attention to the "regally attired" peacock (a common image of beauty in symbolist and decadent verse), the narrator tells us that it is right here, among ordinary animals and "rustic farm implements" that the peacock spends his life, a veritable bird of paradise in the barnyard among the turkeys and the hens, like a captive Andromache spinning her wool among her slaves, except that unlike her he has left behind none of the splendors of royal insignia and crown jewels, a radiant Apollo, recognizable always—even when he guards Admetus' flocks. (Dupee 103).

Thomas à Kempis

Thomas à Kempis's *The Imitation of Christ* was widely read and cited in the 1880s and 1890s. In 1893, Proust went to the trouble of borrowing a copy from Pierre Lavallée, and seems to have been quite affected by it. In a short letter to Lavallée, Proust assured his friend that he would soon return his copy of the *Imitation*, "which I have enjoyed and used very much" (*Corr.* 1: 234). Like Maurice Barrès in *Un Homme Libre* (1889), volume 2 of his trilogy *Le Culte du moi*, Proust found in the *Imitation* an eminently quotable authority on how to live with rectitude in a corrupt social environment that perpetually distracts and attracts the vulnerable individual with its pleasures and refinements. Barrès was moved by the book's arguments for the virtue of solitude and silence (Barrès 16, 135).

Proust used this influential fifteenth-century work as an ideological support for two of his short stories, "*Violante ou la mondanité*," and "*La Confession d'une jeune fille.*" Both are stories of young women who come to an unhappy end: Violante, who survives physically to old age but who dies spiritually at the moment when she rejects her tutor Augustin's advice to seek fulfillment not in worldly pleasures but in doing what she loves with "the deepest tendencies of her soul; and an unnamed young woman who tells her story in the form of a confession to an equally anonymous but sympathetic listener.

In both stories the parental role is important, either by reason of its absence because of an untimely fatal accident (in "*Violante*") or because of a mother's inability to prevent her daughter, the first person narrator, from yielding to her sexual impulses in the arms of a seductive young man (in "*La Confession d'une jeune fille*"). The epigraphs from the *Imitation* are used to emphasize how narrow and hazardous the path to virtue is, and how fearsome the temptations that lie in wait once a young person during her formative years fails to develop the strength of will necessary to maintain her moral equilibrium. Kempis's ascetic thought serves the purpose of placing these two tales in a fabular atmosphere where good and evil, rectitude and sin, are at war with each other, and where what is at stake are the souls of the two protagonists. Stéphane Sarkany speaks in this connection of the "Christian ascetic and medieval morality" of *PJ*

(Erickson and Pagès 115–122). In fact, there is no way of avoiding the conclusion that for young Proust the human soul is a battleground fought over by fiercely opposed forces, in a war that can give no quarter, for the stakes are high and permanent.

The confessional mode has induced some Proust scholars to suspect the influence of Saint Augustine and Rousseau. One could make a reasonable case for the former, inasmuch as Violante's mentor and tutor is named Augustin, who intervenes in one of the exceedingly rare moments in Proust's early fictions where the leading character enters into a dialogic relationship with someone who looks at the world from a different and critical perspective, thus allowing for a more dialectically structured plot. In "*La Confession d'une jeune fille*," however, there is nothing of this sort, only the shocked expression and fatal collapse of the mother when she sees her daughter locked in passionate embrace not with her fiancé but with another young man. As a result of this horrific incident, the girl shoots herself, and it is in this mortally wounded state that she tells her story. Life is thus seen as a perilous adventure demanding the utmost rigor and self-discipline to be lived successfully, from a Christian point of view.

Horace

Proust uses two lines from a Horatian satire to set the tone of "*Un Dîner en ville*," the equal in its humorous effects to similar episodes in the *Recherche*, and the most acute collective portrait in *PJ*. Unlike almost all of the book's other stories and sketches, "*Un Dîner en ville*" lets in some air from the outside world, a refreshing relief from the book's hothouse atmosphere. We are made privy to amusing exchanges between characters, several of whom are servilely attached to various personalities in the Parisian literary world, while the narrator lets the reader in on the little games and secrets of this socially elite but morally degraded group of dinner guests. There is even a soupçon of explicit political commentary in this sketch, rare in Proust's early writing, when the hostess, Mme Fremer, ends a brief discussion about anarchism by asking what such a doctrine could possibly do for the world, since "rich and poor we have always with us." The narrator comments:

> And all these people, the poorest among them having an income of at least a hundred thousand pounds, impressed by the truth of her remark and relieved of their scruples, emptied with beaming cheerfulness their last glass of champagne (Dupee 97).

Racine

The epigraphic quote from Racine's *Phèdre* that introduces "*Mélancolique villégiature de Mme de Breyves*" is taken from the same scene of act 1 to which Proust refers in the dedication. It revolves around the moment in which Phèdre summons up the courage to confess her sexual love for Hyppolyte to her nurse Œnone. In the passage cited here, she compares her stricken heart to the "wound" her sister Ariadne had suffered when she was abandoned by Theseus, now Phèdre's husband, on the island of Naxos. According to the version of the Greek myth used by Racine, Ariadne died after her abandonment by Theseus, and it is this link between love and death that the playwright wanted to underline in the passage quoted by Proust, who in turn treats the theme of love precisely as a wound, as an affliction, a terrible and irrational illness of the soul that consumes its victims. When deep-seated taboos are added to the natural pains of love, the end result is tragic, whether literally as in the story of Phèdre, or spiritually, as in the story of Mme de Breyves.

There is a reason rooted in myth underlying Proust's use of the passage from act 1, scene 3 when Phèdre exclaims: "Ariadne, my sister, by what a love wounded did you die on the shores where you were abandoned!." It shows how carefully Proust arranged his materials in some of these stories, where the form and the theme complement each other in suggestive ways. The end of the long last paragraph of "*Mélancolique villégiature*" picks up again on the theme of a young woman wounded by love:

> If, sometimes, walking along the beach or in the woods, she lets the pleasure of contemplation or of reverie, or even a sweet odor, or a song brought from a distance and muffled by the breeze, gently take possession of her, make her for an instant forget her pain, all at once she feels a terrible blow and a wound in her heart–and above the waves, higher than the leaves, in the misty horizon of woods or sea, she catches sight of the vague image of her invisible and ever-present conqueror, his eyes shining through the clouds, as on the day when he offered himself to her, and sees him vanish with the quiver from which he has taken and let fly another arrow. (Dupee 78)

Baudelaire

Baudelaire was one of Proust's favorite poets from his student days on. A few scholars have suggested the possibility that *PJ* is in effect Proust's *Les Fleurs du mal*. Like *Les Fleurs du mal*, the pieces in *PJ* assumed form and unity only after their author had written most of them prior to the book's definitive status as a collection of disparate writings held together by a unitary vision and by some common themes. More essentially, *PJ*, like the *Les Fleurs du mal*, was a work in which beauty had been wrested and shaped from its source in "evil," i.e. death as well as various forms of social and moral corruption. Keller's thesis that *PJ* is at bottom a "decadent" work exemplifying the concerns of poets and novelists belonging to that school, and Kingcaid's stress on young Proust's obsession with "neurosis," illness, and "fetishism" give such an interpretation some critical authority.

One expression of Proust's deep affinity for Baudelaire was his desire to appropriate some of the qualities of poetry, music, and painting in his prose style. Another was his conviction that criticism was the partner of creativity not its enemy. Both Baudelaire and Proust thought of their writing as having an organic unity. Both were modernist in their sensibilities, yet both were deeply influenced by an essentially Catholic conception of good and evil. Perhaps most important, both attributed primary importance to the notion of an inner self, a core of individuality that they articulated in various ways, as in Baudelaire's belief—one with which Proust certainly agreed—that "there can only be any true, that is to say, any moral, progress in the individual and through the individual himself."[3] In addition, we need to remember that it was not only *Les Fleurs du mal* that enchanted Proust. The *Petits poèmes en prose* (Little prose poems) were also a literary reference point that affected him as it did successive generations of writers, and not only in France.

There were also differences between the two writers. Proust was less prone than Baudelaire to supernaturalism and especially to the idea that evil exists not only in human affairs but in the very constitution of the universe. Baudelaire truly believed that "the cleverest ruse of the devil is to persuade us that he doesn't exist." In *Les Fleurs du mal* the poet oscillates between "the dark abyss into which my heart has fallen" and "the clear fire that fills the limpid spaces." Proust did not see descent into the abyss as a condition for ascent to the realm of the spirit in the same way that Baudelaire did. Yet he did believe, with Baudelaire, that beauty could be extracted from evil and that artistic creation was a means with which to redeem a fallen world.

Proust drew in *PJ* from both *Les Fleurs du mal* and the *Petits poèmes en prose* for images, devices and themes. Two examples of how the former work lived on in the pages of *PJ* are the "*Portraits de peintres*" and the prose poem "*La mer*," while the *Petits poèmes en prose* are present in the short story "*Mélancolique villégiature*" and in the last of the thirty pieces comprising the *"Regrets,"* titled *"Voiles au port"* (Harbor sails).

Baudelaire was a major contributor to the subgenre of poetry about painting in *"Les Phares"* (The beacons), part of the first section of his *Fleurs du mal*. Proust followed his lead in *PJ*, not in a single poem but in four, one of which, on Watteau, recalls Baudelaire's quatrain on the eighteenth-century painter. Baudelaire and Proust both chose to emphasize the "carnivalesque" and theatrical side of Watteau's artistic personality, as seen in his depictions of actors from the Italian and French comic theatre, and in his famous "Embarkation for Cythère," an airy evocation of a *fête galante* that has charmed generations of visitors to the Louvre.

"La mer," mentioned in chapter 3 in connection with Proust's "musical" aesthetic, is replete with Baudelairian imagery, as noted by Anne Henry and Thierry Laget. Baudelaire's *"L'Homme et la mer"* (Man and the sea) is a philosophical poem of the kind that Proust admired, both for what it said and for what it suggested, in the sense that the poem acts as a catalyst for further thought on the part of the reader. It first likens man and the sea, in the depth of their "intimate riches" and "secrets," then alludes to the eons of time during which man and sea have been enemies, both "remorseless" lovers of "carnage and death," and because of this, "eternal combatants, implacable brothers." Baudelaire's poem "Music" is closer in spirit to Proust's "La mer" inasmuch as it explicitly compares the effects of the sea on his state of mind with the effects of music. But Proust does something different with this relationship. Where Baudelaire pictures the sea as expressing both the turbulent and the depressive parts of his personality, Proust begins his little essay by reflecting on the fascination of the sea for those who have known the "disgust of life" and "the lure of mystery" even before sorrow has afflicted them. Unlike Baudelaire, he then dwells exclusively on why the sea, in its vastness and purity, "bears no traces of men's toil and of their lives." In other words, Proust does not follow Baudelaire's cue, at least not in his vision of what the sea symbolizes in human experience, and he uses the poet's evocation of the sea's "musical" enchantment for his own quite different purposes.

Thus, there is nothing crudely imitative in Proust's use of these Baudelaire poems. He seizes upon their imagery and reflects on how music comparable to the sea in its freedom from all worldly taint, but he does not merely ape his predecessor. Intertextual presences in this instance are signs not of subordination on Proust's part to a revered model but of independence grounded in knowledge of what his literary heritage offered him that could be turned creatively to his own ends.

A Profusion of Intertextuality 147

The same is true of Proust's use of Baudelairian images and themes in the story "*Mélancolique villégiature*," which has been studied most intensively by Maria Paganini. At the end of part 4 of this story that mixes fabular and real historical elements, the narrator dwells on a conception of the enraptured lover that is in fundamental respects akin to the state of mind customarily associated with the "intuitive" poet, the "ecstatic" believer, and the "mystically" exalted lover of nature and music, which have their seat in "the mind in its divinest form." Françoise, the story's unhappy heroine, experiences a passion fed by her mind and her imagination that have fixed themselves on an individual who bears little if any resemblance to the figure conjured up by her fantasy. It is this fantasy that gives meaning and purpose to her life, and it is embodied in the rather ordinary figure of Monsieur Jacques de Laléande, a musician associated by Proust with several "Wagnerian" leitmotifs. Part 4 ends with the following portentous words, which comment on Françoise's reviling of that part of her which, in Proust's scheme of things, endows her with a spiritual nobility far more precious than the aristocratic name she has inherited by birth:

> She reviled that inexpressible feeling of the mystery of things when our spirit loses itself in the radiance of beauty like that of the sun when it sinks into the sea, for having deepened her love, for having immaterialized, broadened, infinitized it without, for all that, making it less agonizing, for as Baudelaire says (speaking of the end of autumn days), "there are certain delicious sensations which are no less intense for being vague; and there is no sharper point than that of infinity." (Dupee 75)

The quote is from the prose poem "*Le 'Confiteor' de l'artiste*" (The artist's confession), where Baudelaire uses the sacrament of confession to speak of his tormented desires as a lover and as a poet. It is an exceedingly compressed expression of the "duel" in him resulting from his incessant "study of the beautiful," which makes him, like all artists, "cry with fright before being beaten." Something of this "duel" and this duality is what Proust seems to have been alluding to in the passage quoted above, where he makes use of a Baudelairian concept but applies it to a woman, Françoise, rather than to a man. Françoise is in the grip of a kind of "divine" fury, a struggle that will go on in her soul for as long as her passion for Laléande feeds on itself and its accompanying fantasies and not on the flesh and blood man called Jacques de Laléande.[4]

Another key with which to unlock the secrets of intertextuality in *PJ* is provided by Baudelaire's prose poem "*Le Port*," which Proust assimilates in "*Voiles au port.*" Both of these prose poetic texts fix the mind's eye on the sense of mystery and the unknown that emanates from ships in the harbor, vessels that have traveled the seas and that now enjoy a brief moment of repose before setting sail again to far-off places.

La Bruyère

In the literature of what the French call *mondanité*, dealing with the behavior of men and women in society who act parts assigned to them by their social class but who are also prey to their own ambitions and insecurities, the seventeenth century produced Molière and Pascal, together with La Bruyère, La Rochefoucauld, Fénelon, and others. What La Bruyère brought to the genre of moral and social observation is the ideal of the sincere man, the person who combines elegance, restraint, tact, and good taste in equal measure, and who moves in society with considered regard for himself and others. La Bruyère evaluated his fellow human beings according to this standard and found most of them sadly deficient. He is pessimistic yet modestly hopeful that sound advice, if couched in pleasurable form, as in his own writing, might lead to the correction of foibles and vices that otherwise would fester and deteriorate. He denounced pretense and snobbery and, within limits, argued against some of the more obvious manifestations of inequity and injustice. He was a man of moderate views, a conservative in his thinking, never prone to advocacy of extreme positions. These traits and qualities were what made him attractive to Proust, whose own writings, from *PJ* to the *Recherche*, have an honorable place in the history of French literature about "worldly" people.[5]

Proust's reflections on matters of the heart, on various types of women, on fashion, on social mores and habits, on the faults of the aristocracy, and on such things as the art of conversation, dinner parties, and salons owe much to La Bruyère's treatment of these subjects. Like Proust, La Bruyère did not question the idea of a social hierarchy, but he did point out flaws in the morals underlying that hierarchy. Roger Francillon put the essential elements of the connection between La Bruyère and Proust quite succinctly when he observed that "the most important bases for the relationship between the two writers are: a controlled sensitivity both to the delicacy of feelings and to what is laughable in society, an understanding of the transitoriness of men and things, a rejection of all systems of thought and a stubborn determination to transform the banal and daily stuff of life, by means of style, into a work of art."[6]

A few comparative examples from La Bruyère's *Les Caractères* and *PJ* will have to suffice here. Consider for example what La Bruyère has to say about love and friendship in the section of his book called "*Sur le cœur*" (On the heart):

> Love is born suddenly, without reflection, by attraction or by weakness: a beautiful feature seizes us, and determines us. Friendship on the other hand is formed little by little, with time, through contact, by long interaction. How much intelligence, goodness of heart, commitment, favors and generosity among friends, in order to do in several years much less than is done sometimes in a moment by a beautiful face or a beautiful hand! (La Bruyère 136)

The tone and attitude conveyed by La Bruyère is very close to Proust's understanding of the contradictions and apparent paradoxes that pervade intimate human relationships. What Proust brings to his depictions of these relationships, however, which is entirely missing in La Bruyère, is an intense sensuality and an enjoyment of and need for natural beauty and sensorial expressiveness.

Another feature of *Les Caractères* that appears in *PJ* is a series of "portraits" drawn from life and elaborated with great artistry; they are close in spirit to Proust's portraits of Parisian men and women. Proust's portrait of "*Oranthe*" (an invented name like many of La Bruyère's) is no doubt a pastiche of La Bruyère's manner in describing such characters. It begins by directly interrogating the character, in much the same way that La Bruyère addressed some of his creations:

> So you didn't go to bed last night? You haven't washed this morning?
> But why proclaim it from the house tops, Oranthe? Brilliantly gifted as you are, isn't that enough to distinguish you from common mortals? Must you insist upon acting such a pitiful role besides?
> You are hounded by creditors, your infidelities drive your wife to despair. To put on evening dress would seem to you tantamount to donning a livery, and no one could persuade you to go into society other than disheveled. Seated at dinner you keep your gloves on to prove that you are not eating, and if ever you have a fever at night you call for your victoria and go for a drive in the Bois de Boulogne. (Dupee 43)

"*Contre la franchise*" (Against frankness) is another pastiche in the manner of La Bruyère. Proust introduces three men, Percy, Laurence, and Augustin, calling the latter, who "always tells the truth," a true friend, but we quickly learn that "he is frank, in the same way that Percy is a lecturer, not in your interest but for his own pleasure." The little sketch ends by informing the reader that these three "impudent scoundrels," far from losing favor in society, are the object of applause and keen interest. The three men have hoodwinked an entire social milieu. Little gems similar to this are numerous in the *Caractères*.

The snobs, the roués and sophisticates, the haughty women and pretentious men of the *Caractères* and the people depicted by Proust in "*Fragments de comédie italienne*" are actors performing their parts in ways that, as Proust saw it, remain fixed in the minds of their social peers, thus allowing the individuals who wear these masks in society a wide latitude within which, in their private lives, they can be as outrageous as they wish. Assuming the identities of typical comic characters is the price that real people, unlike the stock characters they imitate, gladly pay for a freedom from restraint that allows them virtually unlimited license to do and say what they want. For Proust, Italian comedy was a convenient metaphor for society itself in its hilarious and tragicomic displays of affectation, foolishness, hypocrisy, self-delusion, cowardice, pretense. Proust's voice in these "*Fragments*" was that of a satirist, a moralist, and a shrewd man of the world.

Tolstoy

Proust's interest in Russian fiction was noted by several of his friends in the early years of the 1890s. He was keenly interested in the moral questions raised by Dostoievsky and Tolstoy, and he turned to them, as he did to certain nineteenth century English novelists, especially George Eliot and Thomas Hardy, for perspectives on the problems of modern society for which the French novel and French poetry did not furnish entirely satisfactory answers. Concern with the interrelations between art and morality was deeply rooted in French literature, but the Russians and the English gave a new immediacy to this concern, and in ways that reflected societies whose social structures and historical experiences diverged radically from those of France. The Russian sense of character and the British flair for social contextualization were among the qualities that attracted Proust to their work.

As far as a Tolstoyan presence in *PJ* is concerned, the case for it has been persuasively argued by Anne Henry and several others, notably Pierre Daum, but Henry should be credited for a discovery and an insight that had not occurred to anyone before her, as far as I know. There is only one unresolved question in her analysis, and it is that she seems to contradict herself on the nature of Proust's attitude toward the two characters, Baldassare and Honoré, the ill-fated but finally redeemed protagonists of the stories that open and close his volume.

Henry argues that "without the story of Ivan Ilych which tells an identical story of revolt and then of inward conversion that allows for a reconciliation with death, "*La Mort de Baldassare Silvande*" could never have been written." To this she adds, apropos of "*La Fin de la jalousie*," that this story too, on the basis of strong internal evidence, "recalls too irresistibly the death of Prince André, also a jealous lover, his slow agony next to the woman who keeps watch over him and who has caused his torment, to allow us to discard the hypothesis of a direct influence of these pages from *War and Peace* on Proust's short story" (1973, 34).

Proust's Baldassare greatly resembles the refined dandy and aesthete, Robert de Montesquiou. He lives surrounded by chrysanthemums, kid goats, and black cats in a circular-shaped living room looking out on the ocean. But in the face of illness and death, he at last renounces his decadent existence, the appurtenances of which Proust describes in considerable detail. In his last days of life, he redeems himself in a way that Henry believes, with good reason, Proust borrowed from Tolstoy. She points out that an anthology of Tolstoyan death scenes titled *La Mort* had appeared in 1886, which contained for the first time in French translation the death scene from Tolstoy's "The Death of Ivan Ilych," plus extracts from already published novels depicting the death of Prince André in *War and Peace*, the death of Levin in *Anna Karenina*, and three other sketches on the same theme titled "The Three Dead." That such writing on a theme that was never far from Proust's consciousness could have affected him deeply makes good sense. Henry notes in support of her thesis that Baldassare, this esthete and viscount in the vaguely named country of Sylvania, after a life of extravagant wastefulness and only occasional musical productivity, of numerous love affairs and lavish banquets, comes to terms with his own spiritual needs in the last moments of his life, like the hero of "The Death of Ivan Ilych."

But in advancing the argument that, after 1893, Proust had shifted in his basic orientation from "vague idealism" to a much more critical and down-to-earth attitude toward his two protagonists, Henry makes us wonder about what exactly the vantage point was from which Proust was treating his death scenes. Were they really "plagiarisms" of Tolstoyan scenes, as she thinks, or were they borrowings for satirical and even caricatural purposes, or perhaps intended to say something about human existence that might differ significantly from what Tolstoy had to say? I would venture to guess that, as was his wont, Proust was making use of another writer, in these two instances Tolstoy, but that he was doing so for reasons of his own, having to do with what Henry herself calls his new understanding that asestheticism was unable to confront the great questions of existence. Thus it is my contention that Proust did not so much imitate Tolstoy plagiaristically as make use of him in a way that lent greater moral authority to his youthful fictional writings.

There is little doubt that Tolstoy helped Proust to shape his death scenes. A comparison of the endings of "The Death of Ivan Ilych" and *"La Mort de Baldassare Silvande"* lends credence to Henry's belief that a usage of some sort was operative. Here is the ending of Tolstoy's story, written in 1886:

> And suddenly it grew clear to him that what had been oppressing him and would not leave him was all dropping away at once from two sides, from ten sides, and from all sides. He was sorry for them, he must act so as not to hurt them: release them and free himself from these sufferings. "How good and how simple!" he thought. "And the pain?" he asked himself. "What has become of it? Where are you, pain?"
>
> He turned his attention to it.
>
> "Yes, here it is. Well, what of it? Let the pain be."
>
> "And death where is it?"
>
> He sought his former accustomed fear of death and did not find it. "Where is it? What death?" There was no fear because there was no death.
>
> In place of death there was light.
>
> "So that's what it is!" he suddenly exclaimed aloud. "What joy"!
>
> To him all this happened in a single instant, and the meaning of that instant did not change. For those present his agony continued for another two hours. Something rattled in his throat, his emaciated body twitched, then the gasping and rattle became less and less frequent.
>
> "It is finished!" said someone near him.
>
> He heard these words and repeated them in his soul.
>
> "Death is finished," he said to himself. "It is no more!"
>
> He drew in a breath, stopped in the midst of a sigh, stretched out, and died. (302)

And now the last scene of *"La Mort de Baldassare Silvande:"*

> At this moment the doctor beckoned everyone to approach, saying, "This is the end!"
>
> Baldassare lay with closed eyes, and his heart listened to the bell which his ears, paralyzed by approaching death, could no longer hear. Once more he saw his mother kissing him as she always did when he came home, then in the evening tucking him in bed, warming his feet in her hands, staying with him if he could not sleep. He remembered *Robinson Crusoe*, and evenings in the garden when his sister sang, and his professor predicted that one day he would be a great musician, and his mother's emotion which she tried in vain to hide. Now there was no more time to realize that passionate expectation of his mother and sister which he had so cruelly disappointed. He saw again the tall linden tree under which he had become betrothed and the day when his betrothal had been broken,

when only his mother had known how to comfort him. He thought he was kissing his old nurse, holding his first violin. He saw it all again through a luminous distance, sweet and sad like the one on which the sightless windows gazed, facing woods and pastures.

All this he saw, yet not two minutes had elapsed since the doctor, listening to his heart, had said "This is the end!" Then, rising, "All is over."

Alexis, his mother, and Jean Galéas knelt down, together with the Duke of Parma, who had just arrived. The servants were weeping in the open doorway. (Dupee 23–24)

Compared with the ending of "The Death of Ivan Ilych," where there truly is a reconciliation of sorts with death, Baldassare's final moments are much more taken up with remembrances of people, places, and emotions associated with his formative years than they are with death. But let's look a bit more closely at the Tolstoyan and the Proustian scenes. There are common features. They are the death sentence itself, pronounced by someone at Ivan's bedside in Tolstoy, by the doctor in Proust; the distortion of the sense of time in both stories, where thought is extraordinarily compressed as death approaches; the presence of family members and friends at the death scene; the image of light, presented in an unadorned way by Tolstoy, in an image, that of "luminous distance," by Proust.

Tolstoy focuses quite closely on the fact of impending death itself, and on how Ivan comes to terms with it through an exceptional moment of reconciliation involving a falling away of pain and, above all, of the fear of death that had always haunted him. In Tolstoy, death has almost a friendly mien; it is what separates Ivan from his family and friends. They cannot comprehend what the dying man is experiencing. Ivan thinks of the world outside his room now as something remote, far off, irrelevant to the great and decisive moment through which he is passing.

In Proust's scene, the emphasis is on life, not death, or at least on Baladassare's still powerful attachment to life, as we see in the series of memories that occur to him as he lies paralyzed in his bed. In fact, we recognize in this ending several of the key components of Marcel's first experiences as recounted in the *Recherche*, but already very much present to Proust's imagination in *PJ*, and in *JS*: his mother's ever comforting presence, his favorite childhood reading, the benevolent aspects of nature that surrounded him. Baldassare is but a projection of Proust's own personality and vision, and what matters in the death scene is the life he is able to recall not the death that is about to take him. Another difference is that the death scene in Proust highlights a failure, a missed opportunity, time spent frivolously, one of the central ideas informing all of Proust's writing and that preoccupied him constantly: the idea that life offers the individual only so many chances, only so many privileged moments, which must be seized in the eternal struggle against loss, waste, and dispersion. Such a failure is especially sad, in Proust's scheme of things, when it involves a person's capacity for creative and artistic expression, which alone, except for the illuminations made possible precisely by death, redeems the otherwise inevitable passing away of all beings and things, great and small. From Tolstoy, we learn something about how death might actually be experienced. From Proust we learn about the value of life, but through sensous and sensory experience, through what memory brings in its wake that is meaningful, through light that truly enlightens the reader about a character's relationship with life much more than about his way of understanding death.

The last scene of "*La Fin de la jalousie*" is a much more authentically Tolstoyan ending than the one in *La Mort de Baldassare Silvande*," in that it is charged with that deep humanitarian feeling of universal fellowship that we associate with the Russian novelist. Both Tolstoy and Proust understood the psychological dynamics of jealousy very well, and it is logical that in this respect Proust owed much to Tolstoy. In any case, jealousy, and the epistemological and moral problems it raises, is a common theme that justifies a comparative study of the two writers.

Intertextual presences in Proust's early writings therefore reflect not only his reading and assimilation of the techniques and devices used by other authors he admired but also his formal education, his philosophical interests and concerns, his family life, his friendships and relationships in Parisian society of the 1880s and 1890s, and his social and class affiliations. In sum, writing for young Proust was the expression of his personal experience and his vision of the world.

In answer to the question of what the ideological implications of Proust's literary borrowings and appropriations are, I would say, first, that his early writing is in large measure a defense of tradition and an assertion of the place he hoped to make for himself in French literary history, which he looked at, however, in a critical and independent manner, often satirically; and second, that he was engaged in an exploration of psychological and philosophical problems to which the genres he was utilizing gave a particular kind of access. Proust was interested not in breaking entirely free from established literary practice, in the manner of the radical avant-garde, but, rather, in respecting what the past had to offer him and that he could then turn to his own purposes. There is nothing in his early writing that presents insuperable problems to most readers. Yet as this chapter has shown, there is a great deal going on in his texts that needs to be studied in detail in order to savor their peculiar stylistic qualities and comprehend their conceptual premises. Nothing in his writing can be taken for granted. One must probe its surfaces to extract the treasure below. He was a conservative thinker, in some respects, but able to see and to reveal the deficiencies of the existing order with considerable verve. His subsequent writing projects—the uncompleted novel *JS*, the essays on Ruskin, and, later, the *Recherche*—build on the foundation he laid in *Les Plaisirs et les jours*.

Part Three

THE CRITIC AND THE NOVELIST

Chapter 9

Critical Principles

> I will always be on guard against an exclusive cult that would attach itself to anything other than the joy that [beautiful flowers] give us, a cult in whose name, through a self-centered return to ourselves, we would make them "our" flowers, and would take pains to honor them by decorating our room with works of art where they are represented. No, I will not find a painting more beautiful because the artist may have painted a hawthorn in the foreground, although I know of nothing more beautiful than the hawthorn, because I want to remain sincere and I know that the beauty of a painting does not depend on the things depicted in it.
>
> Marcel Proust, "John Ruskin"

In this and in the next chapter, my aim is to present an analysis of young Proust's writings during the second half of the 1890s and into the early months of 1900. This is a period in which he devoted himself to the writing of a novel he never finished, after which he turned his attention to the work of the English art historian John Ruskin. There is no doubt that his Ruskin studies, which bore fruit in a series of essays and in two translations,[1] played a key role in his development as a critic and as a novelist. The turn to Ruskin is symptomatic of Proust's ever more intense effort to work out a unified aesthetic philosophy incorporating literature, painting and music. The unfinished novel reflects this effort in curious ways, among which are its focus on subjects dear to the impressionist painters, and in its reverence for images of light, which are pervasive throughout a text that numbers almost 750 pages.

Proust was always a deeply serious writer, yet it seems to me that, in the second half of the 1890s, he moved to a significantly higher level and quality of commitment to creative and critical endeavor, due in part to his reading of Ruskin and in part to a natural process of maturation that we see already manifesting itself before 1895, in certain of the pieces of *PJ*. Proust's encounter with Ruskin and his more than six years of "apprenticeship"[2] to the English writer, was certainly a major event in his intellectual and literary life. It was under Ruskin's tutelage that Proust strengthened his commitment to writing as a mission, as a calling every bit as fateful in its nature and consequences as the one that inspired the great religious prophets of the Judeo-Christian tradition. Proust looked upon Ruskin as a "prophet" equal in power and scope to Nietzsche, Tolstoy, and Ibsen; moreover, even if still implicitly, since he was not yet embarked on the great project of his life—the writing of the *Recherche*—Proust saw himself as only to a limited extent responsible for his choice of mission. On a deeper level, he felt that he, like all committed artists, was but an instrument in the hands of a higher spiritual power, and he looked to that power as the source of his inspiration, much like Homer, Virgil, Dante, and Milton. Translating and interpreting the art criticism of Ruskin was Proust's rite of passage, so to speak, to a realm where he believed that elemental forces were at work shaping and molding the creative lives of poets, painters, composers, all those whose existences were consecrated to realizing themselves in works of art. In sum, Proust was fully prepared to sacrifice life itself for the purpose of realizing himself in his chosen field of literature, for he saw himself now as one of the elect few whose destiny was to light the way to future generations. This does not mean that he suddenly became an anchorite. His schedule of social engagements continued to be full, at least up to the moment in 1907 or 1908 when he began composing the *Recherche*. It means more modestly that his priorities underwent a radical change in emphasis. In the latter part of the 1890s, he was already a man for whom writing was the primary reason and purpose of life, the one and only activity that could give him a feeling of complete fulfillment.

Let's begin looking at this crucial period in Proust's life by considering the meaning and implications of the epigraph to this chapter taken from the most important of Proust's writings on Ruskin prior to the prefaces of 1904 and 1906 (*CSB* 105–141). At first glance, the thought encapsulated in this passage may seem simpler than it is. Its difficulty stems from the fact that it is a highly compressed exposition of concepts that are at once aesthetic, psychological, and philosophical. The operative aesthetic principle rests on the notion that while beauty in nature and beauty in art are, in certain respects, interdependent, they are also, and more fundamentally, different from each other. The beauty that the viewer sees in a flower is itself a creative and subjective perception, not a quality that resides intrinsically in the flower. In this sense, the viewer of the flower and the viewer of a work of art depicting the flower play the same role in the interaction between subject and object, and as such the experiences are similar. Concerning this point, Sartre wrote: "When I am enchanted with a landscape, I know very well that it is not I who create it, but I also know that without me the relations which are established before my eyes among the trees, foliage, earth and grass would not exist at all" (1994, 51–52).

The viewer fixes his aesthetic attention on both the flower in nature and the flower in art with a feeling of pleasure that originates in a gaze that establishes the relations between it and its surroundings. But at the same time, there is a difference between the aesthetic pleasure given by a flower in nature and a flower represented in a painting that one finds beautiful. The former is a pleasure that derives from the object's existence as something independent of human volition, something also that is transitory, of very brief duration, yet destined to return at another time by reason of the seasonal and cyclical rhythms of the universe. On the other hand, the beauty of a flower represented in a painting hinges on a principle that has nothing to do with the natural flower except its outer form, for in the case of the painting, it is what Proust liked to call the "vision" of the artist that determines its peculiar beauty, its power to please and enchant us. It is the artist, the creator, who breathes life into the depicted flower; it is his or her special and unique conception of the object and ability to translate that conception into highly individualized forms that distinguish the painted flower from the natural one. And, of course, art transcends time, it raises the depicted thing or person to a level of autonomy that resists time, even if, ultimately, in the remote future, all things will fade and pass into oblivion. What the flower depicted in a painting possesses that a flower in nature does not is the imprint of an artist's individuality, the mark of a shaping intelligence that renders the objective reality of the flower, to be sure, but the flower as seen by the eyes of a visionary, that is, someone whose unique talent allows him or her to fashion something in a manner unlike any other. This would be as true of a flower rendered abstractly as of one rendered in a more realistic style, since even the most literal painterly realism differs from the photographic image. Proust's appreciation of artistic individuality was a basic component of his ideology as a theorist and practitioner of literary expression; it was what made him such a powerful voice in defense of spiritual values that were threatened, as he and many others like him saw it, by the encroachments of "machinism," by standardization and routine, by what Ruskin and other English Victorians such as Thomas Carlyle judged to be "the leprosy of industrialism and speculation" (Sizeranne 286).

From a psychological point of view, the passage alludes to a phenomenon that has attracted an enormous amount of attention since Marx and Freud conceptualized it, each in his own way, as a basic characteristic of alienated human beings incapable of grasping reality in its dialectical integrity and wholeness: the phenomenon of fetishism. Proust was aware of fetishism as a result of his readings in the works of contemporary experimental sexologists and psychologists, but his grasp of its importance as a trait of modern civilization is every bit as sharp as that of Marx and Freud. He applied it primarily to art, where he noted a widespread tendency to give to works of art, especially paintings, a value that transcended the legitimate bounds of aesthetic appreciation.

Fetishism can manifest itself in various ways: in the desire to appropriate a beloved object, as in the case of a person who adopts a flower or some other natural life form as his own, thus changing a relationship that is essentially spiritual into one that is personal and possessive, or in attributing to that life form "a special force or independent life" in a work of art apart from the vision of the artist who created it (Foster, in Apter and Pietz 253). The latter case is the one especially relevant to Proust's understanding of fetishism. What the cited passage alludes to is the inclination to separate some special feature of a work of art from the vision of its creator. The flower in a painting derives its beauty solely from the shaping vision of the artist, for it is his or her spirit that inhabits and penetrates it. Yet art lovers persist in worshipping the beauty of the things depicted in paintings. Just as, in a Marxian sense, money and commodities in a capitalist system acquire a fetishistic value in and for themselves, considered entirely apart from the complex productive labor process and the social relations that inform them, and as in Freud's investigations, which shed light on why and how human beings attach sexual power not to the totality of the beloved's selfhood but rather to a single feature of that self or to a material object they endow with an animated force of its own, so Proust felt the need to warn himself as much as his readers against the ever present danger of substituting things for human emotions, objects for spiritual presences.

In his Ruskin essays, Proust commented repeatedly, almost obsessively, on the need to distinguish between fetishistic cultism and genuine spiritual identification with an artist or, as in Ruskin's case, with an original critical mind. After Ruskin's death on January 20, 1900, Proust noted, far more people had visited his grave in Coniston than had journeyed to Amiens to see the great thirteenth century cathedral where Ruskin's soul resided, for it was there that the essential part of him was to be found, not in the grave where his physical remains were interred (*CSB* 441). Ruskin's soul lived on in the architectural works to which he consecrated his life, and whose beauty and singularity he described in his writings. The distinction is a crucial one, psychologically and morally; it is what gives to Proust's critical writings in the years 1896 to 1900 much of their intellectual interest.

Proust used his Ruskin essays as a means with which to educate his readers concerning the notion that beauty, when seen in relation to the creative process, should be understood always as a quality residing within the soul of the artist, not in the objects he or she depicts. This idea was closely tied to another, namely that even the greatest works of art, in whatever medium, must not be allowed to take on an independent life of their own apart from historical and moral considerations. History was the record of human strife and enterprise, including that of art, whose purpose, in addition to providing moments of disinterested pleasure, was just as importantly that of illuminating the moral life of humanity, of offering lucid commentary on human affairs, of providing perspectives on problems in human experience that would otherwise remain hidden from consciousness. "Prophetic" writers such as Ruskin, in Proust's view, were the supreme consciences and teachers of humankind; they were, as Thomas Carlyle had believed, the true "heroes" of the ages. Proust's conception of the writer was as exalted as Shelley's, the essence of whose idealistic pronouncement that "Poets are the unacknowledged legislators of the world" Proust assimilated into his own thought.

There is also a philosophical and religious concept present in the epigraph, one that establishes a theoretical link between nature and art as creations emanating from the mind of a creator. In this regard, even if he did not accept in its entirety the immense superstructure of beliefs constituting the Jewish and the Christian world views, Proust did agree essentially with an aspect of Thomas à Kempis's way of articulating the relationship between God and the created world. He saw this relationship as analogous to the relationship between artist and work of art that was first articulated, at least in the early modern era, during the Renaissance. Kempis believed that reverence must always be directed to God the creator, not to His creations; in the same way, as Proust conceived of the question, the reverential attitude so often attached to works of art was in reality misplaced, for it ought to be fixed at all times on the vision emanating from the mind of the artist. Only in this way could human beings protect themselves from aesthetic fetishism. The lofty philosophical idealism that Proust brought to this conception of art was what fed his notion that art as the embodiment of a unique vision of the world belongs properly in the domain of the eternal, where all contingency is transcended. This quasi-religious way of conceptualizing the place of art as being at once in and yet outside the flow of historically measured time was typical of a moment in European history in which poet-philosophers such as Mallarmé gained broad influence in reattaching poetry to metaphysical concerns and anxieties.

What I have said above about Proust's idealist critical principles does not mean that the material world had somehow suddenly vanished from his field of vision. On the contrary, philosophically as well as practically speaking, he never lost sight of the material world, as Randolph Splitter and Mieke Bal have argued, the former in his "psychoanalytical" study of the *Recherche* and the latter in her examination of Proust's "visual poetics." Both scholars show that Proust's aesthetic philosophy and practice can only be appreciated by seeing them as part of a unitary world view, which distinguishes his thought from that of religious philosophers such as Kempis and his followers, regardless of his indebtedness to them.

Proust's many polemical comments about the gross "materialism" of contemporary critics, who looked at the succession of literary and artistic schools of thought as if they were so many changes in government or in fashion (Tadié 166), has induced some scholars to take what the narrator says about the "purely mental character of reality" in the last volume of the *Recherche* as his definitive philosophical position concerning literature and art. But what that passage means, I would argue, is not that the material world plays no role in forming an artist's understanding of reality but instead that the meaning of that reality can only be apprehended by the mind. It was in this context that the narrator declares: "I had realised before now that it is only a clumsy and erroneous form of perception which places everything in the object, when really everything is in the mind" (*In Search of Lost Time* 6: 323) and subsequently insists on "the purely mental character of reality" (326–327).

Unlike Kempis and most other theocentric religious philosophers, Proust did not believe that God the creator existed apart from His creation, just as he did not believe in the Crocean notion that a work of art already exists in the mind of its creator before it assumes concrete form in a poem, a painting, a musical composition. The matter/spirit dichotomy so prevalent in Western philosophy, which assigns an inferior and often shame-ridden role to matter and to everything concerned with the body, while reserving for spirit an absolute purity of origin and purpose, is not entirely absent from Proust's thought, yet I think that Splitter is correct when he observes that "spirit" and "matter," essence and impression, are finally inseparable in Proust's writing, and that he really never lets us forget the inescapable "materiality" of even the most rarefied and "sublime" moments (Splitter 26).

In this regard Mieke Bal is as persuasive as Splitter. Her analysis of Proust's "sensualist epistemology" should discourage the tendency to translate his idealist conception of life into one-sidedly spiritualist terms. Bal argues that Proust's work, culminating in the *Recherche*, is one of the greatest of all testimonies to the power of a "visual poetics" that utilizes techniques of representation and figuration remarkably similar to those of two of his favorite painters, Rembrandt and Chardin. We will be looking at Proust's essay of 1895 on these two painters a little later in this chapter, but it is important to note here, with Bal, that for Proust, it is imagery based on sense experience, and not logical reasoning, that focuses the reader's mind on the significant moments in his narratives; that the image is a place where "affectivity and cognition, epistemology and aesthetics, subject and object, are inextricably mixed" (Bal 198). In the final analysis, therefore, if Splitter and Bal are, as I believe, correct, we can say that Proust does not separate the domain of the mind from that of the body. Where he did adhere to idealist premises was in his virtually lifelong conviction that "truth and beauty" reside within the human subject, not in objects, with the corollary that a work of art, once it is separated from the human mind that created it and given an autonomous value of its own, can only lead to fetishism and idolatry. Art is a world where the "irreducible individuality of the mind is revealed" (Houston 19), not one where material considerations of any kind whatever should be allowed to be determinant.

Some of the same tendencies in Proust's thought concerning the place of literature and art in relation to the principles of idealism and materialism manifest themselves to one degree or another in what he had to say about science and intuition as sources of knowledge, in his views of the proper role and function of criticism, and in his understanding of the relationship between criticism and art. One of the problems we face in trying to untangle these various threads lies, as I have already pointed out several times elsewhere in this study, in the fact that he had an extremely narrow, positivistic, and undialectical notion of what "materialism" means. In a manner tantamount to erecting a proverbial straw man, he almost always attached the word to a series of mundane concerns unworthy of a critic who aspires to achieve what Proust himself saw as the primary aim of criticism, that is, "to help the reader grasp the essential traits of a writer or artist and, if possible, to reconstitute the writer's particular vision of reality" (Strauss 58).

Historical perspective itself, although increasingly acknowledged by Proust, at least in theory, to be a crucial component of all criticism, has at best a perfunctory presence in his writing, even during and after the period of his Ruskin studies (1899–1906). This explains in part why he remained so stubbornly attached to the notion that a writer's life experience was of no essential importance in the process of evaluating his work. In effect Proust trivialized the biographical side of literary study, reducing it to the futile pursuit of external "facts" that bear no relevance whatever to the core values of artistic creativity.

Despite his disregard (or more probably ignorance) of what the great historical-materialist thinkers have contributed to the cause of enlightenment about art, society, and history, Proust was in practice a writer who, while adhering to idealist principles, did not neglect science; who insisted on the differences between creation and criticism, yet never really separated these two realms from each other; and who believed, together with his constant model Baudelaire, that criticism was not only a professional obligation of the writer and poet but also a crucial part of his or her creative life.

What Proust wanted to do, essentially, while not abandoning science and criticism, was to hold the line against the incursions of a mechanistic form of scientism by reclaiming for art and literature a unique and irreplaceable role in human civilization wherein the creative and visionary qualities of the human mind retain their primacy. Unless we keep these two levels of Proust's thinking firmly in mind, it becomes difficult to appreciate why Tadié can speak pertinently of Proust's "medical" and "diagnostic" view of the human condition, while recalling at the same time that Proust was a lifelong idealist thinker. It becomes difficult also to appreciate Malcolm Bowie's comment that the bulk of Proust's writing, whether "creative" or "critical" in nature, occupies an *intermundium* between theory and fiction (1987).

In an important lecture published in 1994 (and reworked in chapter 5 of *Proust Among the Stars*), Bowie returned to this question by making more explicit what he sees as the deeply "ambiguous" side of Proust's moral vision in the *Recherche*. On the one hand, he argues that the *Recherche* has a "distinctive moral architecture," and that Proust deserves an important place in the history of French moral philosophy. Yet on the other hand, Bowie also shows us how complex and ambiguous Proust's meditations on "virtue" and "vice" are in his great work, due in large measure to the quality of "mercy" that ultimately characterizes his vision of human experience and desire. Proust's "deferral of moral judgement," Bowie believes, is evident in his depictions of sexuality, where Proust the stern moralist encounters the equally powerful Proust who sees a certain grandeur in even the most degraded forms of sexual expression. Proust evinces both "a strong-minded normative view of sexual conduct" and an "empathizing and exploratory view." In sum, Bowie thinks that, like many of his predecessors in the history of moral philosophy, Proust was interested in understanding human passions and in rendering them through the depiction of archetypal characters. Proust was at once a "moral scientist" and a compassionate painter of human conduct for whom "the shortcomings and wrongdoings of all social creatures are to be neutralized in a supreme act of forgiveness."

We could argue endlessly about how successful Proust was in integrating critical reflection in his fictional writings, but there is no valid way, in my view, of denying what David Ellison calls "the close relationship of criticism to creativity" in Proust's literary practice (50), a relationship that is especially intimate in the concluding pages of the essay "John Ruskin" and in the final section of the *Recherche*, where an essayistic meditation on art, subjectivity, and imagination brings the novel to a close.

Of the twenty or so critical writings Proust produced during the years 1895 to 1900, seven deserve brief elucidation in this chapter, either because they exemplify broad critical trends and tendencies of the time or because they are exemplary and original in an intellectual sense, as expressions of Proust's visionary idealism. Two deal with literary questions: "*Contre l'obscurité*," published on July 15, 1896, in *La Revue Blanche* and "*La Poésie ou les lois mystérieuses*" (Poetry or the mysterious laws), which is impossible to date precisely; it was not published during Proust's lifetime. Scholars associate it with the years he was most heavily engaged in writing *JS*, 1895–1899. The five others deal with issues in art criticism. One, published posthumously, is devoted to Chardin and Rembrandt; the remaining four are on Ruskin: two brief appreciative obituaries, written in January and February 1900, shortly after Ruskin's death, and two lengthier and more ambitious articles that were later integrated in 1904 and 1906 into the long prefatory and strongly autobiographical essays that Proust wrote for his translations of Ruskin's *The Bible of Amiens* and *Sesame and the Lilies*.

Looking first at Proust's commentary on contemporary symbolism (*CSB* 390–395), one notes in this essay, as in all of his critical efforts during these years, a more personally engaged attitude, coupled with an intense effort to raise the level of critical discourse above polemics to an ideal plane where, he believed, contingency is transmuted into permanent and essential values.

When Proust first submitted "*Contre l'obscurité*" to *La Revue Blanche* in November 1895, he told Pierre Mainguet, the director of *La Revue Hebdomadaire*, that he was taking a considerable risk in letting it circulate openly, and that he feared angry reactions from his friends and associates in the symbolist camp (*Corr.* 1: 446–447). But the article was not published until July 1896, when it appeared suddenly, and in truncated form. Proust was as surprised as anyone else when the essay appeared on July 15th. This was a month after the publication of *PJ* and the minor critical controversy that it had provoked. On July 16th Proust wrote to his mother complaining that the editors of *La Revue Blanche* had published "without consulting me, without advising me, without having sent me the proofs to correct, an article (shortened) that I had submitted six months ago (the article on Obscurity in Poetry) which I had completely forgotten and which I thought had been thrown in the waste basket. Perhaps you find it disturbing that something by me would appear at this moment and because of that I am very upset" (Proust 1953, 68–69). The reason why Proust was worried about his mother's reaction to the article at this moment was that her father had died at the end of June.

Proust had good reason to anticipate a strong critical response to his article from *La Revue Blanche*. With such figures as Mallarmé, Henri de Régnier, Maurice Maeterlinck, and Gustave Kahn on its editorial staff, the review deserved its reputation as a "fortress of symbolism" (Quint 36). What Proust found deficient in symbolist poetry was not really its "symbolism" but what he called its "hermeticism" and its "preciosity," meaning that it used a language that was at once private and pretentious. In a long letter to Reynaldo Hahn a month after the controversial article had appeared, Proust spoke more cautiously and equivocally about symbolist verse. In this letter he said that he found Mallarmé's images to be both "obscure and brilliant," in that they were indeed "the images of things," but "reflected so to speak in a dark and polished mirror of black marble." He noted also to Hahn that Mallarmé tended to pass without warning from "an inflexible and pure classic form, almost naked, to the most insane preciosity." But his overall judgment of the leading exponent of French symbolism was anything but one-sidedly negative. The great pleasure to be extracted from Mallarmean verse, he said, consisted in "finding so much archaism, grandeur, mythology, taste and nature in a sort of brief family letter. That is its charm 'in the final analysis.' It is moreover the charm of Mallarmé and the role of the poet, to lend solemnity to life" (*Lettres à Reynaldo Hahn*, 63–66).

"*Contre l'obscurité*" begins by addressing what Proust calls two types of obscurity in literary composition: obscurity of ideas and images, and grammatical obscurity. He then summarizes what he takes to be the principal rationale for symbolist obscurity, that offered by many young poets and writers who claimed that "in language everything new is obscure," since it reflects new thought and feeling. Proust argues in this respect that too often contemporary writers defend their "obscurity" by connecting themselves to figures in the past who were also at first quite "obscure" to their audiences. But he rejects this line of reasoning, asserting that the obscurity of writers in the past, such as Racine, was very different from its contemporary manifestations, which was really something recent in literary history. Here Proust was speaking of language used in such a way as to wrench it free of all the conventional forms and constraints to which readers are accustomed. His main point in this opening section of the article was that "the laws of the world and of thought" would not change simply because a group of writers wanted them to change, thus allowing themselves to think that "masterpieces from now on would be what they have never been through the centuries: virtually unintelligible."

Proust's argument then takes a turn of considerable theoretical importance, namely that the language of philosophy and the language of literature are two different things. In the former, as seen in the writing of Spinoza, Kant and Hegel, one encounters thought that is as obscure as it is profound, or, better, that is obscure because it is profound. Literary expression, on the other hand, follows a different path, and uses different tools to convey difficult thought. Those who defend the obscurity of symbolist poetry by comparing it with difficult philosophy forget, Proust maintained, that if the writer and the poet can, in effect, go as deeply into the reality of things as the metaphysical philosopher, they do so with other means not based primarily on logical reasoning, which "paralyzes the elan of feeling that alone can take them to the heart of the world." In other words, Proust was saying, literature uses imagery and metaphor to express its conception of life; it uses figurative language drenched in the imaginative and fantasy life of human beings, where "concepts" and "logical reasoning" are felt to be alien presences. Literature is not addressed to our "logical faculties," and it is by other means that such masterpieces as *Macbeth* acquire their "philosophical" power. Philosophy is not absent from literature, but it is philosophy communicated via devices of style, figure, and rhythm that appeal to universal sentiments and concerns.

While philosophy must speak a special language, Proust continued, poetry cannot do so, for words are not pure signs for the poet. Each word contains within itself "the charm of its origin or the grandeur of its past; the poetic word appeals to our imagination and sensibility through an evocative power at least as great as its power of strict signification."

The problem with this point is not that it is groundless but, rather, that it is of limited relevance when we recall the whole history of philosophy and of literature, particularly some of the major trends in nineteenth-century philosophy and literature. Many nineteenth century philosophers employed a language that was basically emotive and imagistic without renouncing the name of philosopher; one thinks, for example, of Emerson, Kierkegaard and Nietzsche. At the same time, philosophical poetry was of fundamental importance in the Romantic movement; without a good grounding in philosophy, understanding Blake, Coleridge, Wordsworth, Shelley, and other English poets of the late eighteenth and early nineteenth century is an impossible task. True enough, these highly conceptual Romantic poets, like their forebears Dante, Milton, and Donne, like Shakespeare and Lope de Vega, made their primary appeal to the emotions, but that does not mean that one can understand their work without a solid foundation in philosophy. In sum, this part of Proust's argument was questionable if taken out of the immediate context within which he entered the debate about symbolism.

The last part of the article argues that symbolism's claim to disregard "the accidents of time and space" in order to show the reader only "eternal truths," failed to grasp another law of life, which was to realize the universal or eternal, but only through the depiction of individuals. Citing *War and Peace* and *The Mill on the Floss* (a rather odd move in an essay devoted mainly to poetry) Proust concluded that it was when these two novels were most themselves that they realized most fully the "universal soul." Tolstoy had illuminated "the deepest mysteries of life and death" by focusing intensely on the lives of specific individuals in specific places and circumstances.

Compagnon's view is that, in "*Contre l'obscurité*," Proust mainly rehashes notions that had already been served up by Gustave Lanson and Ferdinand Brunetière, both of whom, in the name respectively of historicism and cultural traditionalism, were unresponsive to the new trends and personalities in French literature (Compagnon 1983, 216–217). But as Compagnon himself explains, Proust was among the last writers (with Paul Bourget) for whom criticism is still literature, not yet given over to history. In other words, Proust's commentary on symbolism was that of a writer committed to the crucial difference between logical and metaphorical ways of communicating the basic laws and principles of life, as he saw them. Therefore, when it was a question of analyzing the root causes of symbolism's failure to reach any but an initiated reading audience, he resorted to arguments that were at bottom and necessarily Romantic in nature, and adorned them with words of a distinctly imagistic and allusive character. He looked askance at historicism and positivism when applied comprehensively to works of art.

Would a historicist or a positivist say, for example, as did Proust in "*Contre l'obscurité*," that "the poet renounces the irresistible power of awaking so many Sleeping Beauties" in readers if he speaks a language that they do not know? Would historicists and positivists rush to accentuate the difference between "living symbols and cold allegories," or say that all appeals to the vulgar, whether to flatter or to confuse, gave the wrong signal to "the divine archer"? Would they take note, as Proust did, concerning the relationship between the obscure and the visible, that "nature does not hide the sun from us, or the thousands of stars that shine without veils, brilliant and undecipherable to almost everyone's eyes"? Consider the penultimate paragraph of this essay:

> Poets should take inspiration more from nature, where, if the essence of everything is one and obscure, the form of everything is individual and clear. With the secret of life, she will teach them disdain for obscurity. Does nature hide the sun from us, or the thousands of stars that shine without veils, brilliant and undecipherable to almost everyone's eyes? Doesn't nature make us touch, rudely and nakedly, the power of the sea or of the west wind? To each man she gives the ability to express clearly, during his passage on the earth, the deepest mysteries of life and death. Are they for that reason pervaded by vulgarity, despite the vigorous and expressive language of desires and muscles, of suffering, of the flesh rotting or in bloom? And I ought to refer above all, since this is nature's true *time for art*, to the moonlight where for those alone who are initiated, even though it shines so sweetly on everyone, nature, without neologisms, for so many centuries, has made light with darkness and has played the flute in silence. (*CSB* 394-395).

The paragraph is shot through with images, mythical allusions, contrasts, metaphors, in sum a richly expressive language typical of a writer who bridles at the restraints of conventional critical discourse. For this reason, to place Proust in the same category as a Lanson or a Brunetière, despite the similarity of some of his arguments to those of his two older contemporaries, strikes me as somewhat misleading. One senses in this article an urgent impulse to liberate criticism from "logic" in favor of precisely the kind of discourse that Proust claims is typical of the literary imagination.

Mallarmé's reply to "*Contre l'obscurité*" (1945, 382–387) did not mention Proust's name, but it did allude twice to the accusation of "obscurity," which Mallarmé turned back against Proust, and more generally against symbolism's detractors, by reasserting his belief that "there is something occult at the basis of everything," which it is the duty of poets to reveal beneath the surface of things:

> I know, in fact, that [symbolism's detractors] push themselves onto the stage and assume, in their display, a humiliating posture; since to argue on the basis of obscurity—or, no one will grasp it if they don't grasp it and they do not—implies a prior renunciation of the act of judging. (1945, 383)

Mallarmé's critique of Proust's position was based on the assumption that appeals to the need for clarity in writing at all costs were tantamount to adopting a "journalistic" attitude toward language, and in so doing aligning oneself with the benighted readers of the popular press. He reminded Proust of the power of music, which of all the arts made manifest the extent to which human beings sought contact with the mysterious essence of things. Language that aspired to this same power by other means necessarily demanded from the reader an effort of decipherment that the exponents of "clarity" would never appreciate. "I prefer," Mallarmé said, "in the face of this aggression, to retort that our contemporaries do not know how to read" (386).

The lines of battle were drawn, the terms of debate made quite clear, yet I think Tadié is right when he observes that, in reality, Proust and Mallarmé were much closer to each other, philosophically speaking, than either one realized (Tadié 307–308). They differed in their views concerning the role of the writer vis-à-vis the reading public. Where Proust saw universal laws intelligible to all thinking beings, Mallarmé envisioned a more recondite domain where the deepest truths of human life and destiny could only be discovered by moving beyond the limits of ordinary consciousness. Yet they were both fond of the word and the concept of "mystery," which crops up as often in Proust's writing as it does in Mallarmé's. Proust's unfinished essay "*La Poésie ou les lois mystérieuses*" is a case in point. In addition, Proust was just as devoted as Mallarmé to the notion of music as the ultimate expression of humanity's deepest reserves of thought and feeling.

This essay (*CSB* 417–422) is a rambling meditation on the nature of the poet's and the artist's inner life, the "mysterious laws" that exist within the soul of a creator who finds himself quite suddenly in the presence of a thing of beauty, be it something natural or something fashioned by the human hand. In such a presence, the poet or artist establishes a particular relation with beauty, a bond is created between the creative imagination and the thing that attracts it. Proust's point in this strangely meandering piece is that, by virtue of these "mysterious laws" within the poet or painter, the resulting vision will be so complete and persuasive as to make us think that what that particular poet or artist sees is the only beauty in the world, the only truth. But that feeling of exclusiveness is merely the enchantment resulting from participating in a particular vision of things. Proust uses the example of two very different painters, Jean Chardin and Gustave Moreau, to illustrate the fact that each fresh new artistic vision takes possession of us with tremendous force. When one looks at a Chardin, Proust observes,

> not only do you see the beauty of a middle class meal, but you believe that poetry exists only in rustic dinners and you turn your eyes away when you sees jewels. But when you have seen a Gustave Moreau, you look for diamonds and precious stones as things that are just as beautiful, when you have seen a Moreau, after believing that things were only beautiful in their spontaneity like flowers in the field and animals in their life, thus disdaining every kind of art object and leaving them to the rich without imagination, when you have seen a Moreau, you acquire a taste for sumptuous dressing tables, for things turned away from their natural grace and taken as symbols. (418–419).

The "mysterious laws" reside in each and every authentic artist, and they manifest themselves whenever the artist comes upon an "occasion" or situation that prompts him to express them in works of art. This process is "singular and inexplicable"; it unfolds in a manner similar to what occurs in the insect world, where creatures die after laying their eggs. Proust was comfortable with biological analogies whenever they helped to clarify a process rather than an isolated fact. What was at issue here was a process of "procreation" that could most readily be grasped by comparing the creative act of an artist to generative acts in the natural world.

"*La Poésie ou les lois mystérieuses*" provides a good transition to the more ample essay "Chardin and Rembrandt" (*CSB* 372–382), to which Proust was almost certainly referring in a letter of late November, 1895, to Pierre Mainguet, where he says that he had just written "a little study on the philosophy of art in which I try to show how great painters initiate us into the knowledge of the external world. It is the work of Chardin which I take in this study as an example, and I try to show his influence on our life, the charm and the wisdom he diffuses on our humblest days by initiating us to the life of still-life painting" (*Corr.* 1: 446–447). Mieke Bal makes much of this essay, claiming for it an absolutely indispensable place in the evolution of Proust's painterly vision of the world. She believes that this essay prepares us for what was to become the central project of the *Recherche*, which was "to write the image," to employ the visual poetics of Chardin in the literary exploration of private life in the Illiers, the Cabourg, and the Paris of the years leading up to and immediately following World War I. Whether Bal has been entirely successful in relating Proust's poetics so closely to painting is open to question. Her evidence is copious and eloquent with regard to Proust's descriptive and psychological methods in his great novel and the general tenor and direction of her thinking appear to me to be sound. She is convincing in her analysis of how Chardin's famous domestic scenes, especially "The Skate," were utilized by Proust as examples of the kind of transfiguration of ordinary experience he wanted to achieve in the *Recherche*. She makes a comment relevant to our immediate interest when she says, of the essay "Chardin and Rembrandt," that it "should be read as a 'novel': reading in the grain of the text, it seems more like a narrative or a poem than the elaboration of an argument" (50). This is another way of saying what I have earlier pointed out in characterizing Proust's writing in "*Contre l'obscurité*" as often much closer to the language of poetry than to conventional critical or philosophical discourse.

    Bal was not the first to attribute such central importance to Proust's pictorial aesthetics, although her analysis is far more scholarly and rigorous than that of one of the pioneering figures of this critical view, Samuel Beckett, and more detailed in attaching particular features of Proust's method to the work of Chardin and several other painters. In 1931 Beckett put his finger on the painterly nature of Proust's poetics when, after situating him on the "outskirts" of symbolism, and after placing him *grosso modo* in the history of modern relativism and impressionism, he went on to explain that by impressionism, he meant Proust's "anti-intellectual" and "non-logical statement of phenomena in the order and exactitude of their perception, before they have been distorted into intelligibility in order to be forced into a chain of cause and effect" (66). It seems strange to speak of Proust as "anti-intellectual," but this is one way of conveying the idea that he belongs essentially to the culture of Romanticism, for which feelings are of preeminent importance, the imagination is held to be the primary seat of artistic creativity, and art and literature are felt to be instruments of visionary insight into the secrets and mysteries of existence. Here again, Beckett was on the right track when he said that for Proust, as for the painter, style is more a question of vision than of technique.

Another useful study of Proust's poetics in relation to painting is Simone Kadi's *La Peinture chez Proust et Baudelaire*. She discusses the work of many painters who charmed Proust, from Vermeer to Delacroix, from Leonardo to Watteau, from Rubens to Renoir. But her most telling observations as far as the subject of this and the next chapter are concerned, are on Proust and Monet.[3] It was Monet whose painting "*Impression: Soleil levant*" (Impression, sunrise) probably induced Louis Leroy in 1874 to use the word "Impressionist " for the first time (Schapiro 21), which marked a crucial moment in the history of the relationship between painting and a new dynamic concept of light as a manifestation of energy. Between the mid-1870s and March 17, 1905, when Einstein submitted his epochal paper on the interaction of light and matter to the *Annalen der Physik* (Everdell 228), a profound change of perspective concerning the ways in which the personal perception of objects is influenced by the action of light on the senses of the viewer had led to the increased awareness of the subtlety and complexity of visual experience. In the resulting debate between those who adhered to a basically "materialist" conception of light and those who continued to believe that the "impressions" of sensitive artists consisted of more than mere sequences or memories of sensations, Proust stood in the latter camp, and he did so in the name of the "primacy of the spiritual" embodied, as far as he was concerned, in the work of painters such as Claude Monet.

Proust's conception of the new painting reflected, perhaps unconsciously, the notion of "energeticism," which shifted the emphasis in physics away from the centrality of matter to that of energy (Hauser 175). According to this notion, light was a form of energy and could not, therefore, be adequately explained by the "materialist" science of the time. Kadi places Monet at the center of this energeticist current of thought, and she traces Proust's particular affection for him to this current. She probably goes too far in drawing a parallel between what Monet achieved in painting and what Proust was later to achieve in literature,[4] but she is certainly right in saying that Monet contributed decisively to the choice made by the impressionists "to celebrate one of the manifestations of energy that eludes form—light," and that with this choice "we are at the threshold of something new" (228). The "something new" in phsyics was Einsteinian theory, but it can also be said that an equally significant and related breakthrough was being made in the arts, where Monet and Proust were among the leading figures. They gave to the term "impressionism" a psychological and philosophical meaning that, while based on a sensualist epistemology, also transcended it to include the "spiritual" essence and creative powers of the human mind. I would say that this new, energeticist theory of light as energy is as important and as pervasive in Proust's writing as it is pictorially in the work of the impressionist painters. For Proust, as for Dante, images of light are what bind his depiction of the natural and human worlds to the source of all creation: for Proust, the sun; for Dante, God. Metaphorically, in Proust's case, the epiphanic moments triggered by certain sense experiences (the taste of the madeleine soaked in tea, and so on) spring from memories that are "involuntary," they cannot be willed into existence. These sudden illuminations of insight and understanding are indispensable to Proust's world view. Beckett calls involuntary memory in Proust a "brightness" that reveals "what the mock reality of experience never can and never will reveal—the real" (20).

An arresting feature of the essay "Chardin and Rembrandt" is that it forms a bridge precisely between ordinary experience, where a scene such as a dining room that appears "trivial and ugly" to a young man who has just finished his meal and is unaware aesthetically of his surroundings becomes transfigured when that same young man, guided by the first-person narrator of this essay-as-prose-narrative, visits the Louvre and sees for the first time the humble domestic scenes painted by Chardin. If these interiors now seem beautiful to behold, it is because "Chardin found them beautiful to paint." The pleasure that his paintings give the young man is the pleasure distilled from an instant of life that was "studied in depth and eternised" by the artist. But the process of transfiguration does not stop there for Proust. It continues in the subsequent life of the young man who now, having been touched by the genius of Chardin, will look upon ordinary quotidian things with a new appreciation of their ability to "reveal mysteries."

Following this introductory section of the essay, Proust proceeds to give fairly detailed descriptions of some of Chardin's paintings, concentrating especially on his still lifes, and noting, as he does so, that the tourist or pilgrim who allows himself to be guided by Chardin will find in his work the same inspiration and enlightenment that Dante drew from Virgil. He then pauses to consider another master, Rembrandt.[5] Whereas Chardin proclaimed "the divine equality of all things in the presence of the mind, the spirit that looks upon them, in the presence of the light that beautifies them," Rembrandt virtually "surpasses reality." Proust speaks in particular of the paintings "The Two Philosophers" and "The Good Samaritan" as examples of the idea that beauty does not reside in objects, for if that were so, he reasons, beauty would not be so profound and so mysterious. Objects are nothing in themselves, "they are like empty spaces illuminated by the changing expression of light, the reflection given to them by beauty, the divine gaze."

The words "mystery," "obscure power," and "divine" spring from an aesthetic ideology in which Art becomes a substitute for more conventional types of religious faith, a "residence for ideality" rather than a worldly form of production that combines mental and physical labor designed to satisfy human needs and change the quality of consciousness. The essay is a monument to the new exalted status which artistic creation was enjoying at the end of the nineteenth century, when a wedge was driven between the worlds of material and aesthetic production. On the one hand, Proust was attached ideologically to the method of impressionism and its "Heraclitean outlook" (Hauser 169), which treated reality not as being but as a perpetual becoming, yet on the other hand he raised artistic creation to such a lofty plane that it could be said to lose touch with the workaday reality of movement and change. The fact that aesthetic values could, in Proust's philosophy, be translated into worldly terms, where "young men" like the one he introduces at the beginning of the essay constituted a link between art and practical life, saved him, in some measure, from the kind of "idolatry" against which he was to plead eloquently in his early writings on John Ruskin. Proust's philosophy of art was able to accommodate an urgent concern with moral issues, which was one of the aspects of Ruskin's thought that drew Proust to the English art historian.

One of the many things that attracted Proust to Ruskin was the latter's belief that artists and poets were the instruments of a creative force vastly more powerful than they. This was the feeling that led Ruskin, in his *Modern Painters* and elsewhere, to relate "the mental chemistry by which the dream associates its materials" to the "mysterious" process by which creative geniuses receive "new images" that flow from essentially "involuntary remembrances" rather than willed recollections (Ruskin 1964, 13). This was obviously a feature of Ruskin's thought that was congenial to Proust's evolving conception of art and the artist, one that he was to place at the very center of his search for time past. Indeed, the Latin title of Ruskin's autobiography, *Praeterita*, meaning "the past, or things past," found its corresponding expression in the title Proust eventually chose for his novel. Proust was quoted more than once as having said that he knew this work "by heart," as a result of repeated impassioned readings.

Ruskin's religious beliefs and sentiments were Biblically inspired and were far more profoundly Christ-centered than Proust's. At the same time, his feeling for nature was rooted in a pantheistic vision of universal harmony that bespeaks a debt to British romantic poetry that Proust shared, but not to the same degree of intensity as Ruskin. He had a Wordsworthian confidence in the beneficence and fellowship of nature that Proust felt, to be sure, but not as explicitly and as resolutely as Ruskin. Proust gives us the natural world with a strong sense of indebtedness, but his gift does not spring from exactly the same cluster of attitudes that characterized Ruskin. But Ruskin's passion for medieval church architecture was matched by Proust's, as seen in his visits to Venice, Rouen, and Amiens, and in his translation of Ruskin's *The Bible of Amiens*. The two men had a similar reverence for the early centuries of western civilization in the Middle Ages, when, they felt, whole human collectivities participated with religious and civic zeal in the building of cathedrals and in the enactment of social rituals and spectacles that nothing in contemporary life could equal.

Painter (2: 11) and others think that after an early period of enthusiasm for Ruskin, Proust's ardor quickly cooled. Proust did finally distance himself from Ruskin at a certain point, when some of the latter's observations and value judgments struck him as symptomatic of a "fetishistic" attitude toward particular works of art. But these doubts and reservations never changed his basic conviction that Ruskin, despite regrettable faults, was, with Tolstoy and Ibsen, one of the three great "prophetic" figures of the nineteenth century, a man made in the "heroic" mold as that word was used by Thomas Carlyle in *Heroes and Hero Worship*—that is, a person with such enormous creative power (like Dante and Goethe) as to leave the imprint of his personality on an entire epoch in human history. Just as Carlyle had placed poets and philosophers on the summit of human achievement, Proust looked to Ruskin as a veritable beacon to which all lovers of the arts and all people moved by moral passion could look for guidance.

Considering these traits and the interests held in common with the author of *The Stones of Venice*, one of Proust's favorite books, it is certainly no wonder that Proust reacted to Ruskin's death on January 20, 1900, with deep distress but also with the determination to use his literary abilities to make Ruskin better known and appreciated in France. He was not the first to make such a commitment. Like some of his colleagues associated with prominent literary reviews and with the daily press, Proust apparently first learned of Ruskin in the early to mid-1890s, although it is possible that he knew of him well before that. By 1895 Ruskin was so widely known in France that *Le Gaulois* complained in an article of December 1, 1895, that after other fashionable trends had come and gone, Ruskin was still the cynosure of the nation's cosmopolitan intelligentsia. This was said with considerable resentment, since *Le Gaulois*, in keeping with its immovable stand against a revision of the evidence against Alfred Dreyfus, felt that French intellectuals would do well to drop their "faddish" cosmopolitan tastes and return to the pure fount of French national culture. Ruskin was only one of many foreign authors now glutting the literary marketplace with indigestible ideas and silly crazes.

But it was the publication in 1897 of Robert de la Sizeranne's book *Ruskin et la religion de la beauté* that seems to have converted Proust's keen interest into a veritable passion that lasted for seven to eight years, up to and including the two translations of 1904 and 1906. It was Sizeranne's book, supplemented by the help of Proust's mother and an English cousin of Reynaldo Hahn, Marie Nordlinger, both of whom helped him with his readings and translations, that allowed Proust to embark on this new phase of his literary vocation.

The two short obituary notices Proust wrote in the weeks immediately following Ruskin's death stress the English art historian's universality and his role as a "professor of taste." They speak of Ruskin's works as "real breviaries of wisdom and aesthetics," thus manifesting a more and more pronounced tendency to transfer religious sentiments to the realm of art. The same tendency appears in the title Proust gave to the second of these brief notes, "Ruskinian pilgrimages in France." One cannot help but think of the reverential (but "idolatrous") feelings aroused in the narrator's young heart in the *Recherche* by the mere mention of certain French and Italian cities renowned for their painting, sculpture and architecture.

In two much longer and intellectually more significant articles[6] that appeared in April and August 1900, and that, as already indicated, were later incorporated into the introductory essays to the translations of *The Bible of Amiens* and *Sesame and the Lilies*, Proust's affinity for Ruskin takes some intriguing turns.

First of all, Ruskin's writings helped young Proust to clarify his own understanding of art and nature as two irreducible yet interrelated "worlds" wherein "the universal plan within which our individuality is shaped" becomes apparent to the sensitive eye. Proust emphasizes Ruskin's belief in "the universal laws and patterns of existence," a belief that gave to Ruskin's writings on art an unmistakeable dignity and even, at times, solemnity.

Second, as seen especially in the essay "*Ruskin à Notre-Dame d'Amiens*," we become aware of the extraordinary extent to which Proust identified himself with certain of the techniques and focal points of impressionist painting. This can be seen above all in his evocation of the effects of sunlight as it moves from place to place on the cathedral of Amiens. It is at this point in the essay that we begin to notice that Proust has brought to it not merely a scholarly interest in Ruskin and in the Amiens cathedral but also a real passion that found its natural expression in a first-person narrative. Proust displays no uncertainty at all about taking an autobiographical approach to the material of a critical essay. Just as Ruskin was a "generous and thoughtful guide," so Proust wanted to guide his readers in a manner worthy of his subject, and this could only be in the form of a first-person narrative infused with fresh sensory experience, aesthetic delight, and intellectual enthusiasm. It is Proust's personal involvement in the subject matter of these Ruskin essays that gives them their élan, their exceptional energy.

Third, Proust dwells admiringly on the part of the cathedral that Ruskin called "the Bible," namely its western portal, which he compares with Hugo's literary treatment of the biblical comparison in *Notre-Dame de Paris*, and that he explicitly compares here with Monet's paintings of Rouen Cathedral. As he describes the various biblical figures and episodes carved by the collective labors of thirteenth-century French sculptors and placed lovingly on the western facade, Proust returns to his principal subject, which is only apparently the cathedral and its wondrous works of art. His essential subject is "the soul of Ruskin," which allowed him (Ruskin, that is) to rediscover the spiritual impetus that inspired the thirteenth-century sculptors, even if he did not share all of their doctrinal beliefs. In the last several pages of "*Ruskin à Notre-Dame d'Amiens*," Proust articulates his spiritual conception of art with the following words:

> Understanding badly up to then the scope of religious art in the Middle Ages, I had said to myself, in my fervor for Ruskin: he will teach me, for he too, in some part at least, isn't he too the truth? He will allow my spirit to enter where it had no access, for he is the door. He will purify me, for his inspiration is like the lily of the valley. He will intoxicate and energize me, for he is the vineyard and life. And I felt in effect that the mystical perfume of the roses of Sharon had not yet vanished entirely, because one still breathes it, at least in his words. And in this way the stones of Amiens took on for me the dignity of the stones of Venice, and were like the grandeur of the Bible when it was still the truth in the hearts of men and solemn beauty in their works. *The Bible of Amiens* was, in Ruskin's mind, but the first book of a series titled *Our Fathers Told Us*; and in effect if the ancient prophets of the Amiens portal were sacred to Ruskin, it is because the soul of the artists of the thirteenth century was still in them. Even before knowing that I would find it there, it was the soul of Ruskin that I was seeking there and that he imprinted as deeply on the stones of Amiens as those who sculpted them imprinted theirs, for the words of genius can as well as the chisel give an immortal form to things. Literature too is a "lamp of sacrifice" which consumes itself in order to enlighten posterity. I was conforming unconsciously to the spirit of the title: *Our Fathers Told Us*, in these thoughts and in the desire to read Ruskin's Bible there. Because Ruskin, for having believed in these men of another time, because faith and beauty were in them, had found himself also in writing his

Bible, just as they for having believed in the prophets and the apostles had written theirs. (*CSB* 104–105)

In the conclusion to this essay, Proust returns to the theme of Ruskin as a "prophet whose voice is no longer heard. But that is because he has finished saying all of his words. It is up to future generations to gather them up and sing them in chorus."

Some of the same ideas and perspectives of which I have spoken in this chapter appear also in "*John Ruskin*," but this piece has several other features that deserve mention. One is that Proust's writing displays a regrettable tendency to windy verbiage, a certain vagueness of terminology, and an enraptured tone that now and then gets out of control. Religious analogies are pervasive, engendering in the reader a feeling of surfeit. "Aesthetic pleasure," Proust announces toward the end of this essay, "is precisely what accompanies the discovery of truth," but he is unable or unwilling to attempt an explanation of this phenomenon, limiting himself to the observation that "why this is so is difficult to say; it is itself mysterious." At a certain point this aura of "mystery" and veneration surrounding Ruskin's writings becomes a way to avoid rather than confront the complex philosophical problems inherent in them.

Another unpleasant aspect of this essay is Proust's apparent acceptance of an insidious form of anti-Semitism, insidious because it expresses itself clothed in the garb of an aesthetic judgment. Apropos of Ruskin's thoughts on Tintoretto, Proust cites without any disclaimers or qualifications the philosopher and critic Joseph-Antoine Milsand (1807–1886), one of the earliest French commentators on Ruskin. Milsand had said of Ruskin's analysis of two paintings by Tintoretto, a "Holy Family" and a crucifixion scene, that in Ruskin's view the symbolism and genius of the former painting had shown that the birth of Christ marked "the end of the Jewish economy and the advent of the new alliance," while in the latter, "in the figure of a donkey grazing on some palm leaves in the background of Calvary [Tintoretto wanted] to affirm the profound idea that it was Jewish materialism, with its waiting for a completely temporal Messiah and with the disappointment of its hopes at the time of the entry into Jerusalem, that had been the cause of the hatred unleashed against the Savior and, because of that, of his death" (*CSB* 107)." To cite another writer's thoughts without comment is in effect to make them one's own. Moreover, in his own note to the Milsand reference, Proust spoke of the French thinker as "one of the first to speak of Ruskin, in the order of time, and in the force of his thoughts. He was a sort of precursor, an inspired and incomplete prophet who did not live long enough to see the development of the work he had announced" (107).

The essay also has two features that, although not entirely new in Proust's thought, are expressed with uncommon vigor. One of these is that his moral preoccupations step decisively to the foreground of his field of vision. Calling his age one of "dilettantes and aesthetes," he defends Ruskin against the charge of vaporous aestheticism by distinguishing him from his contemporaries as a man made in the Carlylean mold, a true hero of our time. The other noteworthy feature of "John Ruskin" is the connection Proust makes between self-discipline and freedom, between self-sacrifice and the realization of a purpose more important than one's own individual existence. Here Proust redeems the fuzziness of some of his earlier formulations by holding Ruskin up as a moral and creative example that, implicitly, he intended to follow. "Voluntary servitude," Proust maintains, "is the beginning of freedom. We are free in life, but through having purposes: the sophism of freedom by means of indifference was revealed as such a long time ago." He then makes an assertion that allows us to feel the confidence that Proust had at the age of twenty-nine in his own latent powers:

> The novelist's subject, the poet's vision, the philosopher's truth are imposed on them in an almost inevitable way, as if they were external, so to speak, to their thought. And it is by submitting his mind to rendering this vision, to approaching this vision, that the artist truly becomes himself. (*CSB* 140–141)

What follows these sentences is a paragraph too long for citation here, but whose kernel of thought can be said to reflect the writing of *JS* and to presage the writing of the *Recherche*. Its essential idea is that it is only when certain periods of our life are closed forever and no longer bear any immediate relevance to our present existence that we feel the impulse to gather together at least the ashes of that past life. It is then that our memory of this past tells us: "you were such and such a person" without allowing us to become that person again. By affirming to us the reality of a "lost paradise" instead of giving it back to us, memory allows us at least to describe our past life and to "establish the basis for a true understanding of it."

In the Ruskin essays, Proust wrote as both a critic and a novelist concerned essentially with the same problems of existence. These problems also appeared in the scattered pages of *JS*, which Proust abandoned after more than four years of work. They were found in the late 1940s by Bernard de Fallois, who performed the task of sifting through them and of cobbling up a manuscript that could be said to cohere in some fashion. The final chapter of my study will be devoted to the relations between literary text and ideology in this unfinished work.

Chapter 10

Literary Text and Ideology in *Jean Santeuil*

Critical controversy about *JS* was particularly intense, naturally enough, in or shortly after the years when the two French editions of the book appeared, 1952 and 1971. The contentious issues were the methods used by Bernard de Fallois and Pierre Clarac in preparing their editions, the structure and form of the work, and its place in Proust's development as a writer. There was also disagreement about its dates of composition, some critics believing that the book was composed intermittently from 1895 to 1899, while others, notably Antoine Adam, pointed to historical references in the book to back up their claim that Proust had continued to work on it sporadically as late as 1905.

These controversial issues are reflected in one of the few booklength studies of *JS*, by Mireille Marc-Lipianski (1974). She takes note of the book's fragmented and incoherent treatment of plot and character development, and therefore judges it to be a failure as a novel. She is certainly right, but the basic condition required to fully legitimize her judgment is that this massive work of almost 750 printed pages is in fact a novel that should be evaluated like any other fictional narrative aspiring to take its place in the history of the genre. That this is not the way to read *JS* is borne out, I believe, by several weighty considerations that have been discussed by several Proust scholars.

A basic problem is the extreme and probably insurmountable difficulty that Fallois and Clarac had to cope with in piecing together thousands of fragmentary, often disconnected sheets of paper[1] that were found in the late 1940s in a carton that had been stored away for many years in a basement and presumably discarded by Proust as no longer usable for integration into his novel. Because of the inherent difficulty of this task, Fallois apparently took certain liberties in ordering this material for publication that, it was widely felt, violated accepted standards of literary scholarship. In a thorough and minute examination of the *JS* manuscript (*Saggi e richerche*), Philip Kolb observed that Fallois not only gave a title to the manuscript where there was none, but he also "retouched some passages" which he did not reveal to the reader; added chapter titles that were not Proust's; arranged chapters by theme, a highly questionable type of editorial maneuver; and in effect "betrayed" Proust's intentions by making too many arbitrary changes of name, date, and other such interventions. Kolb's conclusions in his 1963 essay had been anticipated, although not documented in Kolb's fashion, by Antoine Adam, who in 1952 deplored the absence of a critical apparatus in the Fallois edition and accused Fallois of gross negligence in his manipulations of the text. After the appearance of the 1971 edition, Enrico Guaraldo accused Fallois of having made a kind of "collage" of thousands of sheets of paper and then passing them off as a novel. In essence, Guaraldo felt that Fallois had sought to give a homogeneity to *JS* that the work did not have. But Clarac did not escape unscathed either. While praising the considerably more trustworthy 1971 version, Guaraldo pointed out that Clarac had also relied too much on grouping the material in thematic units rather than on a "chronological criterion" of organization that would have taken into account the actual order of composition of the various fragments (Guaraldo 1971, 1972).

The upshot of all this is that, between Proust's own uncertainties concerning the structure and development of his narrative and the frequent editorial interventions by Fallois and Clarac, what the reader had (and still has) in hand in book form are two texts whose amorphousness in some of its parts or, on the other hand, whose fake orderliness, make them unsuitable for most types of literary analysis. Nevertheless, I shall attempt an analysis of some of its passages from a broadly thematic point of view, with emphasis on how Proust transfers essentially political and ideological impulses to the safer realms of family, friendship, and nature.

We know that, as far as Proust himself was concerned, from the time he began writing *JS* in September 1895 (*Corr.* 2: 377 n. 2) to December of 1899, when he told Marie Nordlinger that he had been working for a long time on "a book of large proportions, but without completing anything," (*Corr.* 2: 377) he *was* writing what he thought was a novel, and not simply a series of random jottings about this or that with the hope that, somehow and some way, he would eventually succeed in weaving them together in a formally satisfactory manner. Therefore, if we make Proust's intentions one of our criteria of judgment, we cannot but be disappointed. The only way to avoid such disappointment is by doing what Marc-Lipiansky and others were finally compelled to do, namely to recognize that *JS* does not meet the minimal requirements of the novel genre, and that it makes much more sense to see it as an enormous collection of descriptions, sketches, dialogues and reflections written with the hope that these diverse materials would fall into shape as an organic interconnected whole. This hope was not realized. Therefore Proust ended up by abandoning the project rather than try to reshuffle the more than fifteen hundred pages of his manuscript. In effect, instead of continuing his work on the *JS* manuscript, Proust undertook his Ruskin studies, after which, in 1908, he began composing the *Recherche*, where he reworked or integrated some of the materials of *JS*.

JS has one crucial thread that provides a modicum of narrative continuity. It is the consciousness of the main character, whose "sentimental education" (Flaubert has been mentioned as an influence) is tracked over a period of approximately twenty-five years, from the 1870s to the end of the century. In this respect, it can be argued that the book does tell a story of sorts[2] but it is a story without a plot, a narrative lacking key components of plot development such as do exist in the *Recherche*. In *JS* and in the *Recherche* we follow the hero's life over roughly the same time period, but in the latter the first-person narrator tells us how he comes to commit himself to his vocation as a writer in the context not only of the vicissitudes of his own personal existence but also in that of the society of his time, leading to the intertwining of *The Guermantes Way* with *Swann's Way*, a process of social and cultural amalgamation that marks the end of an era of French social history. It is in these two contexts that all of the characters and episodes take their place as parts of an immense canvas that we can contemplate at any one of the many points of interest along the circuitous trail of Proust's narrative. Nothing of the sort takes place in *JS*. Although Jean, like Marcel, is an aspiring writer and poet, this aspect of his life does not assume the centrality that it does in the *Recherche*. Catherine Anne Baudino explains why this is the case: Jean does not really undergo any decisive changes of outlook and self-understanding. In *JS*, she observes, the various episodes and crises in Jean's life are not interconnected in such a way as to reveal any substantial "change of situation, character or thought" (32–33). Baudino lays stress on the intention signaled by Proust in his preface to the work, namely that he has told the "essence" of Jean's life. In doing so, he relies on episodic incidents that contribute to our understanding of Jean's essential nature but that do not add up to a rounded and complex story of a character's evolution and development. The result of this "essentializing" technique is that the various episodes are as if insulated from each other. The same point was made by Justin O'Brien (1967).

I have already pointed out that there are some advantages to looking at *JS* not as a failed novel but rather as a kind of workshop in which the young Proust took some important steps forward in his craft as a novelist and explored virtually all of the themes, character types, and moral problems that he was to interweave so much more amply and ingeniously in the *Recherche*. By putting aside any preconceived criteria of literary excellence in evaluating *JS*, we can better appreciate some of the book's accomplishments.

First of all, despite the discontinuousness of the episodes, we feel that we understand certain aspects of Jean's character better than we know Marcel, the narrator of the *Recherche*. Jean is a much less complex character than Marcel, yet he is at the same time more palpable and accessible to the reader's imagination. Perhaps this is due to the device Proust used to create distance between the character Jean and the reader. He accomplishes this by beginning his story with an introductory encounter between two young friends on vacation at a seaside hotel in Brittany and the renowned writer C. Several years after this encounter, C falls ill and summons the two friends to his bedside. Their conversation reestablishes the intimacy they had enjoyed at the hotel. For this reason, after C's death the narrator decides to publish a copy of C's unfinished manscript, since no mention was made in the obituary of a novel having been found among C's papers. The manuscript is the story of Jean Santeuil. This conventional and timeworn device of a found manuscript turns out in some respects to yield a more recognizable portrait of the protagonist than does the confessional first-person voice of the narrator of the *Recherche*.

Second, *JS* brings us into touch with the young Proust's reverential conception of nature, a conception that will be amply elaborated in the *Recherche*. Both the differences and the similarities between *JS* and the *Recherche* in this regard have been noted by Georgette Tupinier, Larkin Price, and Catherine Anne Baudino, among others. They were all struck by the connection Proust tries to make in both works between the protagonists' education as apprentice writers and their intense response to the natural world. What these scholars have commented on is the still rather inconclusive manner in which Proust evokes natural forces in *JS*, whereas in the *Recherche* these evocations and descriptions are organically related to the narrator's growing awareness of himself as a writer bent on connecting all manner of phenomena, human and nonhuman, within a single, unifying vision of life. Sensitivity to nature is an integral part of Marcel's aesthetic and philosophical education, while in the scattered pages of *JS* it seems to be an end in itself, almost a descriptive ornamentation. Nevertheless, Price characterizes *JS* as a work in which, excepting a few rudimentary hints in *PJ*, Proust deals seriously for the first time in his writing with "the artist-as-a-young man" theme wherein the evocation of nature, with the sun metaphorically and philosophically at its vital center, forms part of a mythic and essentially symbolist vision of life that drew inspiration primarily from the poetry of Charles Baudelaire.

Third, in *JS* we see the partnership between literature and philosophy in a more elementary way than in the *Recherche*. Philosophically speaking, Anne Henry considers *JS* to be an expression of young Proust's "Spinozist pantheism," which in turn rests on a "dynamic" vision of the universe bound together by laws of existence that are only dimly and partially accessible to human intelligence (1983, 109). She astutely characterizes *JS* as a work whose "deep subject" is the poetic contemplation of the world. This prefigures some of what I shall be saying further on in this chapter concerning the ideological substructure of *JS*, wherein a kind of transfer takes place from the realm of human society to that of nature in such a way that the aporias of otherwise unreconcilable sociopolitical and moral contradictions can in some measure be, if not resolved, then at least held in precarious balance.

Still another aspect of *JS* that deserves brief comment here is that it marks a distinct transitional moment in the evolution of Proust's style, from the relatively simple and lyrical writing of *PJ* to the complex and, at times, tortuous prose of *JS*, in which there are sentences that run on for up to three hundred words. Most scholars agree that it was John Ruskin whose prose style Proust began trying to emulate in *JS*, and which he later perfected (with some inevitable lapses) in the *Recherche*. Enrico Guaraldo called the step that Proust took in *JS* a "stylistic revolution" (1972), one that brought him out of the hothouse world of *PJ* and into the great current of socially and historically grounded narrative fiction.

In the following pages, I shall be quoting from the English translation of *JS* published in 1956. This translation was based on the first French edition published in 1952 by Bernard de Fallois and was therefore subject to the distortions and errors of that edition. Nevertheless, for the purposes of my analysis, I do not think that the Fallois edition is without its merits, especially in the passages I cite to illustrate various points. These belong to six types of writing: "dramatic" scenes of interaction and dialogue between Jean and a long series of individuals with accompanying coordinates of time, place, and circumstance; moral commentary; philosophical reflection; psychological sketches and portraits of Jean, his parents, his friends, and his social acquaintances; evocations of landscapes and the forces of nature; and descriptions of social gatherings and events attended by members of the Parisian upper middle and aristocratic classes.

Many of Jean's most important experiences are mediated by painting and poetry, as we have already seen in the case of Baudelaire. Proust loved sunlight, but it is a light to which he had first been sensitized by French, Italian, and Dutch painters. He loved flowers too, but they are flowers whose special qualities had first been brought to his attention by Robert de Montesquiou. Nature and art are tightly bound to each other in *JS*, as they will be in the *Recherche*. It can be said that in Proust's fictional writing, natural phenomena do not acquire their significance until they are seen and transfigured by an artist's or a writer's creative imagination.

The ideological perspective from which young Proust approached his task as an apprentice novelist in *JS* was in large part that of a writer and thinker imbued with the sensibilities of European Romanticism. Many decades ago, Jacques Barzun and Henri Peyre warned against the pitfalls of the term "Romantic," citing its variegated features and historically diverse meanings and applications.[3] Duly warned, I would nonetheless stand by my choice of the word "Romantic" as well suited to convey the qualities of Proust's portrayal of his hero in relation to the society and customs of his time, his conception of nature, his theory of memory and creativity, his attraction to the idea of a single universal substance animating human beings in all times and places, and his feeling that art and spiritual inwardness alone can redeem a life filled with disillusionment and disappointment.[4]

Jean Santeuil is a romantic hero as Georgy Lukàcs defined such a character, a person whose soul and vision of life are so much larger, so much more expansive and generous than the social order in which he finds himself that, like Goethe's Werther, Foscolo's Iacopo Ortis, and De Vigny's Chatterton, it is all but preordained that he will withdraw into himself or come to a tragic end. Jean, as it happens, does not come to such an end, due to his life-sustaining relationships with family, friends, and intellectual mentors, and to his ability to find beauty in the natural world as an antidote to the prevalent corruption of the sociopolitical milieu in which he lives. Like his three famous literary counterparts just mentioned, Jean is a young man of keen aesthetic sensibilities and lofty ideals. Art and nature are the bedrock of his faith in life and in his own eventual liberation from the snares of a superficial and false optimism based on worldly success, wealth, and social position. But much more intensely than his three counterparts, Jean is also attracted to the very society, the very glitter and elegance that so offend him. He is a person of decisively middle-class background who enjoys moving in aristocratic circles, and often thinks and expresses himself in a worshipful manner when in the company of that class's most gracious and distinguished personalities. Indeed, his closest friend, Henri de Réveillon, is the scion of one of France's ancient noble families. His château in the Marne is the locus of some of Jean's happiest, most blissful moments.

Jean is a Romantic hero in his recourse, ultimately, to a form of extreme individualism that allows him to cope with the many sorrows and disappointments of life by seeing himself as superior to the callousness and hostility of his school companions, the opportunism of some of his hitherto revered political leaders, and the moral compromises of virtually everyone around him, be they businessmen, government workers, landowners, artists, or intellectuals.

In a scene that typifies Jean's discomfort and alienation when confronting individuals who occupy high positions in the government and the professions, we see him walking down the rue Royale in Paris with his father and his dearest friend, Henri. The three happen upon the brilliantly versatile Monsieur Duroc, a young man who has already obtained success in three fields of endeavor, medicine, literature, and Government, specifically the Ministry of Foreign Affairs, where Jean's father is also employed. Seeing Jean's hesitancy when he asks him what he wants to do with his life, Duroc quickly tries to coax Jean into opting for a career in the diplomatic corps, or in some other branch of government service. Jean is uncertain about his future, but he already knows what most Romantic heroes know in their viscera, that his life would be a worthless bore to him if he were to follow the path marked out for him by Duroc. In a long and grandiloquent discourse, Duroc urges Jean to continue writing poetry, but as a sideline, a hobby with which he could escape the pressures of his public life in his time away from the office. The narrator (of uncertain identity, a creation of the novelist C but assuredly not C) observes of Jean at this point that he "had never regarded poetry as some sort of seasoning to be added at will to matters of business." Jean, although intimidated by Duroc's extraordinary eloquence and self-confidence, nevertheless musters up the courage to make a little speech that resonates with the values we have come to associate with Proust: ambivalence toward

"Society," a need to "concentrate my mind, to dig deep into myself," and a commitment to "find out the truth of things, to express the whole of myself, to occupy myself with what is genuine, and not, like what you have been describing, essentially futile" (190–191).

Jean's answer is significant in that it serves to point up Duroc's pretentiousness and pedantry. Duroc sees life as basically a game of power and manipulation, and cannot understand what is going on inside the mind of his idealistic interlocutor. But the scene does not end there. Before Jean leaves Duroc, two things happen. First, Jean reveals that a career in diplomacy would require separating himself from his mother, whom he dearly loves and needs, for she is part of his "soul." On hearing the word "soul," Duroc makes a few snide remarks showing the disdain with which he, a philosophical materialist, holds such ideas. Then, as they are about to take leave of one another, the three men see a policeman arguing with a cab driver and then striking him with such force that the man falls back reeling against a lamppost. Duroc shouts words of encouragement to the policeman, provoking in Jean and Henri "an indescribable sense of discomfort." Two worlds confront each other here, one, that of Duroc, in which law and authority are always right, and anyone who might resist their rule is seen ipso facto as inferior and culpable; the other, that of Jean and Henri, where sensitivity to pain and insult and sympathy for the weak take precedence over their loyalty to the established order of things.

The Duroc encounter is one of various chapters in *JS* that deal, for the first time in Proust's fictional writings, with explicitly political figures and issues. I shall argue later on that it is not really in this explicitly political domain that the most important aspects of Proustian ideology reveal themselves in this work but, rather, in his way of figuring and imagining the natural world; nevertheless, the explicitly political theme in *JS* is of sufficient interest to warrant immediate commentary on how it plays itself out in the work.

Proust's representation of political personalities and issues in *JS* is pervaded by a deep pessimism about the existing social order based on what we have already observed in Jean's remarks to Duroc, namely his devotion to spiritual truth, to interiority, and to his mother, who is not only the central figure in his affective world but also the living embodiment of a conception of life in which familial sentiments and responsibilties are felt to be vastly more essential and important than any conceivable public project, especially if and when, as often happens in *JS*, such a project is contaminated by overweening ambition, self-interest, greed, and dishonesty. It is always by celebrating Jean's love for his parents and for a few close friends and teachers that Proust conveys his fundamental dislike and suspicion of political man, even when political energies are directed to socially beneficial goals. His loyalties are to personal qualities not to political programs, to the unselfishness and durability of a mother's love for her son, and of a son's love for his parents, not to the ideas of politicians. What we are dealing with here is a mixture of Romantic individualism and spiritual idealism that are pitted, in grossly unequal combat (but Romantic heroes are always faced by adversaries far more powerful than they) if considered from a purely material point of view, but a worthy combat since the prize, the entity at stake, is nothing less than the protagonist's soul.

In *JS* Proust recounts a series of politically explosive episodes loosely connected by just one thread, and that is Jean's consciousness of himself as an individual caught between the blandishments of a fairly easily acquired worldly success (since his father has influence at the ministry) and the uncertain outcomes of a life devoted to poetry and moral self-scrutiny. *JS* is a modern version, in some respects, of the medieval morality play. Jean's understanding of good and evil is substantially different from the accepted Christian one,[5] but it unfolds and develops in connection with the same kind of *agon* that occurred in the moral literature of earlier centuries.

The vicissitudes of four characters, one of whom, Colonel Georges Picquart, is a real historical personage, serve to highlight the political and moral conflicts to which I have alluded. The characters who act out these conflicts are the zealous reformer Lepic; the socialist Couzon; the liberal cabinet minister Charles Marie, around whom a financial scandal (based on the Panama scandal of 1891–1893) develops that reinforces Jean's growing pessimism about public life; and Colonel Picquart, whose courageous revelations of the schemes and prevarications that underlay the accusations against Captain Dreyfus were motivated, in Proust's interpretation of those events, as much by his philosophical turn of mind as by his political convictions. It is known that Picquart harbored anti-Semitic attitudes, and that he came to Dreyfus's defense more from scruple as an honest army officer than from principled opposition to discrimination against Jews. Lepic, Couzon, and Marie, regardless of their otherwise laudable political intentions, represent forms of moral compromise that Jean finds unacceptable. Picquart is portrayed with great sympathy and admiration, a reflection, no doubt, of the fact that in the early months of 1898, while working intensively on *JS*, Proust was passionately committed to Dreyfus's defense.

The character Lepic serves to underline one of the fundamental themes of *JS*, that lurking behind the most benevolent public images there are often extremely ugly realities that most people tend to disregard whenever possible. This theme is first announced in connection with the Santeuil family's cook, Ernestine, in a reflective aside that recalls Françoise in the *Recherche*. The aside concerns the tolerance most people display for horrible acts of injustice and cruelty when the satisfaction of their own creaturely needs and comforts is the outcome of these acts. The animals daily slaughtered for the pleasure of refined palates suffer "an agony we endure without giving it a second thought because it is necessary to our enjoyment." To this the narrator adds a remark with implications not dissimilar from a famous comment attributed to Walter Benjamin, that "There is no document of civilization that is not at the same time a document of barbarism." Proust's narrator puts this point as follows:

> And so it is that the sheep, the chickens and the bullocks, whose agony we endure without giving it a second thought because it is necessary to our enjoyment, are not the only guileless victims who we daily allow to be sacrificed. Well-being, vanity, greed and superfluity are pleasant masters whose innumerable crimes, daily committed through the centuries and never punished, ensure the happiness of those who profit from them and guarantee their own continued dominance. (88)

In passages such as this, relatively rare in Proust's writings, one feels the wrath of a conscience offended by the hypocrisy and arrogance of the privileged elite. However, Proust's response to injustice does not remain very long on the level of anger expressed by this passage, which would have had the effect, possibly, of forcing him to be more directly engaged with the victims than he ever showed himself to be. Instead, he chose to address himself to individual cases of injustice, such as that of Monsieur Lepic, whom the narrator describes as a "great reformer" who had always fought for the rights of the downtrodden, yet who, at the same time, in his private life, was "a fool who tyrannized over his wife." Because of his complete indifference to his wife's feelings, in three years of marriage Lepic has made her into a "melancholy, ugly woman turned into herself."

Appearances in *JS* are not only usually false and misleading but also frequently nothing but cover-ups of cowardly and disloyal behavior. The socialist Couzon, for example, is shown at first in a favorable light, as a champion of the working class. But later on, when the Marie scandal breaks out, Jean comes to Couzon in the hope that he will defend the good name, not of Marie, who is under investigation for fraudulent abuse of his office, but of his father, Monsieur Santeuil, who has been dragged into the scandal surrounding Marie because Marie is his closest friend and a man with whom he has worked on numerous committees and other official business. Jean wants Couzon to go on record as believing in Monsieur Santeuil's innocence of any and all charges connected with the Marie affair. Couzon refuses to do what Jean asks, insisting that he must place his "ideas" and party affiliations before personal friendship. For Jean, on the other hand, it is not so much that personal affections and loyalties come before politics as that they are the very essence of what true politics should be all about. He envisions a world in which personal and political values go hand in hand, for the same reasons that led Socrates to sacrifice his life for his conception of loyalty to the Athenian polis. Couzon blames M. Santeuil for having continued to see Marie even after the accusations against him had been made public. Jean replies that it was precisely friendship that had motivated his father's continued association with Marie. Couzon appeals to "the common good," which he says requires that he abstain from all personal intervention in the affair. Jean is appalled at Couzon's failure to make good on the promises and commitments of earlier times. He accuses the Socialist leader of cowering before the blackmail and threats of the scandal sheets, in order to advance his own political career. Furious and deeply hurt at the same time, Jean is concerned above all with the feelings of his mother and father, now victims of a scurrilous daily press that has "turned a great many of the people who read them into evil creatures—and that is perhaps worse!"

As far as Marie is concerned, once again Jean reveals that for him politics can only be understood in moral terms. In this instance, the moral issue is not Marie's guilt or innocence, since he had done some of the things of which he was accused, as a result of which, although avoiding incarceration, he loses his cabinet post. The issue for Jean is whether everything good and socially beneficial that Marie had done in his life was negated by his occasional dishonesty and financial opportunism. Jean thinks not, and develops an argument that shows him to be more amenable to ambiguities than one would think from the way he behaves vis-à-vis Couzon. But in this case he is weighing the public response to Marie's misdeeds against the inherent qualities of Marie's life. Yes, he admits, Marie should pay for his dishonesty, but does this dishonesty warrant "the scorn of a thousand gloating eyes, the drunken frenzy of a million hatreds"? The answer, to Jean, is self-evident, and is based on his belief that, amidst all of this public defamation and scandal, there are personal loyalties to be protected, a private domain of affection that will endure far beyond the limited and contingent considerations of political life. The death of Marie's wife shortly after his removal from office, and soon thereafter of Marie himself, serves to emphasize the polluted moral atmosphere that surrounds Jean and his family.

The Jewish question comes to the fore here in two ways. One hinges on the fact that Marie's wife, a Jewess, had been the closest friend of Jean's mother, who is grief-stricken by her loss. Despite Jean's mother's family's history (unlike Proust's own mother, who was Jewish) that was steeped in anti-Semitism, she had overcome her prejudices through her admiration for Madame Marie's virtue and goodness. The other, of course, is through the Dreyfus Affair, in which Jean's mother is again portrayed as sympathetic to Dreyfus and deeply offended when Colonel Picquart, whom she respects, is vilified by his accusers in the Army and government, and by millions of intransigent French supporters of the Army. The Dreyfus Affair is not as central to *JS* as it is to the *Recherche*, since *JS* lacks the extended scenes of Parisian salon life where discussions about the Affair often reveal aspects of the various characters' political viewpoints in surprising ways. But the Affair is sufficiently present in *JS* to allow the reader to get a fairly good cross-section of opinion at the time.

I have already alluded to the underlying pessimism—even, at times, cynicism—of the view of politics that pervades *JS*. The fact is that in this work, Proust, via his narrator, makes it clear that the only politics he believes in is the politics of the family, the politics of affection and love between human beings who care about each other as individuals, and who give something of themselves to their loved ones that no strictly political act, in the usual sense of the term, can ever give. At about the mid point of the story (as its episodes were arranged by Fallois) the narrator sums up his feelings in this regard by stressing what he takes to be the irremediably tainted nature of the customary political acts that are taken to be signs of civic virtue: voting, campaigning for candidates, signing petitions and manifestoes, forming alliances—in short, the public acts of political man. In Proust's eyes, as we have them voiced by the narrator (if we can assume some degree of congruence between the views of the author and his narrator in this instance) politics almost always takes on a demeaning and degraded character, if for no other reason than that these acts "are strictly speaking of no importance whatever, since nothing of our true selves goes into them" (328). The theory of a genuine "inner self" and of an outer superficial facade that depends for gratification on the rewards of status and wealth has rarely been expressed as clearly by Proust as in this section of the book, which is devoted largely to Colonel

Picquart. To set one's name to a manifesto, asserts the narrator, no matter how fine the sentiments behind it may be, "says nothing that is genuinely personal to ourselves." In contrast, an act of kindness to one's parents or to a friend, although unheralded, will remain a vital force for good in the lives of its recipients. Most publicly acknowledged actions are, in the narrator's opinion, ways of escaping from "the dread necessity of turning our eyes inwards, [they are] refuges from introspection and responsibility" (330).

In *JS*, we have moved to the polar opposite of the classical Ciceronian and Renaissance civic humanist concepts of political engagement as a true sign of moral excellence. The value system that prevails in Proust's fictional world exalts the private and the personal, while mocking or otherwise belittling the political.[6]

There is an interesting alternation not only of moods but of visual and philosophical perspectives in *JS* through which Proust changes his focus abruptly from intense close-up shots to panoramic vistas of vast dimensions. He adjusts his lens in such a way as to never allow the reader to become too sure of his or her bearings, too secure in thinking that this, and this alone, is the point of view governing the fictional universe presented here. For example, an intimate love scene that culminates in an outbreak of jealousy is followed immediately by a passage in which the narrator looks with pity on his lovers who, he reminds us, as in a Shakespeare comedy, are but two poor mortals reenacting a drama whose antecedents go back in time many millennia. Or a crisis in the life of a character is not allowed to speak for itself. The narrator is right there with a commentary that requires the reader to back away from the incident itself to survey the whole sweep of human history, where one observes the sorry spectacle of human beings through the ages forever gloating over the misfortunes of those they claim to esteem but secretly dislike, or even hate, as in the case of Charles Marie. His enemies had had to wait a long time before his star began to fall, until finally, "when as the result of the turn of Fortune's wheel which sooner or later makes every possibility actual—it being the fate of all men and of all human institutions to decay—Marie and his Party fell as resoundingly as the most fantastic hatred could have desired" (311–312).

These sudden shifts in temporal perspective, mixed with the tone of fatalism and resignation to the inevitable follies and miseries of human life that predominates in the explicitly political moments of *JS*, create a rather somber atmosphere that, however, is alleviated and, in a sense, redeemed by the approximately 150 pages in which Proust throws aside all inhibitions and restraints to celebrate his particular poetic vision of the natural world, a vision singularly free of the desolate pessimism and negativity that mark other sections of *JS*. In his evocations of nature in all of its moods and manifestations Proust is able to find a home for his idealism, a safe refuge for hope and optimism. I think that it is in this context of burgeoning nature, where images of light, sweetness, and dynamic energy abound, that we find a more significant expression of Proust's ideological stance as a writer and thinker in late-nineteenth century Europe. All of his passionate longing for spiritual communion and universal harmony, which he was able to envision but which he despaired of finding in human society, is transferred by him to the domain of nature.

But before looking at Proust's way of depicting the natural world, it will be helpful to consider several of the ideas developed by Fredric Jameson in *The Political Unconscious: Narrative as a Socially Symbolic Act* (1981). Whether these ideas are, as Jameson thought in the 1980s, applicable to all of world literature, is far too vast and complex a question to be considered here. What seems to me to be indisputable, however, is the relevance of some of Jameson's insights to Proust's treatment of nature and to his way of investing nature with ideals that had no outlet in the sociopolitical domain.

In his first chapter, "On Interpretation: Literature as a Socially Symbolic Act," Jameson borrows from Northrop Frye in raising "the issue of community" in its various guises in literary texts. What Jameson says about religious sentiment as a repository of "the political unconscious" could be applied equally well to the way in which Proust depicts nature in *JS*. It is in these realms of feeling that we discover

> the symbolic space in which the collectivity thinks itself and celebrates its own unity; so that it does not seem a very difficult next step, if, with Frye, we see literature as a weaker form of myth or a later stage of ritual, to conclude that in that sense all literature, no matter how weakly, must be informed by what we have called a political unconscious, that all literature must be read as a symbolic meditation on the destiny of community. (70)

I am not prepared to argue that the cult of nature served exactly the same purpose in the France of the 1890s as religious belief; that nature was in a sense a refuge of French writers and intellectuals in the same order of magnitude as religion. Yet if we take into account the writers and poets who have an important place in *JS*—Musset and Hugo, Verlaine and Leconte de Lisle, Lamartine and Vigny, as well as the English and American writers Ruskin, Carlyle, George Eliot, and Emerson, and the

Greek pastoral poet Theocritus—we can begin to see that it was the Romantic and neo-Romantic traditions that probably inspired young Proust's striking concentration on nature as a beneficent force, as a reservoir of vital energy, and as a source of wisdom and solace almost in the Wordsworthian meaning of those words. For Proust, as for many of his Romantic predecessors, nature was a great restorative and a spiritual guide in life, not only in its unspoiled, unrestrained manifestations but even in its tamed state, in gardens, parks, and in private residences where one feasts the eye on beautiful life forms in all their freshness and innocence. Lamartine's poems such as "*Le vallon*" (The little valley) and Leconte de Lisle's *Les Poèmes antiques* (Ancient poems, 1852) are filled with the kind of imagery we find in some of Proust's landscapes. Even in the writing of the great realist, Balzac, one can find passages that prefigure Proust's adoration of nature. As he looks out on the countryside of his beloved Touraine, the hero of Balzac's *Le lys dans la vallée* (The lily of the valley), Félix de Vandenesse, addresses the reader with these words:

> If you want to see nature as beautiful and virginal as a betrothed young woman, go there on a spring day; if you want to calm the bleeding wounds of your heart, go back there in the last days of autumn; in the spring, love beats its wings there in the open sky, in the fall one thinks of those who are no longer with us. In that air sick lungs breathe a healthful freshness, one's eyes rest on golden haystacks that communicate their peaceful sweetness to the soul. In this moment, the mills situated on the banks of the Indre gave a voice to this rustling valley, the hovering poplar trees were laughing, not a cloud in the sky, birds were singing, cicadas were chirping, everything was melody there.[7]

Balzac's use of the word "laughing" to designate the poplar trees "hovering" in the air summons up an image of playfulness that has a central role in Proust's own conception of what nature offers to human beings able to appreciate her. The connection between Proust and his predecessors seems clear when we try to interpret the meaning of his exultation in contemplating the natural world around him.

In this literary and philosophical context, Jameson's idea of literature as "a symbolic meditation on the destiny of community" takes on a special pertinence to the writing of young Proust. He found the "community" he was looking for, but only in a very limited way, within the intimate circle of family and a few friends, not in the larger political community. As a consequence of this contradiction, he transferred his frustrated idealism to the realm of nature, where he could freely indulge his fantasy life by investing nature with all of the qualities missing in human society. This point brings up another of Jameson's insights in *The Political Uncon-*

scious that is as relevant to *JS* and to many of Proust's other fictional works. It has to do with the significance of what Jameson calls "the aesthetic act," through which, he argues, we can begin to comprehend the multiple connections between literary texts and ideology; for, Jameson continues,

> the aesthetic act is itself ideological, and the production of aesthetic or narrative form is to be seen as an ideological act in its own right, with the function of inventing imaginary or formal "solutions" to unresolvable social contradictions. (79)

The impulse to "invent" imaginary literary solutions to problems is part of that "unconscious" process by which, in a way analogous to the psychogical role of the unconscious in dealing with unacceptable and unresolved inner conflicts, writers cope with the contradictions posed by the sociopolitical order in which they lead their daily lives. By linking literary texts to this process of unconscious reconciliation, Jameson brings his readers back to the admonition with which he opens his book, that is, to "always historicize!" In other words, if we move from the psychological dimensions of reality and attempt, as Jameson would have us do, to account for broad ideological and social themes in literary texts, we must obviously move beyond the exclusively personal and individualized approach to the task of interpretation and to apply the methods of what Bakhtin called "historical poetics."

Rarely has a modern writer equaled Proust's impassioned enthusiasm in *JS* for natural life, his feeling of exultant joy at the manifold beauty and myriad forms that nature presents to the sensitive eye. In the French tradition, Rousseau, Colette and Jean Giono come to mind. Behind Proust's enthusiasm lay the doctrines of Stoicism and Epicurianism, the simple but profound vision of Saint Francis, the natural philosophy of Renaissance humanists such as Erasmus, the Newtonian concept of nature as an orderly and beneficent whole, the lyrical odes and ballads of European Romanticism. No doubt, whether consciously or not, Proust drew from all of these sources to one degree or another. What he finally assimilated and expressed in his writing was a vision of nature that was essentially poetic and contemplative, and as such similar to the conception of nature that Marx found to be typical and deficient in the thought of Ludwig Feuerbach and his disciples. Marx inaugurated a "materialist" critique of idealism that sought to undermine the foundational principles underlying Feuerbach's (and Proust's) response to nature. Marx interrupted and redirected the long tradition of thought about nature to which I have referred. He did so simply by rejecting the contemplative and sentimental side of Western philosophical idealism, and by developing his argument, in *The German Ideology* and other writings, that nature has no meaning at all unless understood in dialectical relations with the transformative labors of humanity through historical time. For Marx, man always has a double reality before him, an historical nature and a natural history, which interact with one another in the concrete phases and processes of time.

What Proust does is avoid entirely the disturbing and disruptive philosophical effects of Marxism and attach himself to his classical, idealist and Romantic heritages. But not unqualifiedly, as I have noted several times in this study. As evidenced in *JS* and in the *Recherche*, Proust expresses his belief that, in the final analysis, when we stop to consider the millennia of time already transpired in human history, we must see that human beings in modern times are the same as the people of ancient Egypt or the characters of the *Iliad*, that "the basic substance of humanity, often invisible and as though intermitted, is still a living reality to be found where least we expect it" (*JS*, 3–4). He believed also that no matter how persistently the spiritualizing impulses stirring within us may rebel against it, the human spirit is compounded of the same elements as nature. This point of view is expressed in connection with the Charles Marie scandal, where the narrator stops to consider that it is the fate of all men and of all human institutions to decay. The eternal laws of birth and decay, of life and death in the nonhuman world are as evident and unalterable as the laws governing the existence of the human species.

For Proust, nature and spirit are finally parts of one and the same reality, whose elements act and react upon each other in endless cycles from which no life form can escape. Thus, it is not quite accurate to say that Proust entirely abandoned the philosophy of materialism, even if he knew nothing or cared not at all about the thought of Marx and Engels. It is just that he arrived at his conclusions via other pathways, including that of the very scientific positivism he so often rejected, and that is embodied in *JS* in several characters, among whom is Jean's own father. Monsieur Santeuil had been educated by a generation of positivist thinkers in the lycées and universities of mid–nineteenth-century France. In his old age, he modifies his positivist belief system but never entirely discards it. Jean, on the other hand, is the product of a spiritualized generation looking for answers to the great problems of existence in another literature and another body of philosophical thought.

Proust was convinced that all members of the human species share substantially the same joys and sorrows, that they are shaped by common risks, perils, and experiences and, as mortal creatures, share the same fate. This perspective is what gives *JS* and some of Proust's other writings their democratic and humanitarian ethos. It is quite different from the way Marx viewed society and history, yet I would not conclude from this that the philosophical worlds of a Marx and a Proust are so much at odds with each other as to preclude any common point of contact whatever. Still, the differences are plainly evident. Proust's characters do not participate in any kind of collective struggle, as they do, for example, in Zola's *Germinal*. What these characters have in common in Proust's scheme of things is more elusive and spiritual. In a revealing passage of *JS*, the narrator comments on Jean's response to his uncle, who had questioned him about his dreams:

> Jean could no more remember what he had dreamed than what had happened to him when he was two. But it made him happy to think that he *had* dreamed, that his uncle had dreamed, that at certain hours all men, imprisoned by an invincible power in dark, deep beds, within curtains smelling of lavender, all shared in a mysterious life in which the old were but little different from the very young, or from the superstitious inhabitants of the primitive world, and of which He, who had charge of them, was at pains to see that they should remember nothing. (90)

In *JS* (and for that matter in all of Proust's writings), the only time we see human beings engaged in what Marxist thinkers call a "transformative" relationship with nature is through minor working-class characters such as cooks and gardeners. And when we do see them, they are engaged essentially either in artistic production, like the Santeuil family's cook, Ernestine who, prefiguring Françoise in the *Recherche*, is a creator, an inventor of original recipes that delight the palate, or in imitating nature, not dominating her, like Monsieur Santeuil's gardener, whose labor is explicitly compared to that of bees and butterfiles.

The Proustian vision of nature in *JS* is one where human intervention plays hardly any role at all. As vision, it is contemplative, and within the contemplative stance, it is poetic feeling, an effusive lyricism, which predominates throughout. In the three passages cited below we can feel how passionately Proust sought for a congruence between inner feelings and concrete sensual experience. In the book's introductory section, there is a hint of this when one of the two young men who have become friends of the writer C comments during brief amiable conversations with the hotel maid on the pleasure that C takes in his retreat on the Brittany coast. Proust uses the moment to paint a series of highly animated natural scenes. The theme of nature's playfulness and the general atmosphere of wellbeing and gaiety are quite striking:

> It was a great pleasure for C to have her stay with him on these occasions, just as I imagine on mornings when the sun, freeing its smiling face from the early mist, addresses a long and loving welcome to all nature, finding a pleasure in stroking the still empty sea, in warming the beaches, in playing among the branches rustling in the dawn wind, and in letting its friendly gaze rest on the sailor who has been afloat since the first light, filling him with a sense of well-being and happiness. (9)

At another moment, in a chapter titled *"Le jardin des oublis"* (The garden of forgetfulness) we see nature "hard at work" amidst an atmosphere of idyllic freedom. It seems likely that the following passage conceals a secret yearning for a world, a society, where one is free "to fly" wherever one wishes, instead of being compelled to mask one's feelings and desires behind hypocritical conventions:

> "Madame Leduc is not in her garden today, I see," said Monsieur Serciers. Yet one could not truly maintain that the garden was lacking in life. One had the impression that every single corner of it was a living dispensary where leaves were ever at work distilling balm, while all around the flowers gave off their heady perfume. Even at some distance from the railing one could catch a smell, so much more penetrating when gathered from the living plants by the breeze which rocked them, mingled them, composed them in a symphony, blew them apart and gathered them together, turn and turn about, than in the hot steam of infusions, or in a chemist's shop, the scent of lime flowers or acacia. Nature, too, was hard at work, taking advantage of the season and the time of day when every flying thing might go where it willed and the flowers lay open like palaces offering hospitality. (128–129)

The final paragraph of a chapter titled *"Promenades"* (Walks) is illustrative of the extent to which Proust invested natural phenomena with the emotions stirring within him. First, the narrator tells us that Jean had rarely if ever found a perfect correspondence between the pleasures he longed for and the joy that these pleasures actually gave him. But one day he experiences an ecstatic moment of perfect fulfillment, as he contemplates a village and the surrounding landscape. It is in passages such as this that Proust's political unconscious was operative, where he in effect transferred to nature that longing for spiritual communion, for "oneness" with the universal "harmonious" order of things which he had despaired of finding in the social order. It is significant, it seems to me, that such a privileged moment should occur while Jean is walking with his close friend Henri de Réveillon, one of several characters in whom we see traces of Reynaldo Hahn, the "hidden god"[8] of *JS* :

> They went by the way of the vines which, glittering in the sun, seemed flooded with a joy not less than Jean's. They reached the farm where the stones before

the door seemed stroked by the sun, giving back smile for smile. They sat down to drink beneath the apple trees which were now full of ripe fruit, having lost their springtime blossom, though they still retained in the tangled tracery of their delicate branches something of their former charm with its memories of youth. Wild grasses on the wall were carelessly confiding to the wind. Not now did Jean, as once he had done when saying goodbye to Mademoiselle Kossichef, wonder whether he would ever know happiness since nothing ever seemed to give him a pleasure that was whole and perfect, but always fell short of expectation, and no matter how lovely this or that might be, never chimed perfectly with his yearning heart, but made him feel misunderstood and impotent, a prey to misery and despair. Now however in his walks and in his dreaming everything seemed to outstrip the pleasure that he felt within himself and to answer it. The woods, the vines, the very stones, were at one with the brightness of the sun and the unblemished sky, and even when the sky grew overcast, the multitude of leaves, as in a sudden change of tone, the earth of the roads, the roofs of the town, seemed as though caught up in the unity of a brand new world. And all that Jean was feeling seemed without effort to chime with the surrounding oneness, and he was conscious of the perfect joy which is the gift of harmony. (269)

Nature alone has the restorative power to convert Jean's melancholy and loneliness into joy, his alienation into a feeling of comradeship and unity. But just as important is his frequent association of nature with the idea of freedom. Although the freedom involved here is not, of course, political in any ordinary sense, it is not unreasonable to see a political motive in his celebration of the elements when they are thrown into the kind of furious and chaotic turbulence he oberves one day during a storm that breaks out near Beg-Meil, on the coast of Brittany. Here we find a side of Proust's personality that is rarely in evidence, something he calls "the spirit of revolt" that is released when the stormy sea and wind, instead of retreating, advance with renewed fury. At such moments, there is "mingled with our pleasure something of that spirit of revolt which, when a trapped criminal is at the very moment of capture, makes us leap with his leaps and draw his strength into our own bodies so that we long for him to break the fierce circle of his enemies whom he can no longer avoid." The reason for this association between the encircled criminal and the wind is that "One cannot drive away the wind nor encircle it, nor make ourselves its masters. One cannot shoot the waves nor kill the sea. Suddenly the fury drops and calm returns. But until that moment comes, something within us swells in sympathy, towers with the waves to their topmost peak" (484–485). It is of obvious "political" significance that immediately after this evocation of a furious and untamed wind, the narrator thinks of Colonel Picquart, to whom his supporters want to cry out, in sympathy with his struggle for justice, "Don't be discouraged! Don't weaken! Don't, when the Esterhazy case comes on, say you have no opinion, or let yourself be shut away!" The analogy is strained, but eloquent nonetheless.

Proust's vision of nature in *JS* revolves literally and symbolically around the sun, for whose life-giving and life-sustaining presence he finds an abundance of images that appear and reappear throughout the text in many guises and many different moods. The word "sun" and its various derivatives and combined forms—sunset, sunlit, sun beam, sunshine, sunflower—is used about 350 times, which attests to the fascination that light had for Proust. These images, together with many tenderly affectionate allusions to other forms of light—fire, candle, lamp—give to sections of *JS* the character almost of prayer, of religiously inspired meditation. Whether this was Proust's conscious intent is difficult to say. But the fact is that, in accordance with the cyclical conception of life that informs the text, the sun, the moon, and man-made light are all enlisted in a paean of mythical and metaphorical exaltation not essentially different from the spirit that pervades the *Psalms* of David, the *Canticle of Brother Sun* of Saint Francis, and other sacred writings. What Proust brings to this tradition is the free imaginative energy of the modern writer, who is unafraid of diversity, tolerant of contradiction, and enamored of sensuous images that appeal directly to the imagination.

In Proust's created world, the sun in *JS* is a universal yet immediate and almost human presence. It has a "smiling face," it offers a "long and loving welcome" to nature. At dusk, it sets with "a sad and tender smile," and in the morning it brings "its brightness and warmth." It penetrates into our domestic lives, setting the wine glasses "twinkling" and "playing" about the knives and forks on the dinner table. From time to time, it is sent "scurrying" away by the cold, but soon returns with its "message of hope." We even hear "the music of the singing sun" when we feel sad, and we take note of its beams "playing" on the lilac leaves. The playfulness and gaiety of the sun are pervasive, but they are not the only dimensions of the sun's power in Proust's writing. Contrary to human time, the sun is permanent; it possesses a "changeless radiance." The "kingdom of the sun" is the origin of the masterpieces of nature, surpassing all human creations, yet closely allied with those creations, for all creative life has a common source.

An image of particular charm in *JS*, as in Proust's other writings, combines the words "sweet" and "light" in various ways, in order to convey what I think Proust felt was the quintessence of the life force; it is an image used for the sun, the moon, and for domestic light, and occurs on one occasion in what is probably the first reference to electric light in Proust's writing. "Sweetness" is a word used by Proust to describe light, air, music, the sound of church bells, poetry, memory, gaiety, affections, a caress, dreams, childhood, certain names, water, and last, but most primary, Jean's mother. Toward the end of the arranged narrative, in his Paris residence, Jean inadvertently puts on his mother's shawl and instantly becomes aware of "a great sweetness" coming over him. This is one of several revelatory moments in *JS*, where for a brief moment a kind of psychological fusion between mother and son takes place that anticipates the relationship between mother and son in the *Recherche*. To Jean, his mother is the soul of sweetness itself, and it is this quality—connoting softness, tenderness, above all, unselfish love—that he momentarily captures while covered by his mother's shawl.

For Jean, no other love can hope to rival the quality of reciprocal devotion between mother and son, not even his friendship with Henri. Indeed, this absolute commitment of love between mother and son implicitly diminishes the power of all other love relationships, which, in Proust's view of things, are born, grow, reach their apex, and then inevitably decline and die, or at best, linger on but in such muted colors as to be unrecognizeable when compared with the first bloom of passion.

Proust's pessimism about love between men and women flows from the conviction that, like almost everything people claim to hold dear in the world, it becomes "adulterated by life" (582). At one point he compares the "illusions" of love to the fleeting charm that an agate marble held for him when he was a boy. Like love, the beauty of the agate marble was a value projected on to it by his mind and imagination. Far from possessing the requisite qualities that alone can sustain love, it quickly fades when the desired object loses its power to satisfy the lover's craving for fulfillment. A uniformly negative conception of love is one of the book's salient features. As already noted, the friendship between Jean and Henri is serene and even tender at times, but it fails to measure up to the perfect unselfishness that Jean demands of love. The love that Jean professes to feel for several women, chiefly two women of the Parisian upper crust named Françoise and Charlotte, degenerates into tortured jealousy and possessiveness with such tragic inevitability as to fully justify the narrator's classification of it as something worse than an illusion: it is nothing but an "illness," a momentary "fever," an "impossible ideal." *JS* contains several little disquisitions on the subject of love, where one finds a depressing litany of arguments dismantling all of the age-old sentiments on its behalf. Alma Saraydar believes that, in his theory of love, Proust was a disciple of

Stendhal, whose treatise *De l'Amour*, she thinks, was a source of Proust's "materialist" bias on the subject. As Benjamin observed in "The Image of Proust," Proust was a "merciless deglamorizer" of love and of other human "illusions."

Homosexual love in *JS* does not have the opportunity to come out of the closet; it is tainted by scandal and ends in misery and loneliness. The Vicomte de Lomperolles's underground sexual pursuits make him the object of a cruel game of blackmail, to which he succumbs without any hope of clearing his name, since at the time it took special circumstances to allow one to lead the kind of relatively worry-free homosexual life that Robert de Montesquiou led by hiring a live-in secretary who was also his lover. As for the lesbian side of homosexual life, it lies at the center of the tormented misunderstandings between Jean and Françoise, who is finally compelled to "confess" a lesbian relationship she had had years earlier by Jean's obsessively jealous insistence that she tell him everything about herself, even if it were to be deeply hurtful to him. Proust was incapable of depicting homosexual love as a choice of love object like any other, although he certainly deserves credit for bringing the subject into the open. That he always viewed homosexuality as something entirely natural to those born with such inclinations is well documented, but in his writing he was unable to break through the socially and religiously constructed prejudices that surrounded it. In this connection, it is sad to remember the spontaneity and pleasure the adolescent Proust associated with homoerotic love.

The ideological implications of Proust's depictions of love in *JS* are not dissimilar to what we observed about his skepticism concerning public life in general. Love as manifested in society, especially between members of the middle and upper classes, is just as prone to corruption as any other aspect of social existence, and is no more likely to transcend selfish ambitions than is the world of politics. The only available and secure refuges from the painful disappointments of social life remain the intimate family nucleus, together with rare friendships (between men), and nature, whose laws are binding equally on each and every human being, but in a fundamentally beneficent manner that transcends the fear ordinarily surrounding physical decay and death. For these inevitable events in the existence of all life forms are part of a vast design of some sort, made visible to us by signs—the seasons, the tides, the movement of the planets and stars, the "kingdom" of the unmoved sun, with its "changeless radiance," as well as the instinctual impulses of myriad flora and fauna—that connect human beings to Being. It is this idea, this vision of life and death, that lends a certain grandeur to the concluding paragraphs of this otherwise shapeless (and plotless) literary work. It is through death, the narrator asserts in the penultimate paragraph, that every human being "journeys into the infinite and into nothingness." It is the thought of death, the coming of death, that "opens for him a window on the mysteries of eternity." In the book's last sentences, we see Jean and his parents at home. His mother is looking intently at the sleeping figure of her husband, now reduced by old age to a shadow of his former self, breathing quietly, while Jean, suddenly aware of his mother's gaze, also turns his eyes toward his father. The life force still possesses Monsieur Santeuil, he is still sustained by it, and this fact gives comfort to mother and son, although they are aware at the same time how near to the end of his life the old man really is. The even sound of his breathing continues, and the narrator observes, calmly, and with serene detachment: "The work of life and death, the work of time, proceeded on its course without a break."

I have reserved the last section of this chapter for a brief consideration of one of the great themes of Proust's life and work that appears, at least on a conceptual level, in almost a complete form in *JS*, namely the creative process through which the writer acquires the necessary understanding of himself and of the surrounding world to elaborate his or her conception of life. The approximately twenty years in Jean's life described in *JS* are not as unambiguously related to his literary aspirations as are the same period in the life of Marcel in the *Recherche*, especially in the later work's concluding pages. Nevertheless, the essential insights of the *Recherche* are already present in *JS*.

Proust expounds his theory of creativity, memory, and time most vividly in the chapter titled "Impressions regained" in the English translation, and "*Souvenirs de la mer devant le lac de Genève*" in the 1971 Pléiade French edition. The crucial Proustian concept of the difference between a deliberate, conscious attempt to remember an experience, which is bound to have limited resonance, and an involuntary remembrance of the same experience, which opens up not only a particular memory but a whole world of feeling and sensation, is announced in Jean's insight connected with a trip to Lake Geneva. The sudden sight of the lake instantly recalls to his mind an earlier time at Beg-Meil, in Brittany, which he had once despaired of rediscovering because in that initial attempt, only his mind and eyes were involved. "Not to them," the narrator observes, "is it given to receive the message of aesthetic joy." Memory alone cannot recreate the past, something else is needed, the stimulus of a sense experience, to be sure, but reactivated by a power called the imagination. This is how the narrator theorizes this magical moment:

> Between the lake at which he was looking and himself what was it that had come to birth that never had existed between the sea and him, that never would have existed between this lake and him, had not something of the same feeling been present years before at the sea? Could it be that beauty and joy for the poet resides in an invisible substance which may perhaps be called imagination, which cannot work direct[ly] on immediate reality, nor yet on past reality deliberately remembered, but hovers only over past reality caught up and enshrined in the reality now present? It is as though before the eye which sees it now and saw it long ago, there floats divine imagination, which is perhaps the source of all our joy, something that we find in books, but only with utmost difficulty in things around us. What has happened is that behind the indifferent spectacle of the present we have found on a sudden a memory of the past revived, the feeling that filled it, a charm of the imagination which attaches us firmly to life and makes us part of it, as though the past, let slip by happiness, not understood by thought, and only vaguely reproduced by memory, had been recaptured once and for all by contemplation. (407–408)

This memorable passage is followed by another example of creative recollection as related to the sense of smell. When the smell of a house where one had once lived returns to us years later, and we are overwhelmed by a flood of memories, it is as if

> the whole of that period of my life were caught up and made present in that smell. And so it was that when it came to me again I felt a whole life rise up which my imagination had never known, but now after so long a space of time had battened on and savoured. (408)

It is easy to miss the almost imperceptible shift in voice from the third person, where it is Jean about whom the narrator is speaking, to the first person, where the narrator speaks of himself as having experienced this blissful moment of illumination regarding past and present. The shift occurs when the narrator feels compelled to address the reader as the "I" to whom this miraculous event has happened. It is not sufficient for him at this moment to maintain the fiction that he is writing about someone other than himself. He needs a more authoritative voice to say what he wants to say here. Even if hesitantly and perhaps unconsciously, Proust had already taken the step that would lead to his adoption in the *Recherche* of the first person authorial voice with which he will tell the story of Marcel's education from childhood to full maturity.

This same section also deals with the question of time and how the memory of a past event, embodied in sense experiences, can be made to reveal its inner secrets, its core meaning for our lives. This is the complex of thoughts and emotions within which, the narrator says, "I find myself confronted by a reality liberated from the temporal circumstances of my life." What is liberated from time, for Proust, is the imagination, which now has a grasp of reality that no amount of reasoning or intellectual speculation could achieve.

This chapter ends with a meditation on memory, time, and art that expresses the same feeling of certitude and transcendence I noted above in connection with the thought and actuality of death. Death and art are the only experiences that allow the individual to catch a glimpse of eternity, to break through the rigid barriers that otherwise impose upon us what Proust calls, in the concluding sentence of this chapter, "the slavery of the *now*, letting us be flooded with the feeling of life everlasting."

Proust brought a well-grounded education in literature, philosophy, and the arts to the task of investigating the ordinary events of daily life, but always from a transcendent point of view. His was a perspective that kept his mind's eye focused on the eternal questions, while his intense and profound immersion in the life of the body and its sensations kept him attached to the physical universe. Proust's vision was idealist at its core, and rested on premises reaching back to Plato, to Saint Augustine, to seventeenth- century philosophy, to Kant, and to certain thinkers and poets of the Romantic movement. He utilized this tradition for his own highly individualized purposes, striving to remain faithful to the principles and aims he set for himself when still a very young man. This is why a study of his early writings turns out to be so useful for a proper understanding of his later years. *Les Plaisirs et les jours*, the critical writings of the 1890s on various writers and painters, especially those on John Ruskin, and *Jean Santeuil*, while valuable works in their own right, form the matrix within which *A la recherche du temps perdu* could come to fruition.

It has been argued, rather persuasively, by Catherine Ann Baudino and Sylvia Sarah Beerbohm among others, that what primarily motivated Proust to write was, in the final analysis, his need to contrast seeming and being, to let us see the world in terms of the essentially Platonic distinction between the historically contingent realm of flux, change, and appearance and the permanent realm of ideal forms or essences. There are hints of this dichotomy, certainly, in *PJ*, where the embattled soul of various characters struggles mightily to emerge from its corporeal prison and win its freedom or lose it, as the case may be. We see it as well in the critical writings devoted to John Ruskin and, in an especially poignant way, in *JS*, which can be considered the transitional text linking the aesthetisizing literary intellectual of the early to mid-1890s to the mature author of the *Recherche*.

Beerbohm attributes a vast "cosmic vision" to Proust. This is a fair characterization as far as it goes. It is a formulation that is too closely tied, however, in Beerbohm's analysis, to esoteric doctrines that, even if acknowledged to have exerted an influence on Proust's thought, are not the decisive and distinctive mark of his evolving conception of life. We need in addition an approach to Proust's writing that anchors it in history, in its concrete socioliterary context, in its moment of time, within which esoteric doctrines did undoubtedly circulate and probably exerted some influence on Proust's mind. Yet these doctrines were only a small part of a complex congeries of literary movements and intellectual currents to which young Proust responded and some of whose ideas he assimilated and made his own. In this sense, whatever types of esoteric spiritism existed in Proust's social world should be evaluated in historical terms, not simply as independent and autonomous ideas whose impact somehow effaces the particular characteristics of an epoch in Western civilization. The worldliness of Proust's ideas and ideals, even the most exalted and cosmic, is of paramount importance. If these historical considerations are kept in mind, then we can agree with Beerbohm and others who have emphasized Proust's dream of achieving a unifying vision of life in which all the variations, differences, and conflicts marking historical man would fall away, revealing the common core of humanity across time and space. It was this kind of universal perspective that allowed Proust to accommodate both the scientific and the spiritual realms of thought in his philosophy and, consequently, in his creative work.

If we remember to situate Proust securely in his socioliterary context, to anchor his thought in the prevalent intellectual tendencies of his time, to give due consideration to his class affiliations and loyalties, and, finally, to connect him to those of his forebears and contemporaries from whom he derived inspiration, an historical-materialist interpretation of his writing can also appreciate what is distinctive and unique in the totality of his work, including his loftiest flights into the realm of the metaphysical and the transcendent. The universal laws that so fascinated and enchanted him throughout his life and that he tried to integrate into his writing belong at once to the physical universe and to the spiritual forces that animate and inform human existence.

Endnotes

Introduction

1. Among the biographies written during these years that I have found useful in various ways are Richard H. Barker's *Marcel Proust: A Biography*, J. M. Cocking's *Proust*, André Maurois's *Le Monde de Marcel Proust*, George D. Painter's two-volume work *Proust: The Early Years* and *Proust: The Later Years*, Derrick Leon's *Introduction to Proust: His Life, His Circle, and His Work*, and Léon-Pierre Quint's *Marcel Proust: sa vie, son œuvre*.

2. Among these are André Ferré's *Les Années de collège de Marcel Proust* (Paris: Gallimard, 1959), Henri Bonnet's *Alphonse Darlu (1849–1921): le maître de philosophie de Marcel Proust* (Paris: A..G. Nizet, 1961) and *Les Amours et la sexualité de Proust* (Paris: Nizet, 1985), and Joyce Megay's *Bergson et Proust* (Paris: Librairie Philosophique J. Vrin, 1976).

3. Two useful articles on rather little-known Soviet criticism and scholarship on Proust are by Yvette Louria, "Proust and Lunacharskii," *Romanic Review* 62 (1971): 127–132, and Gaston Boitchidzé, "Jugements russes sur Proust," *Europe* 49 (1971): 156–132. The most throrough review of Marxist criticism of Proust, with a section on Soviet criticism, is Ronald Thornton's *Marcel Proust and Marxist Literary Criticism from the Nineteen Twenties to the Nineteen Seventies*, Ph. D. Diss, University of Indiana, 1979.

4. Probably the best source for this aspect of Bakhtin's thought is M. M. Bakhtin and P.N. Medvedev, *The Formal Method in Literary Scholarship: A Critical Introduction to Sociological Poetics* (1978).

5. Especially as these terms are articulated by Marx and Engels in *The Communist Manifesto* and in *The German Ideology*.

Chapter 1

1. Proust was admitted to level 5 of the Lycée Condorcet (still called the lycée Fontanes in 1882, but renamed the Condorcet in 1883) in October 1882, as a nonresident

day-scholar because his poor health required that he live at home. Health problems made it necessary for him to repeat level 2, since he was absent for almost the entire year. He received his *bachelier de philosophie* in July 1889.

In one of his paintings of the years 1902–1903, "La sortie du lycée Condorcet," Jean Béraud, a close friend of Proust, captures the privileged milieu of the Condorcet: well-dressed boys, atttended by their elegantly attired fathers and mothers, the fathers in top hats, emerge happily from the school ready to get into the carriages that await them. No doubt an idealized picture, the painting conveys a mood of self-satisfaction and an air of affluence that seems emblematic of *la belle époque*. This milieu and the areas of Paris associated with it have been described and illustrated recently by Henri Raczymov in *Le Paris littéraire et intime de Marcel Proust* (1997).

2   As evidenced in some of the materials in Jeanne Canavaggia's *Proust et la politique*, and in a letter of July 15, 1887, to Antoinette Faure (*Corr.* 1: 96–97), when he was sixteen years old, Proust evinced a certain attraction to the nationalist revanchism of General Georges Boulanger. The letter begins by revealing that his mother had torn up a first draft because of its atrocious handwriting. But Proust then adds that "Basically I believe that my great praise of our worthy general excited the old Orleanist-Republican sentiments of Madame Jeanne Proust." He also spoke of Boulanger's ability to "stir everything that is primitive, untamed and bellicose in one's heart." Proust was fascinated by the French military tradition, which led him on November 11, 1889, despite his asthmatic condition, to volunteer for military service and to serve for about a year with the 76th Infantry regiment in Orléans.

3   Bizet was the son of the composer and of Geneviève Halévy who, after the composer's death, married Emile Straus. Halévy (1872–1962), son of the playwright and librettist Ludovic Halévy, was an essayist, a collaborator with Charles Péguy on the *Cahiers de la Quinzaine*, an ardent Dreyfusard, and author of many books on French labor and political history. Gregh (1873–1960) was an author of biographical and critical studies of Victor Hugo and of studies on French theatre and poetry. Marquis Robert de Flers (1872–1927) was a playwright and essayist, and author of numerous books on travel and theatre criticism. Robert Dreyfus (1873–1939) was an historian, known especially for his *Monsieur Thiers contre l'empire, la guerre, la commune, 1869–1871* (1928).

4   For a critical examination of misleading and erroneous aspects of "transposition theory" as Proust applied it to his treatment of male and female homosexuality in the *Recherche*, especially his "fantasy of feminine sexuality," see Elizabeth Ladenson's study *Proust's Lesbianism* (Ithaca: Cornell University Press, 1999). Ladenson believes that Proust mistakenly transferred a defensible if inadequate theory of male homosexuality to lesbianism.

5   Despite poor health and long absences from school, Proust was already on the honor roll at the age of fourteen, as indicated in a "*bulletin d'inscription au tableau d'honneur du lycée Condorcet*" dated February 14, 1885 (UI ms. "Proust 102"). In 1888 he won first prize for French composition, and at the end of his last year, 1888–1889, he won first prize in philosophy.

6   For a sampling of Proust's early poetic efforts to express his homosexual feelings, see *Écrits de jeunesse,* 121–151.

Chapter 2

1   Readers should be aware that this article, signed "Laurence," is attributed by scholars to Proust, but some doubts about its authorship remain.

Chapter 3

1   Madeleine Lemaire, born Coll (1845–1928), was widely appreciated in Paris at the time, in part for her unusual devotion to roses, which she cultivated and painted constantly, and in part because of her long relationship with Alexandre Dumas fils, who helped her establish her salon, frequently the site of musical recitals and fancy-dress parties.

2   In his introduction and notes to Marcel Proust, *Mon cher petit: lettres à Lucien Daudet,* Michel Bonduelle informs us that Proust was introduced to Lucien by Hahn in the winter of 1894, at one of Alphonse Daudet's "Thursday salons." During the following year, Proust's romantic attachment to Hahn began to cool, making it possible for him to develop "assiduous" relations with Lucien in November 1895. By the summer of 1896, Proust wrote to his new young lover: "I am not sure of anything—except that I love you, my little Lucien, with all my heart" *(Mon cher petit : lettres à Lucien Daudet,* 88). But Proust's relations with Daudet were no smoother than those with Hahn, despite many common interests. Their love affair (but not their friendship) was over by the spring of 1897.

3   Léon Delafosse, *Six mélodies,* Department of Music, B.N., vol. 7-122117

4   Baudelaire played a leading role, posthumously, in effecting this intimate alliance between the arts in the 1880s and 1890s. See Baudelaire's *"Lettre à Wagner"* and his 1861 article *"Richard Wagner et Tannhauser"* in Charles Baudelaire, *L'Art romantique,* ed. Lloyd James Austin (Paris: Garnier-Flammarion, 1968), 263–300. In his introduction to this volume, Austin notes that "the great article on Richard Wagner is one of those that bring the most honor to Baudelaire the critic. Not only does he define the essential character of Wagner's art, but he discusses the problem of the relations between music and poetry in terms that were to be taken up again by the symbolist generation in France, and above all by Mallarmé" (27).

5   *Le Ménestrel: Journal du Monde Musical,* published by Heugel, Paris, beginning in 1834 (Periodical section of the Department of Music of the B.N.).

6   These were the two Flaubert characters whose names, and something of whose manner of expression, Proust borrowed freely in one of the many *pastiches* in *PJ.*

7   The epigraph reads as follows: "Should I call this book a novel? It is something less, and yet much more, the very essence of my life, with nothing extraneous

added, as it developed through a long period of wretchedness. This book of mine has not been manufactured: it has been gleaned."

8   Flavie was the marquise de Casa-Fuerte, née Flavie de Balsoram.

9   But the characteristically "decadent" habits and predilections of the protagonist are more reminiscent of someone like Robert de Montesquiou than of Hahn.

10 Kolb was unable to be more specific about the date of this letter other than to place it in 1895.

11 Some previously unpublished letters from Hahn to Risler appeared in "Reynaldo Hahn: douze lettres à Edouard Risler (1873–1929)," *BSAP* 43 (1993): 37–57.

12 Loevgren cites a passage from Jean Moréas's *Philosophy of Composition* where one finds an extreme expression of what Proust, faithful to the Zeitgeist, was aiming for in his writing: we are striving to create an art, Moréas said, "which would be vaguely poetry, painting, music, but not simply painting, or poetry—something like a concert of colors, a painting of musical notes—a deliberate fusion of genres" (33).

13 The four poems on painters were recited by Simone Le Bargy, with the piano accompaniment of Edouard Risler playing Hahn's musical settings, on May 28, 1895, at the Paris home of Madeleine Lemaire.

14 None of the dedications that accompanied Proust's writings when they were first published in newspapers and reviews were included in *PJ*. Therefore, without a thorough search, we are deprived in the book of one important means of access to the social world within which these stories and prose poems were written.

15 André Gide's testimony is among the many pieces of evidence reinforcing the conjecture that Proust had no sexual interest in women. Gide spoke with Proust about his sex life on several occasions. A frequently cited entry in Gide's diary for May 21, 1921, written after spending some time the previous evening with Proust, says among other things: "Far from denying his homosexuality, he is open about it and exposes it, I could almost say he brags about it. He says that he has never loved women other than spiritually and that he has never experienced love except with men." Gide was rather startled at this meeting to hear Proust express certainty that Baudelaire was a "practicing" homosexual, for which the available evidence is at best faintly circumstantial. See André Gide, *Journal, 1889–1939* (Paris: Gallimard, 1951), 691–694.

16 As indicated in *CSB*, 935, n. 5, the essay was published for the first time, with the title "Les œuvres de Reynaldo Hahn," in a supplement of the *Annales politiques et littéraires* (December 1, 1923).

17 The Hugo quote is taken from *Hernani*, act 5, scene 2, v. 1964.

Chapter 4

1   The salon as a "social institution" to which the young Proust owed certain of his literary ideals but also his severely critical attitude toward contemporary French

society is discussed cogently by Seth L. Wolitz in *The Proustian Community*. Wolitz attributes considerable importance to the Jewish presence in some of the salons Proust frequented in the 1880s and early 1890s. He explores the intertwined themes of culture and heredity in Proust's writing and his notions about French social hierarchies and affiliations.

2   Bernadette Morand, "L'Aristocratie chez Proust," *Europe*, special issue "*Centenaire de Marcel Proust*," (August/September 1970): 37–46.

3   But the image of a "fashionably" dressed Proust must be modified by the Chaplinesque aspects of his appearance that Jacques-Emile Blanche recalls. Blanche tells us that Proust wore somewhat "baggy trousers" and that "his top hats very soon took on the appearance of hedgehogs or Skye terriers as a result of being brushed the wrong way" (Cited in Brée, *The World of Marcel Proust*, 21).

4   Although for this, as for all other aspects of Proust's life, we need to be careful and to remember that Proust relied heavily on Darwin's teachings and generally on experimental science for his understanding of some human motivations and traits. Among the works he read of this type were Hervey de Saint-Denis, *Les Rêves ou les moyens de les diriger* (1867); Alfred Binet, *Études de psychologie expérimentale: Le fétichisme dans l'amour* (1888); and Pierre Janet, *L'Automatisme psychologique* (1889). Moreover, his brother was a physician and his father's scientific accomplishments gave young Proust ready access to the new experimentally based discoveries in medicine, psychology, and biology.

5   Montesquiou discusses his lineage in *Les Pas effacés*. Through marriages and alliances, he was connected with the greater part of the European aristocracy. Montesquiou's biographer, Philippe Jullian, claims that his family had "the longest geneaology in France," going back to the early eleventh century.

6   However, in his massive study *Les Curiosités esthétiques de Robert de Montesquiou*, 2 vols. (Genève: Droz, 1996), Antoine Bertrand has performed a sort of rehabilitation of Montesquiou, claiming for his subject a preeminent place among French poets and trend-setters of the past hundred years.

7   The word "*maître* " can mean lord, master, and teacher, depending on context. All three meanings seem to be present in Proust's use of the term to address Montesquiou.

8   The 1878 Delaunay portrait appears in Tadié's biography of Proust; the Boldini portrait in André Maurois, *Le Monde de Marcel Proust* 35.

9   Proust's housekeeper, Céleste Albaret, casts doubt on Proust's complete sincerity in paying such extreme homage to his older, illustrious friend. She recalls Proust's reaction to an affectionate letter he received from Montesquiou, probably in 1893, in the following way: "I remember how he laughed, brimming over with joy, the first time he received a letter from Montesquiou where he called him 'My little Marcel.' It wasn't the fact that he had arrived at this familiarity with Montesquiou that enchanted him or flattered him. No, that went along with everything he was telling me about the count. It was an inward laugh. For him, this letter was on the contrary the proof that he been able to captivate Montesquiou, that he had be-

come Montesquiou's master, that Montesquiou would one day become aware that "little Marcel" was superior to him—which is, alas for count Robert and for his mortification, what happened" (Albaret 376).

10. Gregh himself was not immune to the charm of aristocratic names. In *L'Âge d'or: souvenirs d'enfance et de jeunesse*, he confessed: "I still remember the name of one of my school-mates: Fontaine de Rambouillet. The name enchanted me by its sonority, and because of what it evoked" (45). Gregh was probably alluding here to the celebrated château de Rambouillet situated in the forest that bears its name.

11. Under the rubric "Bloc-Notes Parisien," with the title "*Une fête littéraire à Versailles*" and signed Tout-Paris, the article has been positively identified as Proust's and included in *CSB*, 360–365. It appeared originally in *Le Gaulois* (May 31, 1894): 1.

12. As indicated by a letter he sent to Montesquiou (*Corr* I: lxxviii) Proust was furious the day after his article in *Le Gaulois* appeared, since it had included a detailed appreciative description of dresses and gowns that the newspaper had excised. "What slow-witted, unpredicted, mysterious and clumsy hand corrected this article?" Proust exclaimed to his mentor. See *CSB* 882.

Chapter 5

1. Marcel Proust, *Les Plaisirs et les jours* (Paris: Calmann-Lévy, 1896), with original watercolor by Madeleine Lemaire, number 15 of twenty copies printed on Japanese Imperial Paper, B. N. Rés $^m y^2$ 179. I have also looked at two other copies of the first edition, one printed on Chinese rice paper, B.N. Rés mZ 289, and a standard copy printed on supple shiny stock at the manuscript and rare book division of the Columbia University library. My description of the book in this chapter is based on a persual of all three copies.

2. In his excellent study of Proust's "*Portraits de Peintres*," J. Theodore Johnson notes that Hahn's four pieces were reproduced in the 1896 edition not in the printed form in which they had first appeared in the folio album published by *Au Ménestrel* (Heugel Publishers) but, rather, in manuscript form, "no doubt an attempt to carry out even further the theme of 'sketches' that dominates this book both in the literary fragments by Proust and in the emblematic vignettes by Madeleine Lemaire" (Johnson 400). Hahn took the task of fitting his music to the nuances of thought and feeling in the poems with great seriousness. He provided expressive instructions to the pianist, such as "a bit heavy like the croup of Flemish horses" for the piano accompaniment to the poem on Albert Cuyp, and "with elegance and melancholy," which he felt was appropriate to the lives of the men depicted in the poem on Anton Van Dyck. The "Portraits de peintres" appeared originally in *Le Gaulois* (June 21, 1895): 2.

3. Such prodding was a prominent feature of Proust's correspondence from 1894 to the early part of 1896. Lemaire agreed to illustrate the volume in November 1893

but was unable to begin work because Proust had not yet found a publisher. In that same month, Proust wrote his friend Robert de Billy that "this year" he was planning to publish a "collection" of his writings. A year and a half later, in May 1895, perhaps despairing of ever seeing his "little things" in book form, Proust wrote to Lemaire asking her to help him persuade Arthur Meyer, the director of *Le Gaulois*, to publish some of his writings in that newspaper. Uncertainties about how and when the book would be published bothered Proust until the spring of 1896, only a few months before the appearance of the book in June.

4   Shortly after the publication of the second 1924 edition of the book, Henri Jourdan examined the 1896 edition and wrote: "I have under scrutiny the large in-quarto with a pale green cover. On this shiny paper, these anemic flowers by Madeleine Lemaire, and these dreamy figures, on all these platitudinous colors and forms, amidst the fleeting handwriting of Reynaldo Hahn, on this world swooning and swollen with sighs, I see passing before me the images of the *Revue Blanche* and that hothouse atmosphere which Anatole France described in his preface, where sickly orchids live" (Larkin Price, "Materials for a Critical Edition of Marcel Proust's *Les Plaisirs et les jours*," Ph.D. Diss. University of Michigan,1965, 67).

5   Many of these changes are documented in the 1971 edition, pp. 912–916. The 1971 edition reproduces the changes in citations, proper names, and a few other elements as they took place from the "pre-original" text to the 1896 edition, but it also makes additional changes worthy of note.

6   The poems are rendered in prose translations. Keller also includes a bibliography and an index of names. Like other translations of *PJ*, the 1988 German edition includes some of Proust's early writings that were excluded from the collection.

7   Apropos of Proust's characters who do not work, Robert Sayre said it well, in an observation about the *Recherche* that is applicable to *PJ:* "The characters of Proust's world—both grand bourgeois and nobles—have no productive relation to the functioning society" (93).

8   The text of Hesiod I have consulted is *Homeric Hymns-Epic Cycle-Homerica*, trans. Hugh G. Evelyn-White (Cambridge: Harvard University Press, first published 1914).

9   Commenting on the second and fourth sections of *Works and Days*, xviii–xix, Hugh G. Evelyn-White makes a few observations that fit *PJ* equally well. "At first sight," he writes, "such a work seems to be a miscellany of myths, technical advice, moral precepts, and folklore maxims without any unifying principle; and critics have readily taken the view that the whole is a cento of fragments or short poems worked up by a redactor. Very probably Hesiod used much material of a far older date, just as Shakespeare used the *Gesta Romanorum,* old chronicles, and old plays; but close inspection will show that the *Works and Days* has a real unity and that the picturesque title is somewhat misleading. The poem has properly no technical object at all, but is moral: its real aim is to show men how best to live in a difficult world. So viewed the four seemingly independent sections will be found to be linked together in a real bond of unity."

10 It is possible that the word "pleasure" in the title of Proust's book was influenced by Gabriele D'Annunzio's 1892 novel *Il Piacere*, which was widely read in France. D'Annunzio's description of the joys and sorrows of a young Roman aristocrat also had its moral as well as aesthetic purposes.

Chapter 6

1 Douglas W. Alden thought that Proust's challenge to Lorrain was not surprising in a young man who "at the time took feudal society seriously," meaning, in this instance, personal honor and physical courage (1938).

2 On this incident, see Barker 72–73; Price, *Materials* 64, 95–96; and Leon 85–86.

3 Letter to Charles Grandjean, November 13 or 20, 1893, *Corr.* 1: 255–256.

4 Freud's phrase in chapter 3, "Animism, Magic, and the Omnipotence of Thought," of *Totem and Taboo*, ed. and trans. James Strachey, introduction Peter Gay (New York: Norton., 1989), 94–124.

5 See Silvain Monod's very funny pastiche of Proust's style in the *Recherche* called "*A la recherche de Clémentine*," in *Pastiches*, 236–243.

6 In a notebook entry on Flaubert written around 1910 that remained unpublished until 1971, Proust spoke of Flaubert as a "grammatical genius" who, in his own domain, had initiated a "revolution of vision" comparable to the change in thought effected by Kant. "[Flaubert's] revolution of vision, of the representation of the world that flows—or is expressed—from and by its syntax, is perhaps as great as that of Kant in moving the center of knowledge of the world to the soul" (*CSB*, 299–302). Proust looked upon Kant's philosophy as having become so thoroughly incorporated into the mental life of Western civilization as to be an unquestioned reality taken for granted by its beneficiaries. It should be recalled that Alphonse Darlu had introduced Proust to Kant in 1888–1889 in a course of study at the Lycée Condorcet, a course supplemented in private lessons given to Proust at his home by Darlu.

Chapter 7

1 The idea that human beings are subject to laws governing their psychosexual lives appears in various guises in Proust's early writing, especially in those passages where the narrator of his stories stops for a moment to reflect on the implications of actions taken by his characters. For example, in "*La Fin de la jalousie*," the protagonist, Honoré, plagued by a crippling jealousy, begs God to free him of his obsession. He begs also for constancy of love and affection, to no avail:

> "'My God! My God! Grant me by Thy grace that I shall love her forever. My God, this grace alone I ask, my God, Thou who hast the power, grant that I shall love her forever!'.

> Now in one of those purely physical moments when the soul within us hides behind the digesting stomach, behind the skin that still enjoys the recent shower and the sensation of fine linen, the mouth that smokes, the eye that takes delight in bare shoulders and bright lights, he repeated his prayer with less conviction, no longer really believing in the miracle that would reverse the psychological law of his inconstancy, just as difficult to circumvent as the physical laws of gravitation or of death" (Dupee 144).

2 Charles I and the Duke of Richmond were beheaded in 1649 at the culminating moment of the Civil War in England.

3 The words between brackets were omitted from the 1949 translation.

4 I have taken the liberty of changing Manheim's translation here and there when I felt that a different wording would be more faithful to the original. The French original is in *Corr.* 2: 76–77.

5 For Proust's respectful but cautious attitude toward theosophy, see his letter of April 28, 1918, to Lionel Hauser in *Corr.* 17: 213–214.

6 This conception of truth-seeking is cogently analyzed by Benedetto Fontana in "Politics, Philosophy, and Modernity in Gramsci," *The Philosophical Forum* 29, nos. 3–4, (Spring/Summer 1998): 104–118, and in an as yet unpublished essay, "What is Truth: Modernity and Hegemony in Gramsci," presented at the International Gramsci Conference, Cagliari, Sardinia, April 15–18, 1997.

7 The conceptual origins of the idea of a "*moi intérieur*" can be traced, in Proust's case, primarily to Pascal and to Henri Bergson.

8 This key idea of Marx in the *Grundrisse* is nicely developed by Sayre in his *Solitude in Society*.

9 The first of Baudelaire's *Petits poèmes en prose* is titled "*L'Étranger*," and is quite different from Proust's in its conception of what is "strange" or foreign; there is a connection nonetheless between the two, which is their emphasis on the primacy of the spiritual: in Proust, through the concept of the soul, in Baudelaire, in the evocation of clouds as evanescent symbols of spiritual longing and beauty.

10 Frank Lentricchia's phrase where he describes "logocentrism" as aimed at "protect[ing] the ideality of meaning by inventing a residence for ideality--the interior of a consciousness shielded from all exterior contaminations" (1980, 177).

Chapter 8

1 As cited by Jonathan Culler in *Structuralist Poetics,* p. 139, where he mentions Kristeva's *Semiotiké: Recherches pour une sémanalyse* (Paris: Seuil, 1969), 146.

2 *Le Mercure de France* (June 1894): 117–122.

3 Baudelaire as cited and translated by John Middleton Murry in "Baudelaire," in Henri Peyre ed., *Baudelaire: A Collection of Critical Essays* (Englewood Cliffs.

N. J.: Prentice-Hall, 1962), 107. In a letter of 1918, Proust expressed this idea with virtually the same words as Baudelaire. In praising his correspondent, Lionel Hauser, Proust wrote that "another reason why praise is due you is that you have understood that all reform would be vain if it were not first a reform of the individual himself, if it were not an interior reform" *(Corr* 17: 212).

4 Another short story by Proust with a theme similar to that of "*Mélancolique villégiature*" is "*L'Indifférent*" in which we find a treatment of love as degrading obsession that foreshadows Swann's "love" for Odette in the *Recherche* and the narrator's emotional involvements first with Gilberte and then with Albertine. Evidently Proust did not think that this story was worthy of inclusion in *PJ* (it appeared in *La Vie contemporaine et revue parisienne* (March 1, 1896): 428–439.

5 In 1888 the seventeen-year-old Proust won a de luxe edition of the *Œuvres de La Bruyère* ed. Gustave Servois Album (Paris: Hachette, 1882) as a school prize for French composition (*Marcel Proust*, Usuels de la Réserve, 14).

6 Roger Francillon, "Proust und La Bruyère," in Marcel Proust, *Bezüge und Strukturen: Studien zu Les Plaisirs et les Jours*, ed. Luzius Keller, 52–74.

Chapter 9

1 John Ruskin, *La Bible d'Amiens*, trans. and ed. Marcel Proust (Paris: Mercure de France, 1904), and John Ruskin, *Sésame et les lys*, trans. and ed. Marcel Proust (Paris: Mercure de France, 1906).

2 The term is used by Richard Macksey in his Introduction to Marcel Proust, *On Reading Ruskin* (New Haven: Yale University Press, 1987), xv.

3 Proust met Monet on at least one occasion, in July 1895, when with Reynaldo Hahn he visited Madeleine Lemaire in Dieppe and was introduced to the great impressionist painter: *Album Proust: iconographie réunie et commentée par Pierre Clarac et André Ferré* (Paris: Gallimard, 1965), 145–146. A trace of this meeting and of the effect on Proust of the Normandy landscape in the summer of 1895 can be seen in the prose poem "Sous-Bois" ("Forest scene" in the Dupee edition of *PJ*), which is dated "Petit-Abbeville (Dieppe), August 1895."

4 In his essay "*Ruskin à Notre-Dame d'Amiens*," Proust, like Monet studying the cathedral of Rouen, dwells lovingly on the effects of sunlight on the cathedral of Amiens at different times during the day.

5 This is not the only article Proust devoted to Rembrandt. See "Rembrandt" (*CSB* 659–664).

6 I refer here to "*Journées de pèlerinage: Ruskin à Notre-Dame d'Amiens, à Rouen, etc.*" and to "*John Ruskin*," *CSB* 69–105 and 105–141. The first appeared originally in *Le Mercure de France* (April 1900): 50–88, the second appeared in the *Gazette des Beaux Arts* (April 1900): 310–318, and (August 1900): 135–146.

Chapter 10

1 A photocopy of these fragments, in three volumes, is in the Kolb-Proust Archive for Research at the Library of the University of Illinois in Urbana. The originals are kept in the manuscript room of the B.N.

2 The narrator of *JS* stops on a number of occasions to remind us that his basic task is to tell a story. Two examples occur in chapters titled "Henri de Réveillon" (167) and "From Sea to Mountain" (398).

3 Jacques Barzun, "To the Rescue of Romanticism," *The American Scholar* 9: (1940):147, and Henri Peyre, *Romanticism and the Modern Ego* (Boston: Little Brown, 1943).

4 This "Romantic" reading of Proust was brilliantly articulated by P.-V. Zima, in his *Le Désir du mythe: Une lecture sociologique de Marcel Proust* (Paris: Nizet, 1973). One of the points Zima makes about Proust's romantic sensibilities is that, like so many of his counterparts in nineteenth-century European literature, the character Jean Santeuil turns away from the world of "reality and action" in order to realize himself in the realm of the spirit, in art, philosophy, and meditation. He is caught by the "antinomy" between the "objectivity of the real and the subjectivity of the dream." In the clash between concrete reality and the dream, one must reverse relations to save the dream, hence the inevitable withdrawal from practical political concerns. But Zima's larger and overarching point is that *JS* is presided over throughout by what he calls "a realm of myths where the birth and the death of myth are the essential events, the principal subjects of the novel's discourse" (94). Proust's world in *JS*, Zima concludes, does not really have the solidity of a Balzacian construction, but rather is composed of "myths, illusions, fabrications, and an attachment to form." The "mythic" formulations that dominate *JS* also affect the treatment of social classes, where the characteristic features of these classes tend to become absorbed by a sort of all-encompassing "feudal" atmosphere and mystique that blur the real historical distinctions involved.

5 Proust's conception of good and evil in *JS* is a rather narrow one, especially if considered in relation to what we have come to know as evil in the twentieth century. It is expressed indirectly towards the end of the book, where Proust introduces the figure of a middle-aged writer named Silvain Bastelle, whose musings on life and art are sprinkled with reflections on good and evil that probably come close to Proust's own views on the matter. For Bastelle, the narrator tells us, "evil" is whatever "dries up" the sources of creative inspiration, while "good" is whatever does not weaken it. What he calls "the real, the basic evil" is the squandering of time on trivial social amusements: "Evil for him became what hardened the spirit by making it prey to noble names, witty talk, material facts, formulae learned parrot-wise, commonplace desires, aimless to-ings and fro-ings, and idle chit-chat" (718–719).

6 An Italian critic, Alberto Beretta Anguissola (1971) caught this aspect of Proust's world view quite well when, in response to the 1971 Pléiade edition of *JS*, he cited Proust's mistrust of political thought and action. For Proust, the intellectual

considered as a "creator of universality and history" had to "make himself ignorant" in order to realize himself in the spiritual and creative domains. Looked at in a broad sense, Anguissola said, what was at work in Proust was "a real refusal of the political and social dimension of human existence." See Alberto Beretta Anguissola, "Storia, scienza, e società in Proust," *Paragone* 22: 260 (October 1971): 61–89.

7   Honoré de Balzac, *Le Lys dans la vallée*, ed. Nicole Mozet (Paris: Flammarion, 1972), 61–62. My translation.

8   In a letter to Hahn dated March 1896 by Kolb, Proust alluded to "the beginning of his novel" in the following manner: "How good you are Reynaldo. Mother was touched by your kindness and I thank you and embrace you with all my heart. I had brought you some little things by me and the beginning of the novel which Yeatman himself, at whose home I was writing, found very poney. You'll help me to correct what would be too much of that. I want you to be in it all the time but like a god in disguise that no mortal recognizes. Without [such a device] you would be obliged to write 'tear this up' all over the novel." *Corr.* II, 52. "Poney" was one of the words Hahn liked to use to designate Proust.

Bibliography

A. Manuscripts and Rare Books

Proust, Marcel. *Les Plaisirs et les jours*. B.N. Reserved and rare book division: Rés ^{m}y^2 179. Paris: Calmann Lévy, 1896.

———. Manuscript of *Les Plaisirs et les jours*. B.N. Manuscript division: 16612.

———. Proof pages of *Les Plaisirs et les jours*. B.N. Manuscript division:16614

———. *Marcel Proust*–Usuels de la Réserve. B.N. Reserved and rare book division, 1965.

———. Manuscript of *Jean Santeuil*. Kolb-Proust Archive for Research, Room 429 Main Library of the University of Illinois, Urbana.

———. Manuscripts and other materials in the Rare Book and Manuscript room of the University of Illinois Library, Urbana.

Delafosse, Léon. *Six Mélodies*. B.N. folio Département de la Musique: Vm7 12117

B. Works by Proust consulted other than *Les Plaisirs et les jours*

Proust. Marcel. "Pendant le carême." *Le Mensuel*, 5 (February 1891): 45.

———. "Choses normandes." *Le Mensuel*, 12 (September 1891): 5–7.

———. "Souvenir." *Le Mensuel*, 12 (September 1891): 7–9.

———. "L'Irréligion d'Etat." *La Revue Blanche*, 3 (May 1891): 91–92.

———. La Conférence parlementaire de la rue Serpente." *La Revue Blanche*, 7 (February 1893): 220–222.

———. "Avant la nuit." *La Revue Blanche*, 26 (December 1893): 381–385.

———. "Contre l'obscurité." *La Revue Blanche*. (July 15, 1896).

———. "Necrologie."*La Chronique des Arts et de la Curiosité*, V 4, (January 27, 1900): 35–36.

———. "Notes et souvenirs: Pèlerinages ruskiniens en France." *Le Figaro*. (February 13, 1900): 5.

———. "Ruskin à Notre-Dame d'Amiens." *Le Mercure de France*. 24, (April 1900): 56–88.

———. "John Ruskin." *La Gazette des Beaux Arts*. (April 1, 1900): 310–318.

———. "John Ruskin." *La Gazette des Beaux Arts*. (August 1, 1900): 135–146.

———. *Chroniques*. Ed. by Robert Proust. Paris: Gallimard, 1927.

——— and André Gide. *Autour de la Recherche-lettres*. Préface de Pierre Assouline. Paris: Editions Complexes, 1949.

———. *Jean Santeuil*. 3 vols. Ed. by Bernard de Fallois. Paris: Gallimard, 1952.

———. *Correspondance avec sa mère, 1887–1905*. Ed. by Philip Kolb. Paris: Plon, 1953.

———. *Contre Sainte-Beuve-nouveaux mélanges*. Ed. by Bernard de Fallois. Paris: Gallimard, 1954.

———. *Jean Santeuil*. Trans. by Gerard Hopkins. New York: Simon and Schuster, 1956.

———. *Lettres à Reynaldo Hahn*. Ed. by Philip Kolb. Paris: Gallimard, 1956.

——— *Textes retrouvés*. Ed. by Philip Kolb and Larkin B. Price. Urbana: University of Illinois Press, 1968.

———. *Jean Santeuil*. Ed. by Yves Sandre. Paris: Gallimard, 1971.

———. *Contre Sainte-Beuve, précédé de Pastiches et mélanges et suivi d'Essais et articles*. Ed. by Pierre Clarac and Yves Sandre. Paris: Gallimard, 1971.

———. *Correspondance*. 21 vols. Ed. by Philip Kolb. Paris: Librairie Plon, 1976–1993. . .

———. *L'Indifférent*. Ed. by Philip Kolb. Paris: Gallimard, 1978.

———.*Selected Letters 1880–1903*. Ed. by Philip Kolb, trans. by Ralph Manheim. Garden City: Doubleday, 1983.

———. *On Reading Ruskin*. Trans. and ed. by Jean Autret et al. New Haven: Yale University Press, 1987.

———. *A la recherche du temps perdu*. 4 vols. Ed. by Jean-Ives Tadié et al. Paris: Gallimard, 1987–1989.

———. *Ecrits de jeunesse 1887–1895*. Ed. by Anne Borrel et al. Illiers-Combray: Institut Marcel Proust International, Société des Amis de Marcel Proust, 1991.

———. *Mon cher petit-lettres à Lucien Daudet (1895–1897, 1904, 1907, 1908)*. Ed. by Michel Bonduelle. Paris: Gallimard, 1991.

———. *In Search of Lost Time*. 6 vols. Trans. by C.K. Scott, Terence Kilmartin, D.J. Enright. New York: Random House, 1992.

C. Editions and Translations of *Les Plaisirs et les jours*

1. French editions
Proust, Marcel. *Les Plaisirs et les jours*. Paris: Calmann Lévy, 1896.

———. *Les Plaisirs et les jours*, préface par Anatole France. Paris: Nouvelle Revue Française, 1924.

———. *Œuvres complètes de Marcel Proust*, tome 9, *Les Plaisirs et les jours*. Paris: Gallimard, 1935.

———. *Les Plaisirs et les jours*. Paris: Gallimard, 1950.

———. *Jean Santeuil précédé de Les Plaisirs et les jours*. Ed. by Pierre Clarac and Yves Sandre. Paris: Gallimard, 1971.

———. *Les Plaisirs et les jours suivi de l'Indifférent et autres textes*. Ed. by Thierry Laget. Paris: Gallimard, 1993.

2. Translations
a. English
———. *Pleasures and Regrets*. Preface by D.J. Enright, trans. by Louise Varese. London: Peter Owen, 1948 (subsequently republished 1976 and 1986).

———. *Pleasures and Days and Other Writings by Marcel Proust*. Ed. by F. W. Dupee, trans. by Louise Varese et al. Garden City: Doubleday Books, 1957.

b. German
———. *Tage der Freuden*. Trans. by Ernst Weiß. Berlin: Proplyäen Verlag, 1926.

———. *Freuden und Tage, und andere Erzählungen und Skizzen aus den Jahren 1892–1896*. Ed. and trans. by Luzius Keller. Frankfurt-am-Main: Suhrkamp Verlag, 1988.

———. *Freuden und Tage*. Ed. and trans. by Luzius Keller. Frankfurt-am-Main: Insel Verlag, 1997.

j. Greek
———. *Diavazontas*. Trans. by Petros Papadopulos and Koster Tsitaraku. Athens: Estia, 1985.

i. Hebrew
———. *Ta 'anugot we-yamin-kitavim*. Trans. by Yoram Bronovsky. Tel Aviv: Zmora-Bitan-Modan, 1979.

e. Italian
———. *I piaceri e i giorni*. Trans. by Marise Ferro. Milan: Ultra, 1946.

———. *I piaceri e i giorni*. Trans. by Marise Ferro. Milan: Sugar, 1968 (reprinted in 1976 by Garzanti).

d. Japanese
———. *Tanoshimi To Hibi*. Trans. by Han'ya Kubota. Tokyo: Kadokawa Shoten, 1960. Reprinted in 1965, 1972, 1975, 1986, the last published by Fukutake Shoten.

h. Portuguese
———. *Os praceres e os días*. Trans. by Fernando Py. Rio De Janeiro: Nova Fronteira, 1983.

f. Slovak

———. *Rozkose a dni.* Trans. by Anton Vantuck. Bratislava: Slov. spic, 1969.

g. Spanish

———. *Obras completas.* Trans. by Consuelo Bergés et al. Barcelona: Plaza & Janés, 1971.

———. *Los placeres y los días. Parodias y miscelánea.* Trans. by Consuelo Bergés. Madrid: Alianza Editorial, 1975.

c. Swedish

———. *Noveller.* Trans. by Karin Bong. Stockholm: Tiden, 1956 (reprinted in 1965).

D. Selected Criticism on *Les Plaisirs et les jours*

Bailey, Ninette. "Couleur picturale et couleur poétique dans *Les Plaisirs et les jours.*" *BSAP*, 16 (1966): 411-422.

Brée, Germaine. "Une Etude du style de Proust dans *Les Plaisirs et les jours.*" *The French Review*, xv, 5 (1942): 401–409.

Costil, Pierre. "La Construction musicale de la *Recherche.*" *BSAP*, 8 (1958): 469–489, and 9 (1959): 83–110.

———. "Proust et la poésie de la fleur." *BSAP*, 13 (1963): 20–41.

Daum, Pierre. *Les Plaisirs et les jours de Marcel Proust–étude d'un recueil.* Paris: Nizet, 1993.

Fraisse, Luc. "Discours sur le style: Marcel Proust lecteur de Buffon." *BSAP*, 38 (1988): 29–36.

Gicquel, Bernard. "La Composition des *Plaisirs et les jours.*" *BSAP*, 10 (1960): 249–261.

Henry, Anne. "*Les Plaisirs et les jours*: chronologie et métempsychoses." *Cahiers Marcel Proust* 6 (1973): 69–93.

Johnson, Jr., J. Theodore. "Proust's Early Portraits de Peintres." *Comparative Literature Studies*, iv, 4 (1967): 397–408.

Keller, Luzius, ed. *Bezüge und Strukturen–Studien zu Les Plaisirs et les jours.* Frankfurt-am-Main: Insel Verlag, 1987.

Kingcaid, Renée A. "A Hothouse of Orchids: Proust's *Les Plaisirs et les jours*." diss., Ohio State University, 1982.

———. *Neurosis and Narrative–The Decadent Short Fiction of Proust, Lorrain, and Rachilde*. Carbondale: Southern Illinois University Press, 1992.

Paganini, Maria. "Intertextuality and the Strategy of Desire: Proust's 'Mélancolique Villégiature de Mme de Breyves'." *Yale French Studies*, 57 (1979): 136–163.

Placella, Paola. *Motivi proustiani. Da Les Plaisirs et les jours alla Recherche*. Naples: Giannini editore, 1976.

Price, Larkin B. *Materials for a Critical Edition of Marcel Proust's Les Plaisirs et les jours*. diss., University of Wisconsin, 1965.

Rolli, Alexandre. "A propos des illustrations de Proust." *BSAP*, 21 (1971): 1178–1179.

Sarkany, Stéphane. "Pragmatique et réception de *Les Plaisirs et les jours*," in *Proust et le texte producteur*, ed. John D. Erickson and Irène Pagès. Guelph, Ontario: University of Guelph, 1980.

Weiss, Véronique. *Les Plaisirs et les jours ou l'écriture double*. diss., New York University, 1995.

E. Selected Criticism on *Jean Santeuil*

Adam, Antoine. "Notes sur deux livres récents: Marcel Proust, *Jean Santeuil*." *Revue des sciences humaines*. (October–December 1952): 359–365.

Anguissola, Alberto Beretta. "Storia, scienza e società in Proust." *Paragone*, 22, 260 (October 1971): 61–89.

Baudino, Catherine Anne. "A Narrative Analysis of *Jean Santeuil*." diss., London University, 1976.

Bell, William Stewart. "The Prototype for Proust's *Jean Santeuil*." *Modern Language Notes*, 53, 1 (January 1958): 46–50.

Brée, Germaine. "From *Jean Santeuil* to *Time Regained*." *Bucknell Review*, 6, 3 (December 1956): 16–21.

———. "*Jean Santeuil*: An Appraisal." *L'Esprit Créateur*, 5, 1 (Spring 1965): 14–25.

Carassus, Emilien. "L'Affaire Dreyfus et l'espace romanesque: de *Jean Santeuil* à la *Recherche du temps perdu*." *Revue d'Histoire Littéraire de la France*. 5–6 (1971): 836–853.

Guaraldo, Enrico. "Per una storia del *Jean Santeuil*." *Paragone*, 22, 260 (October 1971): 89–126.

———. "Il volto nuovo del *Jean Santeuil* di Proust." *Paragone*, 23, 272 (October 1972): 51–67.

Hokari, Mizuho. "Proust et Gustave Moreau–à propos de l'échec de *Jean Santeuil*." *Etudes de Langue et de Littérature Françaises*. 4 (1969): 34–48.

Kolb, Philip. "Proust's Portrait of Jaurès in *Jean Santeuil*." *French Studies*, xv, Oxford: Basil Blackwell, 338–349.

———. "Historique du premier roman de Proust." *Saggi e ricerche di letteratura francese*, iv. Turin: Bottega d'Erasmo, 1963, 215–277.

Marc-Lipianski, Mireille. *La Naissance du monde proustien dans Jean Santeuil*. Paris: Nizet, 1974.

Mauriac, Claude. "Naissance de Proust." *Hommes et idées d'aujourd'hui*. Paris: Albin-Michel, 1953, 219–243.

O'Brien, Justin. "*Jean Santeuil*." *The French literary Horizon*. New Brunswick: Rutgers University Press, 1967, 29–32.

Placella, Paola. "Motivi della *Recherche* dans *Jean Santeuil* and *Contre Sainte-Beuve*."*Trimestre*, vii, 1-4 (January–December 1973): 1–36.

Price, Larkin B. "Marcel Proust's 'Dieu déguisé': The Artist Myth in *Jean Santeuil*." *L'Esprit Créateur*, 9, 1 (Spring 1971): 61–73.

Saraydar, Alma. "Proust disciple de Stendhal–les avant-textes d'un Amour de Swann dans *Jean Santeuil*." *Archives de Lettres Modernes*. Paris: Lettres Modernes, 1980, 1–88.

Tupinier, Georgette. "La Digitale de *Jean Santeuil*." *Revue d'Histoire Littéraire de la France*. 5–6 (1971): 950–964.

F. Biographical, Critical, and Historical Works Consulted

Abrams, M.H. *A Glossary of Literary Terms*, 6th ed. New York: Holt, Rinehart and Winston Inc., 1981.

Adam, Antoine. "Notes sur deux livres récents: Marcel Proust, *Jean Santeuil. Revue des sciences humaines.* (October–December 1952): 359–365.

Albaret, Céleste. *Monsieur Proust: Souvenirs recueillis par Georges Belmont.* Paris: Editions Robert Laffont, 1973.

Alden, Douglas W. "Proust's Duel." *Modern Language Notes*, 2 (1938): 104–106.

———. "Proust." *Gay and Lesbian Literature.* Ed. by Sharon Malinovski. Detroit-London: St. James Press, 1994.

Althusser, Louis. *Lenin and Philosophy and Other Essays.* Trans. by Ben Brewster. London: New Left Books, 1971.

Anguissola, Alberto Beretta. "Storia, scienza e società in Proust." *Paragone*, 22, 260 (1971): 61–89.

Apter, Emily and William Pietz, eds. *Fetishism as Cultural Discourse.* Ithaca: Cornell University Press, 1993.

Arvon, Henri. *Marxist Esthetics.* Trans. by Helen R. Lane. Ithaca: Cornell University Press, 1973.

Auchincloss, Louis. "Proust's Picture of Society." *Partisan Review*, 4 (1960): 690–701.

Aurier, G.-Aubert. "Le Symbolisme en peintre: Paul Gauguin." *Le Mercure de France.* (March 1891): 189–191.

———. "Renoir." *Le Mercure de France* . (August 1891): 103–106.

Autret, Jean. *L'Influence de Ruskin sur la vie, les idées et l'œuvre de Marcel Proust.* Geneva-Lille: Drozet Fiard, 1955.

Bailey, Ninette. "Couleur picturale et couleur poétique dans *Les Plaisirs et les Jours.*" *BSAP* (1966): 411–422.

Bakhtin, M.M., and Medvedev, P.N. *The Formal Method in Literary Scholarship.* Trans. by Albert J. Wehrle. Baltimore: Johns Hopkins University Press, 1978.

―――. *The Dialogic Imagination*. Ed. Michael Holquist, trans. by Caryl Emerson and Michael Holquist. Austin: University of Texas Press, 1981.

Bal, Mieke. *The Mottled Screen: Reading Proust Visually*. Trans. by Anna-Louise Milne. Stanford: Stanford University Press, 1997.

Bardèche, Maurice. *Marcel Proust Romancier*, vol. 1. Paris: Les Sept Couleurs, 1971.

Barker, Richard H. *Marcel Proust: A Biography*. New York: Criterion Books, 1958.

Barnes, Susan J. and Arthur K. Wheelock, Jr. eds. *Van Dyck 350*. Washington: National Gallery of Art, 1994.

Barrès, Maurice. *Un Homme libre*. Paris: Emile Paul, 1912 ed.

Barthes, Roland et al. eds. *Recherche de Proust*. Paris: Editions du Seuil, 1980.

Baudelaire, Charles. *L'Art romantique*. Ed. by Lloyd James Austin. Paris: Garnier-Flammarion, 1968.

―――. *Petits poèmes en prose—Le Spleen de Paris*. Paris: Classiques Garnier, 1980.

―――. *Les Fleurs du mal*. Paris: Larousse, 1993.

Baudino, Catherine Anne. "A Narrative Analysis of *Jean Santeuil*." Diss. London University, 1976.

Beauchamp, Louis de. *Le Petit groupe et le grand monde de Marcel Proust*. Paris: Editions Nizet, 1990.

Beckett, Samuel. *Proust*. New York: Grove Press, 1970; (originally published 1931). Reedited by John Calder.

Beerbohm, Sylvia Sarah. "The Cosmic Vision of Marcel Proust in *A la recherche du temps perdu*." Diss. Columbia University, 1968.

Bell, William Stewart. "The Prototype for Proust's *Jean Santeuil*." *Modern Language Notes*, 53, 1 (1958): 46–50.

Benjamin, Walter. *Illuminations*. Ed. Hannah Arendt, trans. Harry Zohn. New York: Shocken Books, 1969.

———. *Understanding Brecht*. Trans. by Anna Bostock. London: New Left Books, 1973.

Billy, Robert de. *Marcel Proust: Lettres et conversations*. Paris: Editions des Portiques, 1930.

Blanc, Olivier. "Un ami de cœur de Marcel Proust: Clément de Maugny." *BSAP*, 45 (1995): 48–61.

Blanche, Jacques-Emile. *Mes Modèles: Barrès, Hardy, Proust, James, Gide, Moore*. Paris: Librairie Stock, 1928.

Bodei, Remo. *La Filosofia nel Novecento*. Rome: Donzelli Editore, 1997.

Boitchidzé, Gaston. "Jugements russes sur Proust." *Europe*, 49 (February–March 1971): 156–166.

Bonnet, Henri. *Alphonse Darlu 1849–1921: le maître de philosophie de Marcel Proust*. Paris: A.G. Nizet, 1961.

———. *Marcel Proust de 1907 à 1914*. Paris: Nizet, 1971.

———. *Les Amours et la sexualité de Proust*. Paris: Nizet, 1985.

———. "La Théorie d'Hans-Robert Jauss confrontée à l'esthétique proustienne." *BSAP* 36 (1986): 451–468.

Borrel, Anne, Alain Senderens, Jean-Bernard Naudin. *Dining with Proust*. New York: Random House, 1992.

Bottomore, Tom et al. eds. *A Dictionary of Marxist Thought*. Cambridge: Harvard University Press, 1983.

Bourget, Paul. Review of Maurice Barrès's *Sous l'œil des barbares*. *La Plume* (May 15, 1890): 83–87.

Bowie, Malcolm. *Freud, Proust and Lacan: Theory as Fiction*. Cambridge: Cambridge University Press, 1987.

———. *The Morality of Proust*. Oxford: Clarendon Press, 1994.

———. *Proust among the Stars*. New York: Columbia University Press. 1998.

Brée, Germaine. "Une Etude du style de Proust dans *Les Plaisirs et les jours*. *The French Review* , 5 (1942): 401–409.

———. "From *Jean Santeuil* to 'Time Regained'." *Bucknell Review.* 6, 3 (December 1956): 16–21.

———. "*Jean Santeuil:* An Appraisal." *L'Esprit Créateur.* 5, 1 (1965): 14–25.

———. *The World of Marcel Proust.* New York: Houghton Miflin, 1966.

Brown, Christopher. *Van Dyck.* Ithaca: Cornell University Press, 1983.

Brunel, Pierre. et al. eds. *Histoire de la littérature française, XIXe et XXe siècle.* Paris: Bordas, 1972.

Brunet, Etienne. *Le Vocabulaire de Proust.* Geneva-Paris: Slatkine-Champion, 1983.

Bucknall, Barbara J. *The Religion of Art in Proust.* Urbana: University of Illinois Press, 1969.

Buisine, Alain. *Proust et ses lettres.* Lille: Presses Universitaires de Lille, 1983.

Buttigieg, Joseph A. *A Portrait of the Artist in Different Perspective.* Athens, Ohio: Ohio State University Press, 1987.

Cahiers Marcel Proust nouvelle série, 3, *Textes Retrouvés.* Ed. by Philip Kolb with a bibliography of Proust's published writings from 1892 to 1971. Paris: Gallimard (1971): 379–408.

Canavaggia, Jeanne. *Proust et la politique.* Paris: Librairie Nizet. 1986.

Carassus, Emilien. *Le Snobisme et les lettres françaises de Paul Bourget à Marcel Proust.* Paris: A. Colin, 1966.

———. "L'Affaire Dreyfus et l'espace romanesque: de *Jean Santeuil* à la *Recherche du temps perdu.*" *Revue d'Histoire Littéraire de la France.* 5–6 (1971): 836–853.

Carter, William C. *The Proustian Quest.* New York: New York University Press, 1992.

———. *Marcel Proust—A Life.* New Haven: Yale University Press, 2000.

Caudwell, Christopher. *Illusion and Reality: A Study of the Sources of Poetry.* New York: International Publishers, 1937.

———. *Romance and Realism: A Study in English Bourgeois Literature*. Ed. by Samuel Hynes. Princeton: Princeton University Press, 1970.

Cattaui, Georges. "Marcel Proust and the Jews". *The Jewish Review* 3 (1932–1933): 66–75.

———. ed. *Entretiens sur Marcel Proust*. Paris and La Haye: Mouton & Co., 1966.

Caws, Mary Ann and Eugène Nicole eds. *Reading Proust Now*. New York: Peter Lang, 1990.

Chaleyssin, Patrick. *Robert de Montesquiou mécène et dandy*. Paris: Editions d'art Somogy, 1992.

Chantal, René de. *Marcel Proust critique littéraire*, vol. 1. Montréal: Les Presses Universitaires de Montréal, 1967.

Clarac, Pierre and André Ferré eds. *Album Proust: Iconographie réunie et commentée*. Paris: Gallimard, 1965.

Clermont-Tonnerre, Elizabeth de. *Robert de Montesquiou et Marcel Proust*. Paris: E. Flammarion, 1925.

Cocking, J.M. *Proust*. New Haven: Yale University Press, 1956.

Collet, Georges-Paul. "Marcel Proust et Jacques-Emile Blanche." *BSAP*, 24 (1974): 1839–1864.

Compagnon, Antoine. *La Troisième République des lettres*. Paris: Editions du Seuil, 1983.

———. *Proust entre deux siècles*. Paris: Editions du Seuil, 1989.

———. *Proust between Two Centuries*. Trans. by Richard E. Goodkin. New York: Columbia University Press, 1992.

Costil, Pierre. "La Construction musicale de la *Recherche*." *BSAP* 8 (1958): 469–489, and 9 (1959): 83–110.

———. "Proust et la poésie de la fleur." *BSAP* 13 (1963): 20–41.

Courtial, Marie-Thèrese. "La Vision impressioniste de la mer dans la *Recherche du temps perdu*." *BSAP* 25 (1975): 267–276.

Craig, David Ed. *Marxists on Literature: An Anthology*. New York: Penguin, 1975.

Culler, Jonathan. *Structuralist Poetics*. Ithaca: Cornell University Press, 1975.

Curtis, Jean-Louis. "Proust et Ruskin." *BSAP* 45 (1995): 9–18.

Daniel, George P. "Marcel Proust, le Moyen Âge et Pierre Chastellain." *BSAP* 18 (1968): 703–706.

Daum, Pierre. *Les Plaisirs et les jours, de Marcel Proust: étude d'un recueil*. Paris: Nizet, 1993.

De Botton, Alain. *How Proust Can Change your Life*. New York: Pantheon, 1997.

Deffoux, Léon. *Le Pastiche littéraire des origines à nos jours*. Paris: Librairie Delagrave, 1932.

Delage, Roger. "Reynaldo Hahn et Marcel Proust." *BSAP* 26 (1976): 229–246.

Deleuze, Gilles. *Proust et les signes*. Paris: Presses Universitaires de France, 1964.

De Man, Paul. *Allegories of Reading*. New Haven: Yale University Press, 1979.

Dombroski, Robert. *L'Esistenza ubbidiente: letterati italiani sotto il fascismo*. Naples: Guida editori, 1984.

———. *Properties of Writing: Ideological Discourse in Modern Italian Fiction*. Baltimore: The Johns Hopkins University Press, 1994.

Doubrovsky, Serge. *La Place de la madeleine: écriture et fantasme chez Proust*. Paris: Mercure de France, 1974.

Dreyfus, Robert. *Souvenirs sur Marcel Proust, avec des lettres inédites de Proust*. Paris: Simon Kra, 1926. (also published by Grasset, 1926)

Duby, Georges ed. *Histoire de la France de 1852 à nos jours*. Paris: Larousse, 1989.

Dynes, Wayne R. and Donaldson, Stephen eds. *Homosexual Themes in Literary Studies*. New York and London: Garland Publishing Co., 1992

Eagleton, Terry. *Marxism and Literary Criticism*. Los Angeles: University of California Press, 1976.

———. *Criticism & Ideology: A Study in Marxist Literary Theory.* London: Verso, 1978.

———. *Ideology: An Introduction.* London-New York: Verso, 1991.

Eco, Umberto. *Opera aperta.* Milan: Bompiani, 1976.

Eliot, T.S. *Selected Essays.* New York: Harcourt, Brace and Co., 1950.

Ellison, David R. *The Reading of Proust.* Baltimore: Johns Hopkins University Press, 1984.

Emerson, Ralph Waldo. *Self-Reliance and Other Essays.* New York: Dover Publications, 1993.

Erickson, John D. and Pagès, Irène. *Proust et le texte producteur.* Ontario: University of Guelph Press, 1980.

Europe: Centenaire de Marcel Proust. (August–September 1970).

Everdell, William R. *The First Moderns.* Chicago: The University of Chicago Press, 1997.

Everman, Anthony Albert. *Lilies and Sesame: The Orient, Inversion, and Artistic Creation in A la recherche du temps perdu.* New York: Peter Lang Publishing, Inc., 1998.

Ferré, André. *Les Années de collège de Marcel Proust.* Paris: Gallimard, 1959.

Fiser, Emeric. *Le Symbole littéraire: essais sur la signification du symbole chez Wagner, Baudelaire, Mallarmé, Bergson et Proust.* Paris: Librairie José Corti (no publication date given).

Foucault, Michel. *The Archaeology of Knowledge & The Discourse on Language.* Trans. A.M. Sheridan Smith. New York: Harper and Row, 1972.

Fraisse, Luc. "Discours sur le style: Marcel Proust lecteur de Buffon." *BSAP* 38 (1988): 29–36.

Francis, Claude and Fernande Gontier. *Marcel Proust et les siens.* Paris: Plon, 1981.

Fromentin, Eugène. *Les Maîtres d'autrefois: Belgique-Hollande.* Ed. Jacques Foucart. Paris: Le Livre de Poche, 1965.

Frye, Northrop. *Anatomy of Criticism—Four Essays.* Princeton: Princeton University Press, 1957.

Gane, Mike. *The Critical Path: An Essay on the Social Context of Literary Criticism*. Bloomington: Indiana University Press, 1971.

———— ed. *Ideological Representation and Power in Social Relations: Literary and Social Theory*. London: Routledge, 1989.

Gavoty, Bernard. *Reynaldo Hahn le musicien de la Belle Epoque*. Paris: Buchet-Chastel, 1976.

Gay, Peter. *Pleasure Wars*. New York: W.W. Norton, 1998.

Genette, Gérard. *Figures III*. Paris: Seuil, 1972.

Gicquel, Bernard. "La Composition des *Plaisirs et les jours*." *BSAP*, 10 (1960): 249–261.

Gide, André. *Journal 1889–1939*. Paris: Gallimard, 1951.

————. *Journal 1939–1949*. Paris: Gallimard, 1954.

————. *The André Gide Reader*. Ed. by David Littlejohn. New York: Knopf, 1971.

Giorgi, G.. "Proust en Italie," *BSAP* 17 (1967): 591–602.

Girard, René ed. *Proust: A Collection of Critical Essays*. Englewood Cliffs: Prentice Hall, 1962.

Goldmann, Lucien. *The Hidden God: A Study of the Tragic Vision in the Pensées of Pascal and the Tragedies of Racine*. Trans. by Philip Thody. London: Routledge and Kegan Paul. New York: The Humanities Press, 1970.

Goodkin, Richard. *Around Proust*. Princeton: Princeton University Press, 1991.

Gourmont, Rémy de. "Là-bas et ailleurs." *Le Mercure de France*. (June 1891): 321–325.

Graham, Victor E. *Bibliographie des études sur Marcel Proust et son œuvre*. Genève: Librairie Droz, 1976.

Gramsci, Antonio. *Selections from The Prison Notebooks*. Ed. and trans. by Quintin Hoare and Geoffrey Nowell-Smith. New York: International Publishers, 1971.

————. *Selections from Cultural Writings*. Ed. by David Forgacs and Geoffrey Nowell Smith, trans. by William Boelhower. Cambridge: Harvard University Press, 1985.

———. *Prison Notebooks*, Vols. I and II. Ed. and trans. by Joseph A. Buttigieg. New York: Columbia University Press, 1992 and 1996.

Grasselli, Margaret Morgan, and Pierre Rosenberg eds. Trans. Thomas D. Bowie. *Watteau 1684–1721*. Paris: Editions des Musées Nationaux, 1984.

Gregh, Fernand. *L'Age d'or: Souvenirs d'enfance et de jeunesse*. Paris: Grasset, 1947.

———. *Mon Amitié avec Marcel Proust*. Paris: Grasset, 1958.

Guaraldo, Enrico. "Per una storia del *Jean Santeuil*." *Paragone* (October 1971): 89–126.

———. "Il volto nuovo del *Jean Santeuil* di Proust." *Paragone* (October 1972): 51–67.

Hahn, Reynaldo. *Notes: Journal d'un musicien*. Paris: Plon, 1933.

———. *Du Chant: Pour la musique*. Paris: Gallimard, 1957.

———. "Douze lettres à Edouard Risler." *BSAP* 43 (1993): 37–57.

Halévy, Daniel. *Pays parisiens*. Paris: Grasset, 1932.

Hanne, Michael. *The Power of the Story: Fiction and Political Change*. Providence and Oxford: Berghahn Books, 1994.

Harrison, Charles, and Paul Wood, *Art in Theory 1900–1990: An Anthology of Changing Ideas*. New York: Blackwell, 1992.

Hassine, Juliette. *Esotérisme et écriture dans l'œuvre de Proust*. Paris: Librairie Minard, 1990.

Hauser, Arnold. *The Social History of Art*, vol. III. Trans. by Stanley Goodman. New York: Vintage Books, Inc., 1957.

Hayes, Jarrod. "Proust in the Tearoom." *PMLA* (October 1995): 992–1005.

Henry, Anne. "*Les Plaisirs et les Jours*: chronologie et métempsychoses." *Cahiers Marcel Proust* 6 (1973): 69–93.

———. *Marcel Proust: Théories pour une esthétique*. Paris: Klincksieck, 1983.

Henrich, Dieter. *Aesthetic Judgment and the Moral Image of the World: Studies in Kant*. Stanford: Stanford Universityy Press, 1992.

Hesiod-Homeric Hymns-Epic Cycle-Homerica. Ed. and trans. by Hugh G. Evelyn-White. Cambridge: Harvard University Press, 1936.

Hirsch, E.D. Jr. *Validity in Interpretation*. New Haven and London: Yale University Press, 1967.

Hokari, Mizuho. "Proust et Gustave Moreau: A propos de l'échec de Jean Santeuil." *Etudes de Langue et de Littérature Françaises*. 4 (1969): 34–48.

Houston, John Porter. *The Shape and Style of Proust's Novel*. Detroit: Wayne State University Press, 1982.

Huas, Jeanine, *L'Homosexualité au temps de Proust*. Donclau: Dinard, 1992.

Hughes, Edward. "The Mapping of Homosexuality in Proust's *Recherche*", *Paragraph* (July 1995).

Huysmans, Joris-Karl. Preface to *A Rebours*. (Paris: René Fasquelle, 1920) i–xxi.

Iacono, Alfonso M. *Le Fétichisme: histoire d'un concept*. Paris: Presses Universitaires de France, 1992.

Isaac, Jules et al. *L'Histoire: La Naissance du monde moderne/1848–1914*. Paris: Hachette, 1961.

Jackson, Elizabeth R. *L'Evolution de la mémoire involontaire dans l'œuvre de Marcel Proust*. Paris: A.G. Nizet, 1966.

Jackson, Anne B. "Les Critiques de la *Revue Blanche*," in *La Revue des Lettres Modernes: Histoire des idées et des littératures*. 4, 25–26 (1957): 1–47.

———. *La Revue Blanche (1889–1903): Origine, influence, bibliographie*. Paris: M.J. Minard-Lettres Modernes, 1960.

Gane, Mike ed. *Ideological Representation and Power in Social Relations: Literary and Social Theory*. London: Routledge, 1989.

Jacobs, Carol. "Walter Benjamin: Image of Proust." *Modern Language Notes*, 86, 6 (December 1971): 910–932.

James, William. *The Varieties of Religious Experience*. New York: The Modern Library (no date of publication)

Jameson, Fredric. *The Political Unconscious: Narrative as a Socially Symbolic Act*. Ithaca: Cornell University Press, 1981.

Jaquillard, Pierre. "Le Paris de Marcel Proust." *BSAP* 7 (1957): 283–306.

Johnson, Jr., J. Theodore. "Proust's Early Portraits de Peintres." *Comparative Literature Studies* 4 (1967): 397–408.

Jullian, Philippe. *Robert de Montesquiou, a fin-de-siècle prince*. Trans. John Haylock and Francis King. London: Seeker and Warburg, 1967.

Kadi, Simone. *La Peinture chez Proust et Baudelaire*. Paris: La Pensée Universelle, 1973.

Kant, Immanuel. *Critique of Pure Reason*. Trans. by J.M.G. Meiklejohn. London: Dent, 1934.

———. *Analytic of the Beautiful: from the Critique of Judgment*. Ed. and trans. by Walter Cerf. Indianapolis and New York: Bobbs Merrill Co., 1963.

———. *Critique of Judgment*. Ed. and trans. by Werner S. Pluhar. Indianapolis: Hackett Publishing Co., 1987.

Keller, Luzius ed. *Bezüge und Strukturen: Studien zu Les Plaisirs et les Jours*. Frankfurt-am-Main: Insel Verlag, 1987.

Kempis, Thomas à. *The Imitation of Christ*. Ed. Harold C. Gardiner, S.J. New York: Doubleday, 1989.

Kingcaid, Renée A. "A Hothouse of Orchids: Proust's *Les Plaisirs et les jours*." diss., Ohio State University, 1982.

———. *Neurosis and Narrative: The Decadent Short Fiction of Proust, Lorrain, and Rachilde*. Carbondale: Southern Illinois University Press, 1992.

Koivisto, Juha, and Veikko Pietilä. "Ideological Powers and Resistance: The Contribution of W.F. Haug and Projekt Ideologie-Theorie." *Rethinking Marxism*, 9, 4 (1996–1997): 40–59.

Kolb, Philip. "Proust's Portrait of Jaurès in *Jean Santeuil*." *French Studies*, XV. Oxford: Basil Blackwell, 338–349.

———. "Historique du premier roman de Proust." *Saggi e ricerche di letteratura francese*, vol. IV. Turin: Bottega d'Erasmo (1963): 215–277.

———. ed. *Cahiers Marcel Proust: Le Carnet de 1908*. Paris: Gallimard, 1976.

Kopp, Richard L. *Marcel Proust as a Social Critic*. Rutherford: Fairleigh Dickinson University Press, 1971.

La Bruyère, Jean de. *Les Caractères précédés des Caractères de Théophraste*. Ed. by Robert Pignarre. Paris: Garnier-Flammarion, 1965).

LaCapra, Dominick. *History and Criticism*. Ithaca: Cornell University Press, 1985.

———. *History, Politics, and the Novel*. Ithaca: Cornell University Press, 1987.

Ladenson, Elisabeth. *Proust's Lesbianism*. Ithaca: Cornell University Press, 1999.

Lagarde, André and Laurent Michard eds. *XIX Siècle: les grands auteurs français du programme—anthologie et histoire littéraire*. Paris: Bordas, 1985.

Landy, Marcia. *Film, Politics, and Gramsci*. Minneapolis: University of Minnesota Press, 1994.

Larrain, Jorge. "Ideology." *A Dictionary of Marxist Thought*. Ed. Tom Bottomore et al. Cambridge: Harvard University Press, 1983.

Lemaître, Henri, et al. *Dictionnaire Bordas de Littérature Française*. Paris: Bordas, 1994.

Lentricchia, Frank. *After the New Criticism*. Chicago: Chicago University Press, 1980.

——— and McLaughlin, Thomas, eds. *Critical Terms for Literary Study*. Chicago: The University of Chicago Press, 1990

Leon, Derrick. *Introduction to Proust: His Life, His Circle and His Work*. London: Kegan Paul, 1940.

Lesage, Laurent. *Marcel Proust and his Literary Friends*. Urbana: University of Illinois Press, 1958.

Linn, John Gaywood. *The Theater in the Fiction of Marcel Proust*. Columbus: Ohio State University Press, 1966.

Loevgren, Sven. *The Genesis of Modernism: Seurat, Gauguin, Van Gogh, and French Symbolism in the 1880s*. Bloomington: Indiana University Press, 1971.

Louria, Yvette. "Proust and Lunacharskii." *Romanic Review* 62 (April 1971): 127–132.

Lukács, Georg. *Realism in Our Time: Literature and the Class Struggle*. New York: Harper, 1964.

———. *History and Class Consciousness: Studies in Marxist Dialectics*. Trans. by Rodney Livingstone. Boston: MIT Press, 1971.

Mallarmé, Stéphane. *Œuvres complètes*. Ed. by Henri Mondor and G. Jean-Aubry. Paris: Gallimard, 1945.

———. *Œuvres*. Ed. by Y.-A. Favre. Paris: Bordas classiques Garnier, 1992.

Marc-Lipianski, Mireille. *La Naissance du monde proustien dans Jean Santeuil*. Paris: Librairie Nizet, 1974.

Martin-Deslias, Noël. *Idéalisme de Proust*. Paris: Les Editions Nagel, 1952.

Martines, Lauro. *Society and History in English Renaissance Verse*. Oxford: Basil Blackwell, 1985.

Marx, Karl and Engels, Frederick. *The German Ideology. Collected Works*, vol 5. New York: International Publishers, 1976.

———. *On Literature and Art*. Moscow: Progress Publishers, 1976.

Mauriac, Claude. "Naissance de Proust." *Hommes et idées d'aujourd'hui*. Paris: Editions Albin-Michel (1953): 219–243.

Maurois, André. *Le Monde de Marcel Proust*. Paris: Hachette, 1960.

Mayer, Denise. *Marcel Proust et la musique d'après sa correspondance*. Paris: La Revue Musicale, 1978.

Mayer, Arno J. *The Perisistence of the Old Regime: Europe to the Great War*. New York: Pantheon, 1981.

McNeece, Lucy Stone. *Art and Politics in Duras' "India Cycle"*. Gainesville: University Press of Florida, 1996.

Megay, Joyce. *Bergson et Proust*. Paris: Librairie Philosophique J. Vrin, 1976.

Michaud, Guy. *La Doctrine symboliste: documents*. Paris: Librairie Nizet, 1947.

Milly, Jean. *Les Pastiches de Proust*. Paris: Armand Colin, 1970.

———. *Proust dans le texte et l'avant-texte*. Paris: Flammarion, 1985.

———. *Proust et le style*. Geneva: Slatkine reprints, 1991 (1st Ed. 1970)

Monod, Silvain. *Pastiches*. Paris: Henri Lefebvre Editeur, 1963.

Montesquiou-Fezensac, Robert de. *Les Chauves souris*. Paris: G. Richard, 1893.

———. *Le Parcours du rêve au souvenir*. Paris: Bibliothèque-Charpentier, 1895.

———. *Les Hortensias bleus*. Paris: Fasqulle, 1896.

———. *Roseaux pensants*. Paris: Fasquelle, 1897.

———. *Les Pas effacés*, 3 Vols. Paris: Emile Paul, 1923.

Moore, Gene M. *Proust and Musil: The Novel as Research Instrument*. New York: Garland Publishing Co., 1985.

Muhlfeld, Lucien. "Chronique de la littérature." *La Revue Blanche* (January 1892): 53–61.

Nattier-Natanson, Evelyn. *Les Amitiés de la Revue Blanche et quelques autres*. Vincennes: Les Editions du Donjon, 1959.

Nattiez, Jean-Jacques. *Wagner Androgyne: A Study in Interpretation*. Trans. by by Stewart Spencer. Princeton: Princeton University Press, 1993.

Nietzsche, Friedrich. *The Birth of Tragedy and Other Writings*. Ed. by Raymond Geuss and Ronald Speirs, trans. by Ronald Speirs. Cambridge: Cambridge University Press, 1999.

Norris, Christopher. *Deconstruction: Theory and Practice*. New York and London: Methuen, 1982.

O'Brien, Justin. "Albertine the Ambiguous: Notes on Proust's Transposition of Sexes." *PMLA* 5 (1949): 933–952

———. "*Jean Santeuil*." *The French Literary Horizon*. New Brunswick: Rutgers University Press (1967): 29–32.

Paganini, Maria. "Intertextuality and the Strategy of Desire: Proust's 'Mélancolique Villégiature de Mme de Breyves.'" *Yale French Studies* 57 (1979): 136–163.

Pagès, Alain. *13 janvier 1898: J.Accuse . . .!* Paris: Librairie Académique Perrin, 1998.

Painter, George D. *Proust: The Early Years*. Boston-Toronto: Little Brown, 1959.

———. *Proust: The Later Years*. Boston: Little Brown, 1965.

Peyre, Henri. *The Contemporary French Novel*. New York: Oxford University Press, 1955.

———, ed. *Baudelaire: A Collection of Critical Essays*. Englewood Cliffs: Prentice-Hall, 1962.

———. *Marcel Proust*. New York: Columbia University Press, 1970.

Phelan, James ed. *Reading Narrative: Form, Ethics, Ideology*. Columbus: Ohio State University Press, 1989.

Pinto, Paolo and Giuseppe Grasso eds. *Proust e la critica italiana*. Rome: Newton Compton editori, 1990.

Piroué, Georges. *Proust et la musique du devenir*. Paris: Editions Denoël, 1960.

Placella, Paola. "Motivi della *Recherche* dans *Jans Santeuil e Contre Sainte-Beuve*." *Trimestre* 1–4 (January–December 1973): 1–36.

———. *Motivi proustiani. Da Les Plaisirs et les Jours alla Recherche*. Naples: Giannini editore, 1976.

Plato. *Symposium*. Trans. by Robin Waterfield. Oxford: Oxford University Press, 1994.

Pommier, Jean. *La Mystique de Proust*. Geneva: Librairie Droz, 1968.

Poulet, Georges. "Proust and Human Time." *Proust: A Collection of Critical Essays*. Englewood Cliffs: Prentice-Hall, Inc., 1962.

Price, Larkin B. *Materials for a Critical Edition of Marcel Proust's Les Plaisirs et les jours*. Diss., University of Wisconsin, 1965.

———. "Marcel Proust's 'Dieu déguisé': The Artist Myth in *Jean Santeuil*." *L'Esprit Créateur*. 9, 1 (1971): 61–73.

———. ed. *Marcel Proust: A Critical Panorama*. Urbana: University of Illinois Press, 1973.

———. *A Check List of the Proust Holdings at the University of Illinois Library at Urbana-Champaign*. Urbana: A Joint Publication of the University of Illinois Library and the Graduate School of Library Science, 1975.

Quint, Léon-Pierre. *Marcel Proust: sa vie, son œuvre*. Paris: Simon Kra, 1925.

Raczymov, Henri. *Le Paris littéraire et intime de Marcel Proust: photographies de Martine Mouchy*. Paris: Editions Parigramme, 1997.

Raimond, Michel. "Proust et Balzac." *BSAP* (1967): 742–769.

Renauld, Pierre. "Psychologie proustienne et conscience mythique."*BSAP* (1971): 1157–1164.

Rièse, Laure. *Les Salons littéraires parisiens du Second Empire à nos jours*. Toulouse: Privat Editeur, 1962.

Rivers, Julius Edwin. *Proust and the Art of Love: the Aesthetics of Sexuality in the Life, Times, and Art of Marcel Proust*. New York: Columbia University Press, 1980.

Robert, Louis de. *Comment débuta Marcel Proust: Lettres inédites*. Paris: Gallimard, 1925.

Rolli, Alexandre. "A propos des illustrations de Proust." *BSAP* (1971): 1178–1179.

Rosenberg, Pierre. *Chardin, 1699–1779*. Bloomington: Indiana University Press, 1979.

Ruskin, John. *The Art Criticism of John Ruskin*. Ed. by Robert L. Herbert. Garden City: Doubleday, 1964.

———. *Praeterita*. Ed. by Kenneth Clark. New York: Oxford University Press, 1989.

Said, Edward. *The World, the Text and the Critic*. Cambridge: Harvard University Press, 1983.

———. *Culture and Imperialism*. New York: Alfred A. Knopf, 1993

Saint-Pol-Roux. "De l'art magnifique." *Le Mercure de France* (February 1892): 97–104.

Saraydar, Alma. "Proust disciple de Stendhal: les avant-textes d'un Amour de Swann dans *Jean Santeuil*." *Archives de Lettres Modernes*. Paris: Lettres Modernes, (1980): 1–88.

Sarkany, Stéphane. "Pragmatique et réception de *Les Plaisirs et les jours*," in *Proust et le texte producteur*, ed. by John D. Erickson and Irène Pagès. Guelph, Ontario: University of Guelph, 1980.

Sarraute, Nathalie. *L'Ere du soupçon*. Paris: Gallimard, 1956.

Sartre, Jean-Paul. *Qu'est-ce que la littérature?*. Paris: Gallimard, 1948

———. *Literature and Existentialism* (original title *What is Literature?*).Trans. Bernard Frechtman. New York: Carol Publishing Group, 1994.

Sayre, Robert. *Solitude in Society: A Sociological Study in French Literature*. Cambridge: Harvard University Press, 1978.

Schapiro, Meyer. *Impressionism:Reflections and Perceptions*. New York: George Braziller, 1997.

Schom, Alan. *Emile Zola: A Bourgeois Rebel*. London: Macdonald Queens Anne Press, 1987.

Schopenhauer, Arthur. *Philosophical Writings*. Ed. Wolfgang Schirmacher. New York: Continuum, 1996.

Sedgwick, Eve Kosofsky. *Tendencies*. Durham: Duke University Press, 1993.

——— ed. *Novel Gazing: Queer Readings in Fiction*. Durham: Duke University Press, 1997.

Shattuck, Roger. *The Banquet Years: The Origins of the Avant-Garde in France 1885 to World War I*. Garden City: Anchor Books Doubleday: 1961.

Sizeranne, Robert de la. *Ruskin et la religion de la beauté*, 10th ed. Paris: Librairie Hachette, 1920.

Soupault, Robert. "Robert Proust: Frère de Marcel." *BSAP* (1967): 553–568.

Spagnoli, John J. *The Social Attitudes of Marcel Proust.* New York: Columbia University Press, 1936.

Spitzer, Leo. "Le style de Marcel Proust." *Etudes de Style.* Paris: Gallimard, 1970.

Splitter, Randolph. *Proust's Recherche: A Psychoanalytic Interpretation.* London: Routledge & Kegan Paul, 1981.

Sprinker, Michael. *History and Ideology in Proust: A la recherche du temps perdu and the Third French Republic.* New York: Cambridge University Press, 1994.

Stambolian, George, and Elaine Marks, eds. *Homosexualities and French Literature: Cultural Contexts, Critical Texts.* Ithaca: Cornell University Press, 1979.

Strauss, Walter A. *Proust and Literature: The Novelist as Critic.* Cambridge: Harvard University Press, 1957.

Tadié, Jean-Yves. *Proust et le roman.* Paris: Gallimard, 1971.

——. *Marcel Proust.* Paris: Gallimard, 1996.

Taylor, Elizabeth Russel. *Marcel Proust and His Contexts: A Critical Bibliography of English language Scholarship.* New York: Garland, 1981.

Thomas, Francis-Noël. *The Writer Writing: Philosophic Acts in Literature.* Princeton: Princeton University Press, 1992.

Thornton, Ronald. "*Marcel Proust and Marxist Literary Criticism from the Nineteen Twenties to the Nineteen Seventies.*" Diss. Bloomington: University of Indiana, 1979.

Tolstoy, Leo. *Great Short Works of Leo Tolstoy.* Trans. by Louise and Aylmer Maude. New York: Harper & Row, 1967.

Tuchman, Barbara W. *The Proud Tower: A Portrait of the World before the War 1890–1914.* New York: The Macmillan Company, 1966.

Tupinier, Georgette. "La Digitale de *Jean Santeuil.*" *Revue d'Histoire Littéraire de la France* 5–6 (1971): 950–964.

Van Tieghem, Pierre ed. *Dictionnaire des littératures.* 3 vols. Paris: Presses Universitaires de Paris, 1968.

Various. *Entretiens sur Marcel Proust.* Paris and La Haye: Mouton & Co., 1966.

Various. Preface by Jean-Yves Tadié. *Index général de la correspondance de Marcel Proust, d'après l'édition de Philip Kolb.* Kyoto: Presses de l'Université de Kyoto, 1998.

Vásquez, Adolfo Sánchez. *Art and Society: Essays in Marxist Aesthetics.* Trans. by Maro Riofrancos. New York: Monthly Review Press, 1973.

Viers, Rina. "La Signification des fleurs dans l'œuvre de Marcel Proust." *BSAP* (1975): 153–176.

Vigneron, Robert. *Etudes sur Stendhal et sur Proust.* Paris: A.G.Nizet, 1978.

Vogely, Maxine A. *Italy in the Life and Works of Marcel Proust.* Urbana: Illinois University Press, 1969.

Weiss, Véronique. *Les Plaisirs et les jours ou l'écriture double.* Diss., New York University, 1995.

White, Edmund. *Marcel Proust.* New York: Penguin Books, 1999.

Williams, Raymond. *Marxism and Literature.* Oxford: Oxford University Press, 1977.

———.*Writing in Society.* London: Verso, 1980s (date of publication not given)

Wilson, Edmund. *Axel's Castle: A Study in the Imaginative Literature of 1870 to 1930.* New York: Charles Scribner's Sons, 1931.

Wolitz, Seth L. *The Proustian Community.* New York: New York University Press, 1971.

Young, Ian ed. *The Male Homosexual in Literature: A Bibliography*, 2nd ed. Metuchen and London: The Scarecrow Press, 1982.

Zima, P.-V. *Le Désir du mythe-une lecture sociologique de Marcel Proust.* Paris: Editions A.-G. Nizet, 1973.

G. Periodicals

American Proust Association Newsletter

Le Banquet (1892–1893). Genève: Slatkine Reprints, 1971.

Bulletin de la Société des Amis de Marcel Proust (BSAP)

Cahiers Marcel Proust

Comparative Literature Studies

L'Esprit Créateur

Europe

The French Review

Le Gaulois

La Gazette des Beaux Arts

Le Mensuel

Le Mercure de France

Modern Language Notes

Paragone

La Plume

PMLA

La Revue Blanche

La Revue des deux mondes

Revue des Sciences Humaines

Revue d'Histoire Littéraire de la France

La Revue Hebdomadaire

Tout Paris

Yale French Studies

Index

Action Française, 57
Adam, Antoine, 185–186
Admetus, 140, 142
aesthetics and aestheticism, 2, 10, 11, 16, 23, 28, 45, 48–50, 57, 60, 69–70, 72, 86, 101, 107, 110–112, 115–116, 119, 128, 133, 135, 141, 151, 160–162, 164, 173, 179, 200–201, 208
"À la recherche de Clémentine," 220n6
À la recherche du temps perdu, 1, 3, 4, 5, 9, 12–14, 18, 19, 20, 32, 37, 42, 44, 51, 70, 71, 76, 81, 84, 95, 96–97, 101, 106, 108, 110, 117, 131, 143, 148, 153, 155, 160, 166–167, 174, 177, 179, 182, 187, 190, 196, 206, 208–210, 214n4, 219n7, 220n5, 222n4
Albaret, Céleste, 103, 217n9
Albertine (character in the Recherche), 16, 117, 222n4 (ch. 8)
Alden, Douglas, 220n1
Alexis (character in "La Mort de Baldassare Silvande"), 153
Alice Doesn't: Feminism, Semiotics, Cinema, 16
Alighieri, Dante, 51, 77, 160, 170, 176, 178
Alphonse Darlu (1849–1921): le maître de philosophie de Marcel Proust, 213n2

The American Scholar, 223n3
Les Amours et la sexualité de Proust, 213n2
Althusser, Louis, 10–13, 39
"Analytic of the Beautiful," 112
anarchism, 55, 143
André, Prince (character in War and Peace), 151
androgyny, 20
Andromache, 142
Album Proust: iconographie réunie et commentée par Pierre Clarac et André Ferré, 222n3 (ch. 9)
Anguissola, Alberto Beretta, 223–224n6
"Animism, Magic, and the Omnipotence of Thought," 220n4
Annalen der Physik, 175
Les Ann ales politiques et littéraires, 216n16
Les Années de collège de Marcel Proust, 213n2
anti-Semitism, 61, 79, 181, 193, 196
Apollinaire, Guillaume, 57
Apollo, 140–142
L'Après-midi d'un faune, 45, 46
À Rebours, 43
Ariadne (mythical character), 144
L'Art romantique, 215n4
L'Assommoir, 43
Augustin (character in Violante ou la mondanité), 133–134, 142
Augustin (character in "Contre la franchise"), 149

Augustine, Saint, 107, 143, 210
Aubert-Aurier, G., 122
L'Aurore, 61
Austen, Jane, 130
L'Automatisme psychologique, 217n4
"Avant la nuit," 18, 32, 49, 58–60
Axel's Castle: A Study in the Imaginative Literature of 1870 to 1930, 5, 46, 139

Bach, Johann Sebastian, 85
Bailey, Ninette, 96
Bakhtin, Mikhail, 5, 7, 19, 200, 213n4
Bal, Mieke, 114, 164–165, 173–174
Balsoram, Flavie de, 68, 216n
Balzac, Honoré de, 8–9, 93, 99, 223n4, 224n7
Le Banquet, 51–56
The Banquet Years, 52
Banville, Théodore de, 64
Barbusse, Henri, 51
Bardèche, Maurice, 2–3
Barker, Richard H., 213n1
Barrès, Maurice, 57–58, 85, 142
Bartet, Julia, 85
Barthes, Roland, 19, 117
Barzun, Jacques, 190, 223n2
Bastelle, Silvain (character in *JS*), 223n4
Baudelaire, Charles, 21, 22, 35, 44, 46, 80, 122, 139, 144–148, 165, 189–190, 215n4, 216n15, 221n9, 221n3 (ch. 8)
Baudelaire: A Collection of Critical Essays, 221n3 (ch. 8)
Baudino, Catherine Anne, 187–188, 210
Beaulincourt, Countess de, 75
Beckett, Samuel, 100, 174, 176
Beerbohm, Sylvia Sarah, 210–211
Beethoven, Ludwig van, 85–87
la belle époque, 28, 52
"La belle Olympia," 79
Benjamin, Walter, 5, 12, 87, 99, 194
Béraud, Jean, 85, 102, 214n1
Bergson, Henri, 221n7

Bergson et Proust, 213n2
Berkeley, George, 114
Bernhardt, Sarah, 85–86
Bertrand, Antoine, 217n6
Bezüge und Strukturen: Studien zu Les Plaisirs et les jours, 222n6 (ch. 8)
Bibesco, Princes Antoine and Emmanuel, 78
Bibesco, Emmanuel, 128
La Bible d'Amiens, 222n1
The Bible of Amiens, 167, 178–180
Bibliothèque Nationale, 52, 96
Billy, Robert de, 78, 127, 219n3
Binet, Alfred, 217n4
Bizet, Georges, 64
Bizet, Jacques, 31–33, 51–52, 75, 103, 214n3
Blake, William, 170
Blanche, Jacques-Émile, 34–35, 83, 217n2
Blum, Léon, 51
Boitchidzé, Gaston, 213n3
Boldini, Jean, 82, 217n8
Bonaparte, Princess Mathilde, 64, 75
Bonduelle, Michel, 215n2
Bonnard, Pierre, 56
Borda, Gustave de, 102
Borrel, Anne, 32
Boulanger, General George, 214n2
Boulangism, 27
Bonnet, Henri, 213n2
Bourdieu, Pierre, 9
bourgeoisie (middle class), 10, 27, 30, 32, 39, 75–76, 117, 134, 191, 207
Bourget, Paul, 53, 64, 84, 170
Boutroux, Émile, 41, 115–116
Bouvard et Pécuchet (Flaubert characters), 67, 94, 108
Bouwens Van der Boijin, Otto, 48
Bowie, Malcolm, 2, 13, 166–167
Brancovan, Prince Constantin de, 78
Brantes, Mme Sauvage de, 104–105
Brée, Germaine, 5, 37, 99, 138
Breyves, Françoise de (character in *Mélancolique villégiature*), 144

Brunetière, Ferdinand, 170–171
Buisine, Alain, 83
Burne-Jones, 79
Buttigieg, Joseph, 112

Cahiers de la Quinzaine, 214n3
Caillavet, Mme Arman de, 74, 75, 99
Calmann-Lévy (publisher of *PJ*), 92, 95
Canavaggia, Jeanne, 214n2 (ch. 1)
The Canticle of Brother Sun, 205
capitalism, 46, 76, 87, 162
Les Caractères, 149–150
Carassus, Emilien, 5, 37, 75, 83, 96, 134
Carlyle, Thomas, 161, 163, 178, 182, 198
Catholicism, 29, 31, 54–55, 145
Céline, Ferdinand, 52
Cerf, Walter, 112
Cessac, Louise de (maiden name of Mme Sauvage de Brantes), 105
Champaigne, Philippe de, 66
Chardin, Jean, 65–66, 116, 165, 167, 173–176
Charles I, King, 120, 221n2 (ch. 7)
Charlotte (character in *JS*), 206
Charlus, Baron de (character in the *Recherche*), 14, 21, 117
Le Château de Réveillon (first title of *PJ*), 67, 98, 135
Le Château de Réveillon (Lemaire residence), 93
Chatterton, 190
Les Chauves-souris, 80
Chavanne, Pierre Puvis de 79,
Le Chef des odeurs suaves, 80
Chekhov, Anton, 57
Chenier, André, 85
Chevigné, Countess Laure de, 74
Chevilly, Pierre de, 78
Chopin, Frédéric, 70, 85
"*Choses normandes*," 49–50
Choublier (professor at the Lycée Condorcet), 32
Cicero, 197
Le Cid, 28

Clarac, Pierre, 95, 185–186
Clemenceau, Georges, 61
Clermont-Tonnerre, Duchess Elizabeth de, 74
Cobban, Alfred, 12
Cocking, J.M., 213n1 (Introd.)
Cocteau, Jean, 65
Coleridge, Samuel Taylor, 122, 170
Colette, 200
Collière, Marcel; 122
Comédie Française, 86
The Communist Manifesto, 213n5
Compagnon, Antoine, 5, 18–21, 76, 170
"*La Confession d'une jeune fille*," 81, 94, 142–143
"*Le 'Confiteor' de l'artiste*," 147
"*Contre la franchise*," 149
"*Contre l'obscurité*," 19, 58, 167–172, 174
Contre Sainte-Beuve, 53
"*Conversation et sous–conversation*," 47
Coppée, François, 64, 85
Corneille, Pierre, 27–28, 102
Costil, Pierre, 101
Couzon, M. (character in *JS*), 193–195
Criticism and Ideology, 84
Critique of Judgment, 112
Critique of Pure Reason, 110–112
Croce, Benedetto, 164
Culler, Jonathan, 221n1 (ch. 8)
Le Culte du moi, 57, 142
Les Curiosités esthétiques de Robert de Montesquiou, 217n6
Cuyp, Albert, 70, 218n2

D'Annunzio, Gabriele, 43, 220n10
Darlu, Alphonse, 28, 33, 36, 52, 70, 115, 120, 138, 220n6
Darwin, Charles and Darwinism, 18, 217n4
Daudet, Alphonse, 64, 72, 77, 85, 102, 215n2
Daudet, Mme Alphonse, 74
Daudet, Léon, 66
Daudet, Lucien, 63, 102

Daum, Pierre, 93, 96, 109, 150
"*The Death of Ivan Ilych*," 151–154
Debussy, Claude, 42, 46, 64
decadentism, 21, 97, 107, 120, 141, 145, 151, 216n9
La Défense de l'Europe contre la peste, 30
Deffand, Mme Du, 73
Deffoux, Léon, 108
Degas, Edgar, 79
Delacroix, Eugène, 175
Delafosse, Léon, 64, 85–86, 215n3
Delage, Roger, 70–71
De l'Amour, 207
Delaunay, Elie, 82, 217n8
De Lauretis, Teresa, 16
Deleuze, Gilles, 3
De Man, Paul, 13
Derrida, Jacques, 15, 112
Desbordes-Valmore, Marceline, 64
Le Désir du mythe: Une lecture sociologique de Marcel Proust, 5, 223n4
"*Un Dimanche au Conservatoire*," 86
"*Un Diner en ville*," 94, 143
Le Disciple, 53
Dominique (character in *L'Étranger*), 132
Donne, John, 170
Dostoyievsky, Fyodor, 115, 150
Dreyfus, Robert, 31, 51, 103, 214n3
Dreyfus, Captain Alfred, 39, 61, 76, 102, 178, 193
Dreyfus Affair, 13, 76, 78, 135, 193, 196
Dreyfusards and Dreyfusism, 18, 61, 214n3
Du Chant, 66
The Duke of Richmond, 120, 221n2 (ch. 7)
Dumas fils, Alexandre, 120, 215n1 (ch. 3)
Dupee, F.W., 97–98
Durand-Ruel art gallery, 57
Duroc, M. (character in *JS*), 191–192
du Roux, Marie, 78

Eagleton, Terry, 9–10, 84, 130
Echnagucia, Elena Maria, 64
Écrits de jeunesse, 215n6 (ch.1)
Écrits pour l'Art, 57
Einstein, Albert, 175
Eliot, George, 150, 198
elitism, 120–127, 131
Ellison, David, 167
"*Éloge de la mauvaise musique*," 71
"*Embarkation for Cythère*," 146
Emerson, Ralph Waldo, 139–142, 170, 198
Engels, Frederick, 6, 201, 213n5
Enright, D.J., 97
Erasmus, 200
L'Ère du soupçon, 46
Ermitage, 57
Ernestine (character in *JS*), 194, 202
Esotérisme et écriture dans l'œuvre de Proust, 127
L'Esprit chrétien et le patriotisme," 53
Estherhazy, Marie Charles Ferdinand (mentioned in *JS*), 205
"*L'Étranger*" (sketch by Proust in *PJ*), 109, 130–133
"*L'Étranger*" (poem by Baudelaire in *Petits poèmes en prose*), 221n9
Études de psychologie expérimentale: Le fétichisme dans l'amour, 217n4
Evelyn-White, Hugh G., 219n9
Everman, Anthony Albert, 5, 116–117
existentialism, 123

Faculty of Law and Political Science (in Paris), 41–42, 50
Fallois, Bernard de, 182, 185–186, 189
"*Famille écoutant la musique*," 71, 94
Faubourg Saint-Germain, 73–74, 85
Faure, Antoinette, 38, 214n2
Fauré, Gabriel, 42, 64
Febvre, Lucien, 19
feminism, 16

Index

Fénelon, Bertrand de, 78, 128, 148
Ferré, André, 213n2
"*Une fête littéraire à Versailles,*" 218n11
fetishism, 20, 145, 162-163, 165, 178
feudalism, 77, 117, 220n1, 223n4
Feuerbach, Ludwig, 200
Fifth Symphony of Beethoven, 85-86
Le Figaro, 95
Film, Politics, and Gramsci, 15
"*La Fin de la jalousie,*" 93, 140, 151, 220n1 (ch. 7)
Finaly, Horace, 51
Flaubert, Gustave, 18, 54, 94, 108, 187, 215n6 (ch. 3), 220n6
Flers, Marquis Robert de, 31, 51, 78, 214n3
Les Fleurs du mal, 144-145
Floressas des Esseintes, Jean de (character in *À Rebours*), 43
The Formal Method in Literary Scholarship: A Critical Introduction to Sociological Poetics, 213n4
formalism, 18-19, 113, 124
Fontana, Benedetto, 221n6
Foscolo, Ugo, 190
Foucault, Michel, 17, 125
"*Fragments de comédie italienne,*" 93-94, 106, 130, 138, 140, 150
France, Anatole, 35, 36, 43, 70, 75, 78, 93, 95, 99, 102-104, 107-108, 120, 138
Francesca da Rimini (character in *The Divine Comedy*), 51
Francillon, Roger, 148, 222n6 (ch. 8)
Francis, Claude, 61
Francis of Assisi, Saint, 200, 205
Franck, César, 64
Franco-Prussian War, 27
Françoise (character in "*Avant la nuit*"), 58-59
Françoise (character in the *Recherche*), 37, 194, 202
Françoise (character in "*La Fin de la jalousie*"), 93

Françoise (character in *JS*), 206-207
Mme Fremer (character in "*Un Dîner en ville*"), 143
French aristocracy, 10, 13, 30, 32, 35, 37, 39, 43, 73, 75-78, 81, 83, 85-87, 105, 126,134, 148, 191, 217n2, 217n5, 218n10
French Revolution, 11, 14
Freud, Sigmund, 28, 115, 162, 220n4
Freuden und Tage, 98-100, 107
Frye, Northrop, 198

Galéas, Jean (character in "*La Mort de Baldassare Silvande*"), 153
Gallimard (French publisher), 95
Gaucher, Maxime, 27
Gauguin, Paul, 46, 122
Le Gaulois, 85-86, 95, 134-135, 178, 218n11, 218n12, 218n2, 219n3
Gautier, Théophile, 64, 79
La Gazertte des Beaux Arts, 91, 222n6 (ch. 9)
The German Ideology, 201, 213n5
Germinal, 43, 202
Gesta Romanorum, 219n9
Gicquel, Bernard, 93, 96-97, 101, 107-108
Gide, André, 47, 56, 57, 131, 216n15
Gilberte (character in the *Recherche*), 222n4 (ch. 8)
Giono, Jean, 200
Gluck, Christoph von, 70
Godebska, Misia, 57
Goethe, Johann Wolfgang von, 178, 190
Goncourt brothers, 46
Gontier, Fernande, 61
"*The Good Samaritan,*" 176
Gorky, Maxim, 57
Gounod, Charles-François, 64
Gourmont, Rémy de, 45, 58, 122
Gramsci, Antonio, 5, 7, 15, 19, 37, 56, 77, 123
Grancey, Count Charles de, 120
Grandjean, Charles, 220n3

Greffulhe, Countess Elizabeth
Gregh, Fernand, 31, 35, 51–53, 83, 103, 214n3, 218n10
Greslou, Robert (character in Bourget's Le Disciple), 53
The Grundrisse, 221n8
Guaraldo, Enrico, 186, 189
The Guermantes Way, 187

Hachette Almanac, 104
Hahn, Carlos, 64
Hahn, Reynaldo, 22, 63–72, 86, 92–93, 98, 102, 104, 107, 120, 127, 139, 168, 179, 203, 215n2, 215n9, 215n11, 216n13, 218n2, 219n4, 222n3 (ch. 9), 224n8
Halévy, Daniel, 31, 32, 33–35, 51, 83, 214n3
Halévy, Fromental, 75
Hamsun, Knut, 57
Harlequin, 93
Hardy, Thomas, 150
Hartmann, Karl von, 115
Hassine, Juliettte, 127
Hauser, Lionel, 221n5, 222n3 (ch. 8)
Heath, Willie, 93, 120–121
Hegel, G.W.F., 169
hegemony, 7, 13
Heilbrun, Carolyn, 32
Heine, Heinrich, 64
Henraux brothers, 128
Henrich, Dieter, 113
Henry, Anne, 4, 96, 110, 114–116, 127, 137, 146, 150–152, 189
Heroes and Hero Worship, 178
Hermant, Abel, 84
Hernani, 216n17
"Herodiade," 45
Herzen, Alexander, 57
Hervieu, Paul, 84
Hesiod, 98–100, 135, 137–139, 219n8, 219n9
historical materialism, 5, 7–8, 12, 15, 18, 19, 28–29, 111, 130, 166, 211

"History," 139–140
History and Ideology in Proust: A la recherche du temps perdu and the Third French Republic, 5, 12
The Holy Bible, 120
"Holy Family" (Tintoretto painting), 181
M. Homais (character in Madame Bovary), 54
Homer, 120, 122, 160
Homeric Hymns-Epic Cycle-Homerica, 219n8
Un Homme libre, 142
L'Homme et la mer, 146
homosexuality, 17–18, 31, 32–34, 38, 52, 58–59, 68, 71, 78, 117, 207, 214n4, 215n6 (ch. 1), 216n15
Honoré (character in "Violante ou la mondanité), 99
Horace, 139, 143
Les Hortensias bleus, 79
Hugo, Victor, 64, 72, 180, 198, 214n3, 216n17
The Human Comedy, 93
Huysmans, Joris-Karl, 21, 43, 122
Hyppolyte (character in Phèdre), 144

Ibsen, Henrik, 160, 178
Icarus (mythical son of Daedalus), 70
ideology and ideological criticism, 1–23, 27–29, 37, 39, 55–56, 72, 75, 76, 82, 91, 98, 109, 129, 131, 137, 142, 161, 186–211
The Iliad, 201
"L'Île du rêve," 64
"The Image of Proust," 5, 87
Imitation of Christ, 100, 132, 142–143
"Impression: Soleil levant," 175
impressionism, 8, 45, 46, 50–51, 94, 97, 119, 123, 159, 165, 174–177, 179
"L'Indifférent," 222n4 (ch. 8)

Individuality and individualism, 35, 57, 120, 129, 161, 165, 179, 191–193
intertextuality, 137–155
Introduction to Proust: His Life, His Circle, and His Work (Leon biography), 219n1
L'Irréligion d'État," 53–54
Ivan Ilych (protagonist of *The Death of Ivan Ilych*), 151

"J'Accuse!", 61
Jackson, Anne B., 57, 61
James, Henry, 36
Jameson, Fredric, 14, 198–200
Jammes, Francis, 57
Janet, Pierre, 217n4
Le Jardin de Bérénice, 58
Jean Santeuil, 3, 17, 23, 55, 67, 153, 155, 182, 185–211
Jesus Christ, 140, 177, 181
Jeunhomme, Auguste, 56
Jewish culture and religion, 31, 46, 78, 181, 217n1
"*John Ruskin*" (Proust essay), 167
Johnson, Barbara, 112
Johnson, J. Theodore, 96, 218n2
Jourdan, Henri, 219n4
Journal (Gide's diary), 216n15
Le Journal (newspaper),72, 102
"*Journées de pélerinage: Ruskin à Notre-Dame d'Amiens*," 179, 222n4 (ch. 9)
Joyce, James, 36, 46, 47, 83
Judeo-Christian thought, 17, 53, 60, 79, 99, 112, 129, 142, 160, 163
"*Jugements russes sur Proust*," 213n3
Jullian, Philippe, 85, 217n5
Jupien (character in the *Recherche*), 21

Kabbalah (Spanish), 127
Kadi, Simone, 137, 175
Kahn, Gustave, 45, 168
Kant, Immanuel, 17, 110–113, 116, 169, 210, 220n6

Keller, Luzius, 96, 98–100, 107–109, 138–139, 145, 219n6
Kempis, Thomas à, 100, 107, 132 134,139, 142–143, 163–164
Ker-Roussel, 56
Kierkegaard, Søren, 170
Kingcaid, Renée A., 96–97, 104, 107, 145
Kolb, Philip, 186, 216n10, 224n8
Kolb-Proust Archive, 223n1
Kossichef, Mlle (character in *JS*), 204
Kristeva, Julia, 137, 221n1 (ch. 8)

La Bruyère, Jean de, 108, 131, 139, 148–150
Lachelier, Jules, 115
Ladenson, Elizabeth, 214n 4
Laget, Thierry, 95–97, 99, 146
Lahor, Jean, 64
La Jeunesse, Ernest, 103
Laléande, Jacques de (character in "*Violante ou la mondanité*"), 110, 147
Lamartine, Alphonse de, 198–199
Lambert, Mme de, 73
Landy, Marcia, 15
Lanson, Gustave, 19–20, 170–171
La Rochefoucauld, Gabriel de, 78
La Rochefoucauld (seventeenth-century moralist), 148
La Salle, Louis de, 31, 51
Laurence (character in "*Contre la franchise*"), 149, 214n1 (ch.2)
Les Lauriers sont coupés, 103
Lauris, Georges de, 78
Lavallée, Pierre, 120–128. 142
Lavedan, Henri, 84
Le Bargy, Simone, 216n13
Leclercq, Paul, 56
Leconte De Lisle, Charles-René-Marie, 64, 198
Leduc, Mme (character in *JS*), 201
Lemaire, Madeleine, 63, 67, 74, 75, 78, 79, 86, 92, 95, 98–99, 104, 120, 121, 126, 135,

215n1 (ch. 3), 216n13,
218n1, 218n2, 218n3,
219n4, 222n3 (ch. 9)
Lemaire, Suzette, 63, 86
Lemaître, Jules, 49
Leonardo da Vinci, 66, 80, 120, 175
Leoncavallo, Ruggiero, 72
Lentricchia, Frank, 221n10
Lenvres, Honoré de (character in "*La Fin de la jalousie*), 93, 108, 150, 220n1 (ch. 7)
Leon, Derrick, 213
Lepic, M. (character in *Jean Santeuil*), 193-195
Le Roux, Hugues, 49
Leroy, Louis, 175
lesbianism, 17, 58-59, 207
Leslie (narrator of "*Avant la Nuit*"), 18, 59
Lettre à un lecteur facile, 57
Lettre à Wagner, 215n4
Levin (character in *Anna Karenina*), 151
Librairie Rouquette, 52
Lilies and Sesame: The Orient, Inversion, and Artistic Creation, 5, 116-117
Lippmann, Léontine (maiden name of Mme de Caillavet), 75, 99
Liszt, Franz, 86
Literature and Existentialism, 124
Loevgren, Sven, 46, 216n12
Lomperolle Vicomte de (character in *JS*), 207
Lope de Vega, 170
Lorrain, Jean, 102-103, 220n1
Loti, Pierre, 64, 72
Louis xiv, King, 86
Louria, Yvette, 213n3
Lunacharsky, Anatoly, 5
Lukàcs, Georg, 5, 128, 190
Luynes, Countess de
Lycée Condorcet, 3, 10, 22, 27, 29-31, 33-35, 36, 50-51, 55, 61, 103, 127, 213n1 (ch. 1), 214n1 (ch. 1), 214n5, 220n6
Le Lys dans la vallée, 199, 224n7

Macbeth, 169
Macksey, Richard, 222n2
Maeterlinck, Maurice, 57, 58, 122, 139, 168
Mainguet, Pierre, 168, 173
Mâle, Émile, 128
Mallarmé, Stéphane, 35, 44-45, 46, 57, 65, 66, 72, 79, 84, 98, 116, 122, 164, 168-169, 172, 215n4
Manet, Édouard
Mann, Thomas, 46, 76, 128
Marc-Lipianski, Mireille, 185, 187
Marcel (narrator of the *Recherche*), 187-189, 208-209
Marcel Proust (reference work in B.N.), 222n5 (ch. 8)
Marcel Proust (Tadié biography), 4
Marcel Proust (White biography), 4
Marcel Proust: A Biography (Barker biography), 214n1
Marcel Proust: A Life (Carter biography), 4
Marcel Proust and Marxist Literary Criticism from the Nineteen Twenties to the Nineteen Seventies, 213n3
Marcel Proust: sa vie, son œuvre (Quint biography), 213n1
Marcel Proust: Théories pour une esthétique, 4, 115
Marie, Charles (character in *JS*, 193, 196-197, 201
Marie, Mme Charles (character in *JS*), 196
Martin, Randy, 15
Martines, Lauro, 2, 14-15
Marx, Karl, 6, 28, 162, 200-202, 213n5, 221n8
Marxism and Deconstruction, 15
Marxism and Literature, 6-7, 138
Marxism and Marxists, 7-8, 12, 14, 15, 75, 123, 130, 162, 200-202, 221n8
Marxist criticism, 5-23, 213n3
Mascagni, Pietro, 72
Massenet, Jules, 64

Mauclair, Camille, 122, 139
Maugny, Viscount Clément de, 105–106
Maupassant, Guy de, 128
Maurois, André, 213n1 (Introd.), 217n8
Maurras, Charles, 57
Mayer, Arno J., 76, 86
Medvedev, P.N., 213n4
Megay, Joyce, 213n2
"Mélancolique villégiature de Mme de Breyves," 94, 99, 106, 108–109, 144–147, 222n4 (ch. 8)
Mellot, Marthe, 57
Le Ménestrel: Journal du Monde Musical, 215n5
"Mensonges," 64
Le Mensuel, 48–51
"La Mer," 71, 94, 145–146
Le Mercure de France, 52, 53, 57, 91, 121, 139, 221n2 (ch. 8), 222n6 (ch. 9)
metempsychosis, 125–127
Metsys, Quentin, 79
Meyer, Arthur, 134–135, 219n3
Meyerbeer, Jacques, 64
Middle Ages, 107, 178, 180
The Mill on the Floss, 170
Milly, Jean, 109
Milsand, Joseph-Antoine, 181
Milton, John, 160, 170
modernism, 45, 46–47, 67, 76–77, 119, 122, 145
Modern Painters, 177
Molière, 148
Mon cher petit: lettres à Lucien Daudet, 215n2
Le Monde de Marcel Proust (Maurois biography), 213, 217n8
Monet, Claude, 46, 65, 175, 222n3 (ch. 9), 222n4 (ch. 9)
Monod, Silvain, 220n5
Monsieur Thiers contre l'empire, la guerre, la commune, 214n3
Montaigne, Michel de, 34
Montégut, Émile, 139
Montesquiou-Fezensac, Count Robert de, 10, 43, 64, 74, 77–87, 107, 120–121, 126, 135, 151, 190, 207, 216n9, 217n5, 217n6, 217n9, 218n12
Morand, Bernadette, 74, 217n2
Moréas, Jean, 57, 216n12
Moreau, Gustave, 21, 43, 79, 173
La Mort, 151
"La Mort de Baldassare Silvande, Vicomte de Sylvanie," 68, 71, 94, 107–109, 133, 140, 151
Mort à crédit, 52
Mozart, Wolfgang Amadeus, 70
Muhlfeld, Lucien, 58, 122–123
Musset, Alfred de, 64, 198

Nathanson brothers, 56
Nathanson, Alexandre, 56
Nathanson, Louis-Alfred, 56–57
Nathanson, Thadée, 56
naturalism, 43, 46, 49, 57, 122
Nerval, Gérard de,.35
"the new novel," 47–48
Newton, Sir Isaac, 200
Nietzsche, Friedrich, 52, 55, 57, 160, 170
Noah (Biblical character), 120, 138–139
Noailles, Countess Anne de, 74, 75
Nordau, Max, 57
Nordlinger, Marie, 67, 179, 186
Notes: Journal d'un musicien, 65
Notre-Dame de Paris, 180
Les Nourritures terrestres, 57
La Nouvelle Revue Française, 56
Novalis, 122

O'Brien, Justin, 188
L'Obstacle, 72
"Ode to Versailles," 85
Odette (character in the *Recherche*), 13, 68, 222n4 (ch. 8)
Odette (character in "*Souvenir*"), 50–51
Œnone (character in *Phèdre*), 144
L'Œuvre, 46

Œuvres de La Bruyère, 222n5 (ch. 5)
"Les œuvres de Reynaldo Hahn," 216n16
Offenbach, Jacques, 64
"Olivian," 130–131, 138–139
On Reading Proust, 222n2
L'Opéra Comique, 64
"Oranthe," 108, 149
Orcagna, 79
Our Fathers Told Us, 180

Paganini, Maria, 147
Painter, George, 83, 85, 178
Pantalone (commedia dell'arte character), 93
Le Paris littéraire et intime de Marcel Proust, 214n1 (ch. 1)
Les Pas effacés, 217n5
Pascal, Blaise, 49, 55, 148, 221n7
Pastiches, 220n5
patriotism, 12, 27, 37, 54–55
Patriotism and the Christian Spirit, 54–55
peasant and working classes, 14, 37, 54–55, 75
Péguy, Charles, 214n3
La Peinture chez Proust et Baudelaire, 137, 175
"Pendant le carême," 49–50
Percy (character in "Contre la franchise"), 149
"Personnages de la comédie mondaine," 93
Petits poèmes en prose, 145, 221n9
Peyre, Henri, 190, 223n3
"Les phares," 146
Phèdre, 144
Philosophy of Composition, 216n12
The Philosophical Forum, 221n6
philosophical idealism, 4, 10, 11–12, 17, 28, 42, 45, 50, 53–54, 76, 87, 106, 110–112, 138, 163–167, 177, 198, 201, 210
philosophy of praxis (Marxism), 19
The Philosophy of the Unconscious, 115

Il Piacere, 220n10
Picquart, Colonel Georges (real person and character in JS), 193, 196, 204
"Pinacothèque," 79
Placella, Paola, 96
Les Plaisirs et les jours, 3, 9, 16, 17, 22, 29, 48, 53, 54, 58, 63, 66–67, 70, 71, 74, 75, 79, 81, 82, 83, 84, 87, 91–155, 159, 168, 189, 210, 215n6 (ch. 3), 216n14, 218n1, 219n6, 219n9, 222n4 (ch. 8)
Plato, 21, 32, 52, 122, 210
Pleasures and Regrets (Enright's title for PJ), 99
Plotinus, 122
La Plume, 52, 57, 91, 121
Poe, Edgar Allan, 46, 122
Les Poèmes antiques, 199
"La Poésie ou les lois mystérieuses," 167, 172–173
"The Poet," 139–140
The Political Unconscious: Narrative as a Socially Symbolic Act, 198–200
"Politics, Philosophy, and Modernity in Gramsci," 221n6
"Le Port," 147
Portraits de peintres et de musiciens, 92, 94, 107, 127, 135, 145, 218n2
positivism, 17, 19, 53, 111, 119, 165, 171, 201
postmodernism, 15
poststructuralism, 15
Potter, Paulus, 70
Poussin, Nicola, 66
Praeterita, 177
Price, Larkin, 95, 96, 103, 140, 188–189
The Prison Notebooks, 135
"Promenade," 106, 141
Proust, Marcel:
  biographies of, 4–5, 213n1 (Introd.)
  critical approaches to, 1–23, 46–48, 83–84, 87, 95–100,

104, 113–117, 137–139,
    173–175, 185–189, 206–
    207, 210–211
  Dreyfusism of, 61, 76
  early writings of (1891–1895): 50–
    55, 58–60, 85–87; *Les
    Plaisirs et les jours*, 92–155;
    (1896–1900): on John
    Ruskin, 159–183; *Jean
    Santeuil*, 185–211
  education of, 3–4, 10, 22, 27–39,
    41–42, 50
  elitism of, 120–121, 125–128
  family background of, 10, 30–31,
    36, 41
  and the French aristocracy, 10–11,
    73–87, 105
  heroic ideals of, 27–28, 102–103
  homosexuality of, 17–18, 31–34,
    38, 63–64, 68, 71
  and impressionism, 8, 119, 176–
    177
  and John Ruskin, 7, 23, 159–183,
    189
  Judeo-Christian values of, 17, 54–
    55, 60, 129, 163
  literary-critical ideas of, 2–3, 11,
    18–22, 23, 28–29, 35–36,
    43, 45–46, 49–50, 76–77,
    101–102, 104–110, 113–
    114, 119, 131–135, 138,
    140–155, 159–183
  patriotism of, 12, 27, 37, 54–55
  religious attitudes of, 11, 29, 119,
    127
  Reynaldo Hahn's influence on, 67–
    71
Proust, Adrien (Proust's father), 30,
    104, 217n4
Proust, Robert (Proust's brother), 31,
    60, 87, 217n4
Proust family, 10, 27, 30–31, 33, 36,
    41
Proust (Cocking biography), 213n1
Proust among the Stars, 166
Proust: The Early Years (Painter
    biography vol. 1), 213n1
Proust: The Later Years (Painter
    biography vol. 2), 213n1
Proust et la politique, 214n2)
*Proust and the Art of Love: The
    Aesthetics of Sexuality in
    the Life, Times, and Art
    of Marcel Proust*, 32
The Proustian Community, 5, 217n1
Proust entre deux siècles, 5, 18, 20–21
"Proust et Lunacharskii," 213n3
Proust's Lesbianism, 214n4
Psalms of David, 205
Puccini, Giacomo, 72

queer studies, 16–17
Qu'est-ce que la littérature?, 124
Quillard, Pierre, 64
Quint, Léon-Pierre, 219n1

Rabaud, Henri, 52
Rachel (character in the *Recherche*), 21
Racine, Jean, 21, 27–28, 64, 80, 120,
    139, 144, 169
Raczymov, Henri, 214n1 (ch. 1)
Rambouiller, Fontaine de, 218n10
Régnier, Henri de, 65, 85, 109, 168
"Les Regrets, rêveries couleur du
    temps," 71, 94, 106, 130,
    135, 140–141, 146
Reichenberg, Suzanne, 85
Remembrance of Things Past, 97
Rembrandt, 116, 165, 167, 176,
    222n5 (ch. 9)
The Renaissance, 21, 163, 197, 200
Renan, Ernest, 120
"Rencontre au bord du lac," 109–110
Renoir, Pierre Auguste, 121, 175
"Rêve," 109
*Les Rêves ou les moyens de les
    diriger*, 217n4
Réveillon, Henri de (character in *JS*),
    67, 191, 203, 206
La Revue Blanche, 51, 56–61, 80, 91,
    121–123., 168
La Revue des deux mondes, 52
La Revue Hebdomadaire, 71, 91, 94,
    168

La Revue Indépendante, 57
La Revue lilas, 29
La Revue Moderne, 57
La Revue de Paris, 95
Le Rhône: Nuit étoilée, 46
"Richard Wagner et Tannhauser," 215n4
Rièse, Laure, 75
Risler, Édouard, 69, 215n11, 216n13
Rivers, Julius Edwin, 32–33, 38, 67
Rivière, Jacques, 83
Robinson Crusoe, 152
Roccagiovine, Julie de, 75
Rodenbach, Georges, 66, 85
Romanticism, 21, 115, 170–171, 174, 177, 190–193, 199–201, 210, 223n4
Romanticism and the Modern Ego, 223n3
Rossetti, Dante Gabriel, 52
Rothschild, Henri de, 52
Rougon-Macquart novel cycle, 42
Rousseau, Jean-Jacques, 129–130, 143, 200
Rubens, Peter Paul, 175
Ruskin, John, 3, 7, 20, 23, 155, 159–183, 187, 189, 198, 210, 222n1
"Ruskinian pilgrimages in France," 179
Ryan, Michael, 15

Saint-Denis, Hervey de, 217n4
Saint-Loup, Robert de (character in the *Recherche*), 13, 14, 21, 37
Saint-Pol-Roux, 122
Saint-Saëns, Camille, 42, 64
Sainte-Beuve, Charles-Augustin, 19–20
salons, 12, 22, 73–87, 216n1
Sandre, Yves, 95–96
Santeuil, M. (Jean's father, character in *JS*), 195, 208
Santeuil, Mme (character in *JS*), 195, 208
Saraydar, Alma, 206
Sarkany, Stéphane, 142
Sarraute, Nathalie, 46–48

Sartre, Jean-Paul, 47, 124–125, 161
Saussine, Count Henri de, 78
Sayre, Robert, 5, 219n7, 221n8
Schelling, Friedrich von, 115–116
Schopenhauer, Arthur, 48–49, 58, 110, 113–116
Schumann, Robert, 70
scientism, 42, 49, 166
Séailles, Gabriel, 115–116
Second Empire, 77
Sedgwick, Eve Kosofsky, 16–18
semiotics, 14, 16
Sémiotiké: Recherches pour une sémanalyse, 221n1 (ch. 8)
M. Serciers (character in *JS*), 203
Sesame and the Lilies, 167, 179
Sésame et les lys, 222n1
Sévigné, Mme de, 66
Shakespeare, William, 122, 140, 170, 197, 219n9
Shattuck, Roger, 52
Shelley, Percy Bysshe, 35, 163, 170
"The Skate," 174
"Si mes vers avaient des ailes," 64
"Six mélodies," 215n3
Sizeranne, Robert de la, 179
Le Snobisme et les lettres françaises de Paul Bourget à Marcel Proust: 1884–1914, 5
The Social Contract, 130
socialism and socialists, 54, 75–76, 91, 123
Socialist Ensembles: Theater and State in Cuba and Nicaragua, 15
Society and History in English Renaissance Verse, 14
Socrates, 18, 34, 60, 140, 195
Sodom and Gomorrah, 17, 38, 71
Solitude in Society: A Sociological Study in French Literature, 5, 221n8
"Sonate clair de lune," 71
Sorbonne, 10, 41, 116
The Sorrows of Young Werther, 190
"La Sortie du lycée Condorcet," 214n1

"Sous-Bois," 222n3 (ch. 9)
"Souvenir," 49–51, 58–59
Soviet criticism on Proust, 5, 7, 10, 213n3
Spinoza, Baruch, 169, 189
Splitter, Randolph, 164–165
Sprinker, Michael, 5, 12–14, 37
Stein, Gertrude, 46
Stendhal, 8–9, 207
The Stones of Venice, 178
Straus, Émile, 34, 214n3
Straus, Geneviève (née Geneviève Halévy), 31, 52, 61, 68, 74–75, 214n3
Straus family, 68
Strindberg, August, 57
Structuralist Poetics (221n1 (ch. 8)
surrealism, 123
Swann, Charles (character in the *Recherche*), 13, 20, 67, 222n4 (ch. 8)
Swann's Way, 5, 187
Swedenborg, Emmanuel, 127
Swinburne, Algernon Charles, 52
symbolism, 36, 42–43, 45, 57, 58, 67, 79, 97–98, 101, 111, 116, 119, 122, 141, 146, 167, 169–171, 174, 189, 205, 215n4
The Symposium, 18, 32
System of Transcendental Idealism, 116

Tadié, Jean-Yves, 4, 42, 79, 83, 166, 172, 217n8,
Tage der Freuden (Ernst Weiß's title for *PJ*), 100
Taine, Hippolyte, 42
Le Temps, 95
Tendencies, 17–18
Tennyson, Lord Alfred, 52
La Terre, 43–44
Thalia, 93
Théâtre d'Application, 49
Theocritus, 200
Theseus (legendary son of Aegeus), 144

Third Republic, 11–14, 18
Thornton, Ronald, 213n3
"*The Three Dead*," 151
Tintoretto, 181
"*To the Rescue of Romanticism*," 223n3
Tolstoy, Leo, 52, 57, 93–94, 107, 114, 137, 139, 150–154, 160, 170, 178
Totem and Taboo, 220n4
Touche, Pierre de (Proust pseudonym), 49
Toulouse-Lautrec, Henri de, 56
La Troisième République des lettres, 5, 18–20
Tupinier, Georgette, 188
Twain, Mark, 57
"*The Two Philosophers*," 176

Ulrich, Karl Heinrich, 17
Le Ultime lettere de Iacopo Ortis, 190
Ulysses, 84

"*Le vallon*," 199
Van Dyck, Anton, 70, 79, 120–121, 218n2
Van Gogh, Vincent, 46
Verga, Giovanni, 128
Verhaeren, Emile, 57
verism, 72
Verlaine, Paul, 35, 46, 57, 64, 67, 85, 198
Vermeer, Jan, 175
La Vie contemporaine et revue parisienne, 222n4 (ch. 8)
Vigny, Alfred de, 190, 198
Vinteuil, Mlle (character in the *Recherche*), 21
"*Violante ou la mondanité*," 94, 99, 106, 108–109, 133–134, 142
Virgil, 120, 160, 176
"*Les Voiles au port*," 146, 148
Vuillard, Édouard, 56

Wagner, Richard, 42, 48–49, 64, 80, 147

War and Peace, 8, 151, 170
Watteau, Antoine, 66, 70, 146, 175
Weil family, 30–31
Weil, Jeanne-Clémence (Proust's mother), 30, 69, 71, 79, 103–104, 120, 179, 196, 214n2, 224n8
Weil, Nathé, 30
Weiß, Ernst, 98, 100
White, Edmund, 4, 12
Whitman, Walt, 46
Wilde, Oscar, 57
Williams, Raymond, 6–7, 60, 110, 138
Wilson, Edmund, 5, 46, 139
Wolitz, Seth L., 5, 12, 217n1
Woolf, Virginia, 46
Wordsworth, William, 170, 177, 199
Works and Days, 98–99 137, 219n9
The World of Marcel Proust, 5, 37, 138, 217n3
World War I, 3, 13, 77, 174

Yeatman, Léon, 103, 224n8
Yeats, William Butler, 46
Yturri, Gabriel, 78

Zhdanov, Andrei, 10
Zima, P.V., 5, 12, 223n4
The Zohar, 127
Zola, Emile, 18, 42–44, 46, 61, 202